FAITH

Behind the Fences

A True Story of Survival in
a Japanese Prison Camp

KELLY DISPIRITO TAYLOR

Covenant Communications, Inc.

Cover images: *Dark Starry Sky* © sololos. *Secure Zone* © Benjiecce, courtesy iStockphoto.com. *Map of Indonesia* © Dylan 46, courtesy iStockphoto.com.
Back images of Hanny's childhood and father's gravesite, courtesy Hanny Londt-Schultz. Back images of Hanny and Peggy Londt-Schultz and Kelly Dispirito Taylor, courtesy Summer Potter

Cover design copyright © 2011 by Covenant Communications, Inc.

Published by Covenant Communications, Inc.
American Fork, Utah

Printed in the United States of America
First Printing: February 2011

17 16 15 14 13 12 11   10 9 8 7 6 5 4 3 2 1

ISBN-13: 978-1-60861-063-1

This book is dedicated to my "angel mother," Jackie DiSpirito, who is cut from the same cloth as Hanny's mother, Tina. They are both women of extraordinary faith and love.

ACKNOWLEDGMENTS

Many thanks to Hanny Smith and her sister, Peggy Teiraband, for answering my countless questions about their experiences during WWII, some of which are still tender. I feel like two of the best benefits of this project are the dear friends I made in you.

I sincerely thank my editor, Samantha Van Walraven, who has been a patient mentor to me throughout the publication process. I also express my appreciation to Covenant Communications for seeing the potential in this project and particularly in Hanny's incredible story.

Thank you to Deborah Koehler, who willingly read a very rough first draft of this book and offered enough encouragement to spur me on. Your detailed suggestions were appreciated.

Finally, and most importantly, I am profoundly grateful to my husband, Alan, who believed in me as a writer and in this project as a worthwhile venture. Every writer needs a partner who supports her through the best and worst of times. Thanks, Al, for being that person for me.

CONTENTS

Saint Theresa's Prayer

May today there be peace within.
May you trust God that you are exactly where you are meant to be.
May you not forget the infinite possibilities that are born of faith.
May you use those gifts that you have received
and pass on the love that has been given to you.
May you be confident knowing you are a child of God.
Let this presence settle into your bones,
and allow your soul the freedom to sing, dance, praise, and love.
It is there for each and every one of us.

HANNY'S FOREWORD

ALL THESE YEARS I'VE WANTED my memories written down, so when Kelly offered to write a book, I was grateful. The world should know that God does know each of His children and that He does watch out for them, even in the most destitute of circumstances.

As a child I always asked questions. *Where does God live? Is He with us on the earth? Does He help us in our lives?* They were a child's questions, but I always had them in my mind. I was always looking for answers. When I was about eight, we got a Bible, and I read it a lot. We did not have a church in town, but we celebrated Christmas, Easter, and other Christian holidays. And when I was about thirteen years old, before Pearl Harbor was attacked, I went for a year to a Catholic high school. I learned there that the Holy Ghost, Jesus Christ, and our Heavenly Father were all one spirit, but I could not understand that concept.

Then, six months later, we were taken to a concentration camp. In that camp, we worked hard, served, and shared what we had with the sick children. I had many spiritual experiences during my time in the camps where I felt that we were guided in our misery.

I didn't learn about the Church until years after the war. In coming to understand such a harrowing experience, I did not have the gospel to help me overcome my bitterness and confusion. The only thing I had to rely on was my sweet mother's Christlike example and the change of heart I saw in others around me. It was not until 1955 that we were visited by two Latter-day Saint missionaries, who taught us the gospel.

We learned about the Holy Ghost, Jesus Christ, and our Heavenly Father as three separate beings, and in that moment, something clicked for me. It suddenly made sense. They taught us about Joseph Smith, who translated the Book of Mormon and became a prophet, and I had no problem with it. Even as a young girl growing up in a Catholic school, there was a pope. I thought, *Why wouldn't God have leaders to guide His church on the earth?*

One of the most incredible principles they taught us was that we could talk to Heavenly Father. I had always prayed when I was young, but they had been memorized prayers, like the Lord's Prayer. I liked that I could have personal prayers because that is how I thought we should talk to God. They taught me that no problem was too small to take to our Heavenly Father. And as I learned these truths, I started to look back and saw how through my life, all my prayers had been answered—not right away but in time. I thought about the prison camps, when I was choosing a career after the war, when I found my husband, and many other spiritual questions and experiences, and I realized that all those years I had been guided by the Holy Ghost.

Sometimes I cry that He has watched over me so much. I have had to have my eyes open to accept events in my life as answers and not coincidences. The Atonement of Jesus Christ has helped me over the years to know that through the temple work I have done for my family, I will see my father again and my mother too. It's such a blessing, such a comfort. It's because of Christ that we'll be together forever. That's a beautiful thing.

This is my testimony. The Holy Ghost guides us. Heavenly Father is mindful of us. He loves us. In the name of Jesus Christ, amen.

Hanny Smith

PREFACE

ONCE IN A WHILE, SOMEONE will cross your path and truly change you as a person. I remember sitting in a church service one morning as a bent, elderly woman slowly made her way to the podium and shared with the congregation a story about her time in a prison camp during WWII. It piqued my curiosity because not only was this sister's story moving, but her Asian features also seemed to clash with her Dutch accent. Who was this woman? What was her story? I was immediately intrigued, and I continued to watch her over the next few months.

On several occasions, she shared tidbits about her time in captivity but didn't elaborate. I finally felt compelled to ask about her life. I found that Hanny Smith had been an internee of a Japanese-run prison camp in Sumatra, along with many other European citizens living in Indonesia at the time.

I felt an insatiable curiosity to know more, and I was convinced I wouldn't be the only one interested in her story. I have always loved writing, and I proposed a book project to Hanny, one centered on her time in the camps during WWII. I'll never forget the look she gave me at that moment. Her warm brown eyes lit up. "Lately, I've been praying for someone to write my story. I've always been convinced that it needs to be told," she said. From that point on, I felt it was my responsibility and privilege to see that she achieved her heartfelt desire. After spending many afternoons interviewing Hanny and recording her experiences, I felt that, in a very unique way, I was beginning to understand what she and her family had gone through sixty-five years ago. As we journeyed together, I was changed.

This story is based on the experiences Hanny and her family had while in the Sumatran prison camps of WWII. The events in this book are true, though there are some fictional elements to help create the flow of the novel. The main characters are real, as are their general personalities. However, some of the minor characters have had their names changed or are a compilation of Hanny's and her sister's memories. In short, the essence of Hanny's experiences as a teenager in the camps—struggling to survive and striving to do so through the faith her mother taught her as a child—is true.

This is Hanny's story.

1. Tandjoeng-enim

5. Palembang

2. Moeara-enim

6. Belalau

3. Island of Bangka

7. Lubuklinggau

4. Muntok

8. Lahat

1

Preparations

I AWOKE TO THE RHYTHMIC sound of a hammer. Or was that just the pounding in my head? I had spent a fitful night, tossing and turning and having disturbing dreams. I was usually a sound sleeper, too, which made me wonder what had triggered my restlessness. Rubbing my eyes, my mind traveled back to the previous evening. Without warning, a feeling of dread hit me like a wrecking ball. Of course. I buried my head under the pillow, recalling yesterday's events that could very well change my family's lives forever.

***

Raindrops streaked my window like tears as I finished packing my bag for the trip back to school. My short weekend at home was quickly drawing to a close. It was late Sunday afternoon, and the smoky clouds overhead looked as heavy as my heart felt. At first the rain had tapped softly on the roof, and then it increased into a rap-rap-rap above my head. I sighed as somewhere in my brain it registered that the rainy season here in Sumatra was just around the corner. I was returning to my boarding school in Lahat in a few short hours because with the rainy season came another round of school.

I buckled my bag after a quick glance to make sure I had everything, and then I laid my parasol and school satchel beside it. I heard the sudden soft sounds of piano music lilting through the house and smiled as I made my way to the parlor.

My thirteen-year-old sister, Peggy, was perched on the tapestried piano bench with a look of concentration on her face. Her long, artistic fingers slid confidently across the keys. It was beautiful to watch. Music was one of Peggy's most amazing gifts. The music she evoked by stroking those ivory keys never failed to cheer me.

I watched my sister's face as she played. She was only a year younger than me, and her thick black hair and tan skin mirrored mine in many ways. The only difference was that my hair was cut short, while her hair was wiry and unruly, a fact that niggled and picked at my mother to no end. After the train wreck of a haircut she had inflicted on Peggy last spring, Mammy was not allowed within a ten-mile radius of Peggy's hair when she had a pair of cutting shears. I smiled when I thought of our mantra, *We would trust Mammy with our lives but never with our hair.* Our father had taken over haircutting duties where Peggy was concerned from that day forward. He was the only one she would allow to trim her long tresses.

The Asian features my sister and I shared were inherited from our grandmothers who had both been born on Nias, a small island off the western coast of Sumatra. Their portraits hung near the piano. I glanced over at them, as I had a hundred times before, and saw the family resemblance. Liquid brown eyes and smooth tan cheeks were the features that stood out most to me from their photos, along with the flash of sparkling white teeth in their smiles.

Pictures of my Dutch grandfathers hung beside their wives' portraits. I had been raised European and was a Dutch citizen, thanks to my grandfathers and their influence. My mother called us Eurasians, half Dutch and half Indonesian. Our town of Tandjoengenim welcomed people of all nationalities—Dutch, Germans, Indonesians, Eurasians, and even a few English. We were all there because of the coal mines.

I refocused on the scene at hand when I heard a violin case pop open. My father had his worn violin tucked up to his chin now. I smiled. We all enjoyed musical evenings. Pappy would accompany Peggy on his violin. I remember how pleased he was when Peggy started her love affair with the piano. He would encourage her to practice by keeping time with his violin. They were both gifted musicians, and their playing together later evolved into a beautiful duet of violin strings and piano keys.

Often, Mammy and I would sit and embroider nearby, listening to the music as we painstakingly wove art of our own on the sewing canvas. My younger brothers, Justin and George, would sit on the floor and listen too, sometimes quietly piecing together a puzzle or reading a book. I loved those evenings together. We'd listen to Brahms, Tchaikovsky, and Beethoven—all our old favorites.

Once in a while, Peggy would get playful. With a hint of a smile on her face, she would increased the momentum of her fingers on the piano keys and more popular musical tunes would emerge. Justin and George would perk up, and even Mammy would join in as we sang along to favorites like "Let's Call the Whole Thing Off" or "The Way You Look Tonight."

I caught Peggy's eye as she turned her music sheet. She winked at me, and I suspected that this impromptu musical evening was for my benefit. I think she must have detected my feelings of melancholy at the thought of leaving home the following morning. As usual, she came to the rescue by trying to lighten my heavy heart. Though she was at times a little crusty around the edges to those she didn't know, Peggy would do anything for those she loved.

I felt a warm hand on my shoulder. Mammy smiled at me, her eyes crinkling at the corners as she sat down next to me on the sofa.

"I asked Kokie to bring dinner down here this evening. It will be relaxing. We'll stay cozy and dry while we listen to the rain outside."

"Sounds nice, Mammy. Is this number new? I've never heard Peggy play it before."

"Yes, it's new. She's definitely dedicated to her music—even more so since you've been away at school. But I know if she had the choice, she'd rather be chatting with her sister over a tall glass of lemonade," my mother whispered as she brushed a stray strand of hair away from my face, tucking it gently behind my ear.

A single violin chord sliced through the air. A string of piano notes soon accompanied it, and they blended together in perfect harmony. I closed my eyes as the music washed over me, filling places that had been empty moments before. Mammy's sympathetic hand softly closed over mine. No words were necessary. She understood, and that touched me.

My younger brothers entered the room with Kokie, our cook, teasing her and trying to get a bite of her delicious caramel cake. She smiled and shook her head, obviously pleased at their pleading. I stood up to rescue our dessert from the boys' antics.

I must have grown an inch or two at school because never before had I been able to look at Kokie eye to eye. That's not saying much, though. Our cook was petite in every way, from her tiny wrists and hands to her slight, dancerlike figure that was draped in a pretty, teal-colored sarong. I loved her, just as I loved Nanny, the woman who helped Mammy care for us. They were pure Indonesian women who had worked for our family since we had moved to Tandjoengenim several years ago. Looking at her fondly, I realized how much she meant to me. She and Nanny were like *tantes* to me, aunts in my heart, if not by blood. They were family.

Kokie was just laying out the savory chicken kabobs we were going to eat for dinner when a knock at the door echoed down the hallway. Nanny must have answered it because almost immediately my Uncle Alfred came rushing into the room, his face white and voice breathless, as if he'd sprinted all the way here from his home several streets away. Peggy stopped playing abruptly when she saw the look on his face.

"The radio . . . turn on the radio, Alex. It's happened, just as we feared it might. The Japanese have struck . . . they've attacked the Americans at Pearl Harbor this morning at dawn. It was a complete surprise . . . no one anticipated it!" He stopped to catch his breath, while we all sat silent and bewildered.

"The Japanese air strike was . . . victorious. Most of the American battleships were sunk as well as other U.S. hardware. There was a mass destruction of the U.S. forces in Hawaii. The Japanese disabled them in one fell swoop. I—I am stunned."

Before my uncle could continue, my father bolted out of the door and toward the living room. We all followed after him. As we entered the room, piling on the floor in front of the radio, Pappy adjusted the knob, trying to get the voice from the box as clear as possible so we could hear every word. The best reception he could manage was still scratchy and hollow, but we were so focused on what the newscaster was saying that clarity was the last thing we worried about.

We caught the tail end of the newscast, outlining the attack on the U.S. naval base of operations in Hawaii. The Japanese had launched a well-planned air attack on the base the announcer kept referring to as Pearl Harbor. Five of the eight American battleships stationed there had been severely damaged, possibly even destroyed, as well as most of the Hawaiian-based combat planes. He ended by reiterating that the attack on Pearl Harbor had been completely unexpected and had yielded a lot of destruction. The date was December 7, 1941. What a horrible thing to happen so close to Christmas!

My uncle leaned over and clicked off the radio as a big-band number began to play. He walked over to the window with his hands in his pockets and stared out into the gloom. Pappy sank into his nearby armchair. He covered his face with his hands.

"It's begun," he said wearily.

"What's begun, Pappy?" Justin asked eagerly. Eleven-year-old enthusiasm. Somebody should bottle a little of that energy. They would make a fortune.

"For months the West has cut Japan's oil and coal imports, knowing that the Japanese were allied with Germany in this war being waged in Europe. Since Japan needs petrol and coal to run their military equipment, they are desperate to find it elsewhere. Uncle Alfred and I suspect that Indonesia and Malaysia will be prime targets for the Japanese, as these islands are rich in resources of all kinds. It appears that Japan strategically chose to attack the Americans at Pearl Harbor because now their Pacific fleet is disabled. They can't come to our rescue. Without that threat, Japan has free rein to invade Indonesia, Malaysia, the Philippines . . . anywhere that will restock their oil reserves, coal bins, or what have you."

"Alex, are you saying we may be in danger of invasion?" my mother asked incredulously.

"That's exactly what I am saying." We all sat in silence, contemplating exactly what that meant for us in Sumatra.

"Unfortunately, we're sitting ducks," my uncle chimed in. "We have virtually no military strength with which to protect ourselves, and it could be months before the Dutch can get here to help us. Besides, they've got their own problems fighting off Hitler's Nazis."

"We need to prepare ourselves as soon as possible for invasion," my father said as he raked his fingers through his hair. "I don't mean to alarm anyone, but those that are prepared will have less to fear."

"Pappy, my train leaves for school first thing tomorrow morning. How will I get back home if an invasion should happen?" I whispered. My tone was strangled, even to my own ears. I gulped down a bitter mouthful of fear.

"You won't be going back to school, Hanny. Nobody knows what Japan's timetable is, but we must not split up regardless. Until we know more, you'll stay here at home with us," my father said resolutely.

"But I only brought a weekend bag with just a few things. Everything else is still at school. How will I get my clothes and shoes, all my belongings?" I asked. The enormity of the situation was starting to sink in for me. We were in real danger. There was no way Pappy would postpone my education otherwise. He was scared, and his fear permeated my skin, settling deep into my bones.

"I'm sorry, darling, but you'll just have to make do for now. We'll see if the nuns at the school will send a parcel with your things, but my guess is they'll be busy with other frantic parents. Maybe Peggy has some clothes you could borrow for the time being. What do you say, Peg?"

"Hanny's gotten taller since she's been away. I don't think anything I have will be long enough for her," Peggy said doubtfully.

"I don't think they will be able to share much," Mammy said. "But surely I can whip up a couple of new dresses for Hanny. I've already got one packed away that I'd planned to give her for Christmas, and I have enough extra fabric for two or three more."

"We have a lot to do in the next few days, but, by all means, making Hanny some clothes is a priority." Closing the blinds, my father stood up and stretched. He walked over to my mother and put his hand on her shoulder.

"Let's make an early night of it. Tomorrow's going to be a big day. I'll need the boys' help after breakfast, Tina. Dress in your oldest clothes, boys," Pappy said as he turned to walk my uncle to the door.

"If anyone is interested in dinner, Kokie's kabobs and cake are still set out in the parlor," Mammy suggested halfheartedly.

No one felt very hungry after the news we had just received. Even twelve-year-old George, whose primary goal in life was to eat as much food as humanly possible, declined. No one had the stomach for it.

Our little party broke up. It had begun with high hopes for a relaxing evening but had ended with each of us scared and nervous about what the future held. We were unnaturally quiet as we said good night and departed for our bedrooms. Peggy and I whispered for a few minutes about Pearl Harbor and the Japanese and what it might mean for us, but we knew so little about it that our conversation soon lagged.

After shrugging on my pajamas, I lay in bed, curled into a tense and fearful ball, thinking of the night's events. When sleep finally did visit me, it was not restful. I felt like I had been sucked into a vortex of strange images. Giant metal monsters lay groaning on their sides, wounded by shiny, buzzing birds flying overhead. As the birds hit each monster, the gaping hole would burn, but instead of oozing blood, smoke streamed out of it as the great beasts writhed and sunk down into the cool, dark depths below them. I could hear screams in the distance, and an ever-present buzzing sound as the fatally wounded beasts, colossal and smooth, slipped to their watery deaths.

***

Shaking off the images from my bad dreams, I rolled out of bed and tried to salvage my crumpled dress from the night before. It was the only one I had with me that was still halfway presentable, unless I wanted to wear my scratchy school uniform. I grimaced at the thought. As I looked in the mirror, another thought crossed my mind. A faint shadow of a smile lit my face.

Mammy was meticulous about how we dressed. We always had to look pressed and polished, like we had just stepped out of a bandbox. She was a wonderful seamstress. Mammy prided herself on the fact that we were the best-dressed children in Tandjoengenim. Many afternoons I would find her sitting in the garden, scouring American magazines for a glimpse of what the latest famous actors and actresses were wearing. She could replicate anything.

I wagered Mammy would take one look at my wrinkled shift dress and get busy. I knew she would die rather than allow me to leave the house looking slovenly. Hence, the smile.

I padded down the hallway toward the living room where I saw a side lamp still lit. I silently skidded to a stop as I spotted Mammy asleep on the settee, her glasses perched haphazardly on her face.

In her hands rested a soft, rose-colored dress with tiny sprigs of green peeking through the pattern. At her feet, I spotted a baby blue dress, folded in a neat pile. Any lighthearted teasing I had planned died on my lips when I realized Mammy had been up most of the night fulfilling her promise of providing me with new dresses as soon as possible. My lips trembled at the thought.

Smoothing back a lock of dark hair that had fallen on her face, I leaned down and kissed her cheek. She started awake, catching her glasses as they fell to the side.

"Oh, you startled me, Hanny. Is it eight o'clock already?" she said, stretching. "I must have dozed off. Here, take a look at these dresses. The blue one is finished, and all I need on the pink dress is to gauge how long we want the hem."

I fought back tears, which didn't go unnoticed. Mammy patted my hand, a look of concern wrinkling her brow. I smiled, trying to reassure her that I was fine. My girlish plans of moments ago faded as I thought about what a tremendous woman my mother was—elegant and accomplished to the world and a loving wife and mother at home. I hoped to be half the woman Mammy was when I grew up.

Minutes later, the pounding that had awakened me resumed. I realized it was my brothers and father who were making the noise, not my throbbing head as I had imagined earlier. Mammy and I went to inspect the damage the boys were inflicting with their hammers. The cold cellar was a beehive of activity. The food dishes Kokie often stored in this little shed of a room were shoved aside, and hammers and other curious tools took their place. Pappy waved a hello as we walked through the door. We watched him wipe streams of sweat from his face with a folded handkerchief he'd taken from his pocket before continuing his job of ripping up wooden boards from the cellar floor.

"Hey, Hanny! You've finally come to see what we *men* are up to, have you?" Justin yelled over the banging of George's hammer. He was sticking his chest out, obviously impersonating his favorite film hero, Tarzan. I had to smile. I could count his ribs through the thin shirt he wore. Justin's body hadn't caught up to his mouth yet, but I had to give him credit for trying.

Justin and George were close. There was only a year between them, but while Justin was still a typical boy, George was starting to hit puberty. Within the last few months, he had gained a bottomless pit for a stomach. From what my mother had told me, he had taken to following Kokie around like a lost puppy, always panting after her for a taste of this or another helping of that, batting his big brown, puppy-dog eyes to get in her good graces. Thank goodness our cook was eternally patient.

George had some redeeming qualities as well. Out of the four of us, he was the animal lover. He was always with our animals, watching over them and caring for them.

I learned from Mammy that Pappy and the boys had started their demolition project just after dawn, and, by the looks of it, they were well on their way to completing the hole in the ground. She said Pappy anticipated that the Japanese would ransack our valuables when they invaded Sumatra and my father would do everything within his means to prevent them from stealing our possessions.

"What kinds of things does he plan to bury away, Mammy?" I asked, curious to know how big the hole needed to be.

"I'm not certain of all he plans to stow away down there, but I do want to make sure your grandmother's jewelry is safely hidden. I think I may entrust some of the more precious pieces to a friend, maybe Kokie, but the less valuable jewelry will be fine buried in the hole. In fact, I think I will just go and make sure they are boxed and ready for your father when he needs them," she said as she slipped out the door.

I watched as George fought a vicious brawl with a particularly stubborn board. His flushed face looked as determined as the wooden plank appeared to be. Noticing his scuffle, Pappy lent him a hand. The board then quickly gave way, exposing a new patch of dirt. Pappy dug in his shovel, expanding the hole to about three or four feet in diameter. Justin was in charge of the wheelbarrow, hauling away the boards and dirt as quickly as they were discarded. They were working hard, and I wanted to help.

"Pappy, what can I do?" I called to him over the noise.

"Well, we are almost ready to start burying our treasures, Hanny. Peggy just ran over to Uncle Alfred's house to see if they want anything kept safe. Why don't you go to the kitchen and collect the two sets of china we bought in Holland a couple of years ago? The ones for you girls' hope chests? We'll also need the silverware we picked up there. Kokie can help you carry them out if they're too heavy, okay?"

I nodded and set off on my assignment. As I collected the items my father had asked for, the hard, black seed of fear that had planted itself in my heart last night started to sink its tenacious roots deep into my soul. I knew without a doubt that my quiet, tidy little life was changing forever, and I didn't like it. All of the security we had enjoyed during our time here in Tandjoengenim was being dug up and disheveled, like the dirt and floorboards in the other room. A weight like none I'd ever known loomed over us, balancing haphazardly, threatening to fall—promising to fall.

By nightfall, the hole was finished. Our treasure chest of china, silver, gold, and other items of sentimental value was buried deep in the earth. A freshly laid cement floor hid the hole. I wondered at my father's ingenuity, but my amazement at his resourcefulness would reach new heights the following morning.

I awoke to find him tinkering with an old brown suitcase Mammy used occasionally for weekend getaways. It was dented and dinged. There were black smudges from dirty railway floors on both sides. It was an eyesore; there was no other word for it. I secretly thought Mammy kept it solely because it had been one of the cases she had clutched as a new bride on her honeymoon trip.

"'Morning, Hanny! Hand me that pair of pliers, will you? I just need to pry back this piece of cardboard, and we'll be set."

"Set to do what?" I asked.

"I'm constructing a secret compartment in this case. Just a small area where we can store our important papers—insurance policies, investments, that sort of thing."

I felt the small seed of fear continue to grow, sprouting nasty little vines that began constricting my heart.

"Why would we need that, Pappy? We're not planning a trip, are we?" I asked, yearning desperately for his reassurance that all would be well. A note of fear must have slipped into my question because he glanced at me swiftly before he replied.

"No, dear. We aren't planning a trip, at least not yet. It's just a precaution. That's all."

We were silent for a moment, both lost in our own thoughts. I heard him clear his throat, and when he spoke, his voice was low and soothing.

"Hanny, we have to prepare ourselves for anything. For the past two days we've been preparing ourselves physically, but we need to prepare emotionally, too. Each of us must. We prepare for the worst but always, always hope for the best. Do you understand what I'm saying?"

The vines tightened their grip on my heart until I couldn't breathe. Fear was sucking the air out of me. All I knew was that I had to leave the room. I had to get away from that dingy, old suitcase that had the unknown packed away in it. I turned and ran out of the house and into the sunshine.

I kept running until I reached my father's bird sanctuary. It was a small, fenced-in area at the end of our yard. I wrenched open the door, seeking the solitude and peace my father always seemed to find there. It was one of his favorite haunts.

I heard the flutter of wings as I entered. I imagine the birds weren't accustomed to a noisy teenager entering their quiet domain. There was a little bench on one side where Pappy liked to sit and think. I sat on it, trying to restore the quiet—not just the quiet of the sanctuary but the quiet inside me, too.

Before long, I heard the birds start to twitter and talk to one another. Apparently they had restored their order, but I had not restored mine. I closed my eyes and listened to them chatting like little old ladies at a quilting bee.

A short time later, the door opened quietly. The scent of my father's aftershave wafted toward me as he silently took a seat beside me. The spicy, masculine smell reassured me, as it had since I was a toddler climbing onto his knees after a bad dream. I breathed in the familiar scent, and it gave me strength. I smiled an apology.

"I'm an idiot, Pappy. Sorry about running out like that, as if you don't have enough on your mind. I guess I'm just scared," I said, leaning my head on his shoulder.

"We're all scared, my dear. That's just part of being human."

"You're scared too?"

"Sure I am. Why do you think I am going to all this trouble to prepare? I have to feel as if I can *do* something, that I can control some small corner of our lives," he said quietly as he gazed up at a cockatoo perched high above our heads. He wrapped his arm around my shoulder. We sat in silence, enjoying the chattering of our feathered friends flitting from one branch to another. My mind wandered away from our little bench as if on wings. I drank in the comfort of sitting there securely, my worries taking a backseat for the time being. My father cleared his throat, and it quickly brought me back from my reverie.

"Hanny, will you promise me something? Promise me that no matter what happens you'll always take care of your mother."

I was confused about why he would bring up Mammy at a time like this. I looked up at him, trying to gauge his intentions. His eyes were not easy to read.

"Of course, Pappy. I'll always take care of Mammy. I . . . I love her," I said, my words tumbling out, each dripping with the unspoken question, *Where is this conversation going?* Pappy patted my head absently, as if now his thoughts were taking flight.

"I know you will, my dear. You're a strong person, Hanny, loyal and devoted—stronger than you know, I think. I just needed to hear you say it, that's all." He sighed, looking around the sanctuary.

"Are you ready to head back inside now? I want to finish my work on that suitcase this morning."

"All right, Pappy."

Hand in hand, we headed back to the house to continue our preparations, leaving our conversation and our little bird friends behind for another day.

2

Duty

OUR CHRISTMAS SEASON PASSED PEACEFULLY that winter of '41, with no
threats from outside our borders. Lights and music were the hallmarks of
our holiday celebration. We had our Christmas tree in the living room—
not the traditional evergreen we heard about in storybooks but a deciduous
tree from our island. Evergreens were not to be had on Sumatra anywhere.
Our little Christmas tree was beautiful in its own right, though. With
candles lighting its leaves, it looked luminescent. I wouldn't have traded it
for all the fir trees in the world.

On Christmas Eve, Peggy played traditional carols at the piano: "Away
in a Manager," "O Little Town of Bethlehem," and, my personal favorite,
"Silent Night." Afterward we sat around the Christmas tree, and Mammy
read us the nativity story from Luke 2 by candlelight, as she had each year
since we could remember. Her voice, soothing and soft, almost lulled me
to sleep. Tiredly, I looked around at my brothers. Justin was curled up like
a kitten, sleeping peacefully on the tree skirt. He looked so still lying there;
all the spunk and fervor had been put to rest for the night. I caught Peggy's
eyes, and the two of us smiled. She reached over and grabbed a soft throw
from the settee and gently covered him.

Our little family gathering broke up soon after. Pappy lifted Justin in
his strong arms and carried him to his room, tiptoeing down the hallway.
Peggy and I crawled into our beds as well. Tomorrow would be a busy day,
with guests coming for dinner soon after our noon meal. Mammy always
invited workers from the mine for Christmas dinner. It was usually those
who were without a family nearby with which to share the holiday. She
said holiday dinners always taste better when shared with others.

Peggy and I would help Mammy and Kokie prepare the meal. Traditionally,
we would cut vegetables, stir sauces, or do whatever else was needed. Thoughts

of tomorrow's mouthwatering dinner weaved through my mind until sleep gently took over.

The next morning we all woke early and dressed quickly. There were two dark green dresses hanging on the chair in our room. It was our custom that Mammy sewed Peggy and me a new Christmas dress every holiday season. This year was no exception. Our dresses looked like ones the film stars from America wore, full with clean lines and a playful collar as the focal point.

Sinterklaas had visited late last night after we had all drifted off to sleep. His gifts were simple—a book, new piano music, a ball. Presents were not the emphasis this season. They were just a reminder of the many more precious gifts our family had enjoyed throughout the year.

Peggy and I quickly made our way to the kitchen where Kokie was already in full swing. Mammy was up and about as well. We gave her a quick hug of thanks for our new dresses. Mammy was a gourmet cook, having studied in Paris one of the years we had spent in Holland. She could whip up amazing ragouts, canapés, and all types of succulent dishes. During the holidays, Mammy was in her element. She and Kokie worked together seamlessly, each anticipating what the other was thinking before a word was spoken.

After a morning of trying to help but really succeeding only at getting underfoot, Peggy and I heard laughter and voices in the foyer. After we gave Mammy a pleading look, she gave us permission to go and greet our guests.

Before meeting them, I ran out to the patio where I had stored my centerpiece. It was tradition now that every Christmas season I would hunt through Mammy's garden for the most beautiful flowers in bloom. After careful selection, I would snip them and arrange them into a centerpiece for our dining room table. This year I had found some gorgeous peach-colored dahlias. Knowing they were Mammy's favorite, I'd chosen a handful of those. Yellow and pink roses complemented the rest of the arrangement beautifully, along with some perky little marigolds thrown in for filler. I carefully set the arrangement on the dining room table, admiring my handiwork.

"Your centerpiece looks great, Hanny. Too bad it's so big we won't have any room left on the table for the food," said a muffled voice from under the tablecloth. I could barely make out a familiar snicker.

"George? What are you doing under there?" I softly chided.

"Well, I knew the grown-ups would clam up if I walked into the living room. From under the table, I can eavesdrop perfectly and hear every word they say."

"The question is, why would you want to? Why not go climb a tree or kick around your new ball with Justin or something? Aren't you bored listening to the adults talk about grown-up stuff?" I asked.

"So far it's been pretty dull. I want to hear about the war, though. I keep hoping to catch some word about what's been happening with the enemy. They'll shut right up if they see me snooping around," he whispered from below.

I looked down at my flower arrangement. The skeleton we had all tried to shove under the rug for a few days suddenly showed its bony self, and it was not a pleasant reminder. It seemed as if my family had all made a silent pact that over Christmas we would avoid the topic of war or Pearl Harbor or any impending invasion. I guess we had all just wanted to enjoy a peaceful holiday before facing the uncertainty of the coming year once again.

But the fact was that other countries had already been invaded: the Philippines, Burma, Malay. Each time we read the newspaper, Japan's military influence appeared to extend further, their trophies mounting. It had reached the point where I dreaded seeing the paper sitting on the side table by Pappy's comfy chair in our sitting room. It only brought more worry.

I glanced at George's dark, wavy hair, barely visible beneath the festive tablecloth. My brother, as young as he was, had shown a mature side, a side worried about the future, a side insistent on being informed, even at the risk of being discovered hiding under the dinner table by an unhappy grown-up.

"I won't tell your secret, George. But you better praise my centerpiece to no end at dinner. No cracks about it being too big or too showy or anything like that. And I want to hear about anything you learn on your little reconnaissance mission. Deal?" I asked.

"Fine. Now stop talking and keep moving before someone suspects I'm here."

The rest of the dinner was uneventful. We ate a delectable meal of chicken crepes with all the fixings, and we had elegant desserts to finish—the chocolate torte with raspberry sauce was my favorite. Our guests seemed to enjoy themselves, "oohing" and "aahing" as each course was brought to the table. The conversation never shifted to anything unpleasant, at least not while we children were around. As disappointed as George was that his covert operation hadn't uncovered anything new about the war, I was secretly pleased. No news might mean that things wouldn't happen as Pappy had predicted. Maybe the Japanese had no plans to invade Sumatra. Maybe we were not going to be part of their insidious plans for Indonesia . . . maybe.

***

A few days after the new year, my hopes were dashed. At breakfast my father announced his intention to help the Dutch Indonesian Army in their preparations for invasion.

The Philippines, already supplied with U.S. troops, was barely holding the Japanese at bay. The other nations Japan had attacked had fallen—and quickly. It was the general opinion of all we knew in Sumatra that our peaceful, green island would not sit unscathed in Japan's insatiable lust for resources to aid its war efforts. All able-bodied men at the mines had been ordered to report to Palembang to meet the nearest army regiment. They were to leave that afternoon.

"We have finished doing what we can to prepare here at home. Now it is my duty to help our country," he announced, ladling himself some porridge. We looked at him, wondering what he meant.

"We don't have the same caliber of military hardware the Japanese do—planes and battleships and that type of thing. Sumatra is a peaceful country, and we have naively relied on Holland to defend us if and when needed. Unfortunately, the Dutch troops are busy securing the motherland from Hitler and his regime. For the time being, we are left to our own devices," Pappy explained.

"But Pappy, what can we do? We have a couple of ramshackle old battleships in the harbor. They're nothing compared to Japan's fleet," Peggy said incredulously, her legs crossed like a pretzel as she listened intently to my father's reply.

"You're right, Peg. Our outdated battleships won't do us much good. But while we don't have the traditional means to ward off our enemy, we can hurt them in other ways. I have been asked to lend my expertise to the effort. In fact, I'm scheduled to meet with the officers in charge this afternoon," my father explained, leaning over his steaming bowl of oatmeal. That sounded mysterious.

"Your expertise? What do you think they mean by that?" I asked interestedly, biting into a ripe plum. Pappy smiled.

"Well, I do play a mean game of soccer, but I gather the army is more interested in my geological expertise. I have a feeling I'll be asked to disable some of our local resources." Pappy worked as a geologist at the mines in Tandjoengenim. He knew all about coal and oil and fuel.

"What? That would be ridiculous! Wouldn't that hurt our side? Why would we disable our own resources?" Peggy asked, clearly outraged.

"What do you think Japan's intention would be if they invaded Sumatra? What do we have that they could possibly be interested in?" Pappy questioned in his "instructor" tone of voice. He was notorious for turning our questions into teaching moments.

"Maybe the Japanese just want us on their side," Justin suggested.

"That's a thought, my boy. But we wouldn't make very powerful allies, would we? We don't have many troops, and we just determined that we don't have much equipment that would be useful to them. What *do* we have, though, that Japan might want?"

"Resources," I guessed.

"Bingo, Hanny. Resources. We have oil fields, coal mines, agriculture, gold, and ore. Japan has been in search of resources for some time now— oil to gas their planes, coal to run their ships, metal to build guns and tanks. We have what the Japanese are most in need of." He glanced at us to see if we understood. We did. Sumatra had been blessed with all sorts of assets the Japanese might find useful. Since the 1600s, the Dutch had been skimming the cream off of Sumatra, a land rich in minerals and money crops. Sumatra was the precious ruby in the cap of Dutch imperialism, the means by which the Netherlands had funded many of their expenses. Why wouldn't Japan do the same?

"Your grandfather predicted a decade ago that the Japanese were after our metal ore. They bought quite a bit of our metal back in the 1930s. *Opa* predicted then that we'd get it all back in bombs. It looks like he may have been right," sighed my father, soberly finishing his breakfast.

I looked up to see my mother in the doorway, her arms folded and her body leaning against the frame. She looked lost in thought. She was massaging her forehead, a telltale sign that she was worried. Whenever she was sad or anxious, she would rub her forehead as if to erase the harrowing thoughts that plagued her mind.

I realized Mammy was worried about Pappy leaving this afternoon. They were very close. Like two cogs in a wheel, they fit together perfectly. Maybe she felt that same achy seed of fear in her heart that had planted itself in mine weeks before. I tried to catch her eye, but she had a dreamy look that confirmed her thoughts were not in the present.

"Ah, Tina, there you are," my father called as he noticed her in the doorway. She jumped as she riveted her attention on his voice and away from her thoughts.

"Sorry. I was miles away. Did you all get enough to eat?" Mammy asked.

"Tina, this is important. I am not sure what's going to happen this afternoon. Kretzer and I may be asked to leave with the army directly, though I hope I will be allowed to see you all beforehand. But, if not, I want you to be prepared," Pappy said as he rose to join Mammy at the head of the table.

With his arm around Mammy's shoulder, Pappy continued, "Tina, if the Japanese do come while I am gone, you must remember to take that old brown suitcase at all costs. Our important documents are stored in the secret compartment at the bottom, like I showed you. No matter what time of day or night they come, keep that suitcase handy. Sleep with it next to your bed if you must. If the Japanese make you leave with them, take the case with you—if they will allow it, of course." My father spoke with strains of urgency lacing his voice. Mammy nodded that she understood, a worried look in her dark brown eyes. Then Pappy turned to us.

"Children, you are not to go outside to play if I am asked to leave." He put up his hand to stop the boys' protests before they left their lips.

"It is not safe. I know you've had free rein of this place, but no more. If the Japanese came while you were outside, who knows what they might do. Let Kokie and Nanny go out and get groceries and the things you need. They will be safe from the enemy.

"I am sorry that this is how our lives must be for a while. I just don't trust the Japanese. I've heard stories, rumors from other places . . ." Pappy's voice trailed off.

"Surely, they wouldn't hurt us. Would they, Pappy?" I asked.

"I don't know. Let's just say that I would feel safer if I knew you weren't out roaming around. I hate to even mention it, but, in other places, there are rumors about some of the local women becoming concubines for the Japanese soldiers. Whether or not it is by choice, I don't know." His voice was barely a whisper as he uttered the last of what he had to say. Our gasps stopped him short.

"Alex! My word. What an awful thought," Mammy replied in disbelief.

"I don't mean to frighten you. Honestly, I don't," he said, rubbing Mammy's shoulders. "But you do need to be cautious. We don't know what we may be up against. Just to play it safe, stay as close to home as possible. Please."

Time always seems to run faster when you are trying to hold onto it. Before we knew it, Pappy was kissing each of us good-bye. We ran to our special tree in the front yard and climbed it. I can't count the number of times we had scaled its thick branches to watch for our father coming home from work in the late afternoon. This time we climbed it so we could watch him walk away, his easy, familiar gait taking him who knew where. We kept our eyes glued on him until he looked like a little toy soldier in the distance.

As he walked away, so did some of my security. For someone who wrestled with a shy nature, I took great comfort and reassurance in my father, who always seemed at ease in any situation.

"When will we see him again?" Justin asked as we walked back toward our house. I didn't know quite how to answer. It was the same question that had been reverberating in my mind all morning.

"I wish I knew, Justin. I think the best thing—maybe the only thing— we can do is just what he's asked of us . . . and pray for him. I know that's what Mammy will be doing," I said. I squeezed his hand as we stepped up onto the stoop. Although they weren't regular churchgoers, my mother and father both had a deep and abiding faith in their Heavenly Father.

Turning, I saw Mammy lean over the fence, still facing the direction Pappy had walked, her chin resting on her folded arms. She was surrounded by her flowers, their cheery faces bobbing in the breeze. Her lilac-colored dress blew around her knees. I was tempted to go to her, but watching her expression, I got the feeling she might appreciate a few minutes to herself. I held the door open for Peggy and George and then closed it quietly behind me.

3

The Wait

For the next month and a half, we didn't hear from Pappy. He never returned from Palembang that afternoon in January. We got word from my uncle that Pappy and Mr. Kretzer, his colleague from work, had been directed to join the Royal Netherlands East Indies Army immediately on their trek south. Their operation was covert, which made us feel that Pappy had been right in his guess about what the army wanted from him. Other islands in Indonesia had already practiced the scorched earth policy. They had tried to disable their resources before the Japanese arrived, making it impossible for invaders to benefit from their spoils. Mammy suspected that was what the Dutch Indonesian Army was going to ask of Mr. Kretzer and my father.

The very thought of the wrath they might incur from the Japanese for doing something so blatantly defiant scared my mother. I could tell by her shaky voice as she told us of her suspicions. I saw the way her fingers kept flying to her head to massage away her fears and the dreamy look that would take her thoughts away from us until she was unreachable.

I was afraid too, but I kept my fear trapped inside of me like a caged animal. My brothers and sister looked to me for direction. I couldn't—I wouldn't—let my worry sink its tentacles into them.

In that six weeks or so after Pappy left, Mammy did not waste away, despite her worries. As was typical of her, she set to work. The Red Cross was recruiting women to train as field nurses who would be capable of dressing wounds and doing triage in the event of an invasion. Mammy joined and received her training, like several of the other women in Tandjoengenim. There was only one doctor in our area because we lived in such a remote location. In the event that Tandjoengenim was ever attacked, the women trained in nursing would be worth their weight in gold.

I admired Mammy for trying to help the effort. She was never one to sit back and waste away. She was a doer.

While she was receiving her training, Mammy felt it would be best if we stayed with Mrs. Kretzer in her home. The Kretzers were Mammy and Pappy's best friends, and they didn't have any children of their own. Mrs. Kretzer was lonely with her husband gone and sincerely wanted to be helpful. She was a kind woman, older and a little grandmotherly. I think she enjoyed having us keep her company.

Our days during those months crawled by, slowly and methodically. Time was our adversary, forever holding back the minutes and hours until Pappy returned and we could have our freedom again. We felt a little like captives, holed up inside the Kretzers' home, not able to stretch our legs or come and go at will. Our challenge was to find things to fill the time, but it was too big to fill, stretching on and on. Peggy had the piano, but as much as she loved it, after hours of concentration, even she tired of sitting at the bench plucking those black and white ivory keys.

I spent my time sewing and knitting. I admired Mammy's talent of turning a few simple yards of material into a beautiful, serviceable piece of clothing. I spent those empty weeks sewing and embroidering and trying to improve the knitting I had begun to learn at boarding school.

Sometimes I found myself smiling. Knitting sweaters and scarves seemed so ironic. Who would ever want to wear them here in hot, steamy Sumatra anyway? Still, knitting was a skill, and I wanted to perfect it. Besides, the rhythmic click-clack of the needles was somehow relaxing to me.

The boys read and then looked outside. They drew and then looked outside again. Whatever they did *inside* didn't seem nearly as inviting as being outside where they were used to running and swimming and playing. Being directed to stay inside was probably the most challenging for Justin and George, who yearned to be able to leave the house and play.

"Hanny, *please*. Let us go outside, just for a few minutes. If I read another book, I swear I'll go cross-eyed," pleaded Justin. He grabbed my hand in earnest, making me prick my finger on the needle I was holding.

"Ouch, Justin! That hurt. I'm not your jailer. I wish we could go outside too, but if Pappy asked us to stay inside, we'd better listen," I said for the hundredth time, as I sucked my throbbing fingertip. Even I recognized the petulant tone in my voice.

"I'm worried about Ape and Knorrie," George said, joining us in the window seat. Ape was our pet chimpanzee, and Knorrie, our pig. The boys loved to play with them and tease them. I vividly remembered a time not too long before I left for boarding school that always made me chuckle to think about.

Laughter had drifted through my bedroom window, drawing my attention away from my thoughts to the excitement outside. I poked my head out to find George racing after our pet pig, Knorrie. He was laughing so hard at the short-legged animal that he was falling miserably behind in his attempts to catch him. I yelled my hello, which consequently disrupted the chase, thankfully for the pig. My brother's tan legs crumpled beneath him as he fell to the ground in hysterics.

"George, why are you torturing that poor animal?" I asked, smiling.

"It's not torture, Hanny. The old boy needs his exercise. Knorrie likes our daily game of chase. Without me, he'd be so big that Kokie would be tempted to cook him up for dinner some night," George replied, trying desperately to look innocent.

"That's if he doesn't die of fright first," I said. Then I commented on what a beautiful day it was, breezy and fresh, none of the usual humidity we experienced so often in Sumatra.

George answered distractedly; his attention had already reverted back to Knorrie, who was trying to burrow under the fence with his snout. Silently creeping up behind him, George was on the prowl again. His prey was so busy snorting and scurrying to get out under the fence that he didn't realize his bacon was about to fry. I smiled as I pulled my head back through the window.

George and his pets. He had always loved living things, and he usually had Knorrie chasing at his heels and Ape's long, hairy arms around his neck. He used to carry that chimpanzee around like a toddler. Being away from our pets was particularly hard for poor George.

"What if Kokie forgets to feed them? Or what if they run off or something?" George asked me now, drawing me back to the moment at hand. His voice was anxious. I realized just how worried George was about our animals when I detected a tear glistening in the corner of his eye. Not wanting to embarrass him by drawing attention to it, I stared out the window.

"Kokie is trustworthy, George. She knows how much we love our pets. She will take good care of Ape and Knorrie for us. Did you know Mammy entrusted some of her best jewelry to Kokie before we came here? They were her most precious pieces—the ones she was afraid to bury in the storage room. She wouldn't have done that unless she trusted Kokie completely, would she?" I suggested.

George shook his head silently, still looking out the window. I squeezed his shoulder, knowing he was trying to control his emotions. Justin cradled his head on his folded arms as he too gazed out.

"Where do you think he is, Hanny? Pappy, I mean. It's been almost two months with no word. I guess I didn't think he'd be gone this long."

"I don't know," I replied simply. It was the only answer I had to give him. He'd been asking the same question for weeks now.

"I'm sure he'll be home soon, Justin. All we can do is trust in God to take care of him, like Mammy says," Peggy offered, walking up behind us.

"Yeah, but don't you wonder where he is . . . what he's doing? I mean, it must be important because he would never leave us for this long if the army didn't really need him," George commented.

We all stared out the picture window in Mrs. Kretzer's parlor, each of us wondering where our Pappy was at that very moment and each wishing he were on his way back home to us.

***

The next morning I woke to a dense blackness. Although it was midmorning, outside it looked more like 3:00 AM. An acrid odor filled the room like an ominous cloud. Something was clearly not right, and I was scared. I jumped out of bed, pulled on my robe, and shook Peggy.

"Peggy, wake up, will you? Look outside! It's morning, but it's dark as midnight out there." Peggy groaned as she rolled over.

"What's going on, Hanny? I was just having the most delectable dream about eating chocolate truffles with the queen of Holland. Why are you waking me up already? It's the middle of the night. Go back to sleep."

"Peggy, I'm serious. I checked my watch by the light of the candle in the hallway, which, by the way, is almost burned to a nub. It's 8:20 in the morning!"

Peggy slipped out of bed, and I held out my arm to take hers. Just then we heard Mammy's quiet step outside in the hall.

"Hanny! Peggy, dear. Don't be alarmed. I had to walk here in the dark earlier this morning after my shift at the clinic. Fortunately, it's close by because I had to feel my way along. The air was as black as tar. Before I left the clinic, we received word that the oil fields nearby have been sabotaged. Someone has set the oil on fire so the Japanese can't benefit from it when they come," Mammy whispered.

"Was it Pappy's doing?" Justin's small voice questioned in the dark.

"I don't know, sweetheart. I suspect Pappy might have been involved, but I really don't know for sure. Let's go light some of Mrs. Kretzer's candles. Until we know more, we need to stay in and try not to breathe the fumes from outside. Surely they can't be healthy."

I felt my way along the hall until I joined Mammy and the others in the sitting room. The dirty smell of burning oil enveloped me like the noxious breath of death. It was all I could do to keep from gagging.

Darkness covered our area of Sumatra for nearly three days. The gloom outside settled into our hearts. We lived in a sunny part of the world and generally never went more than a day or so without the sun peeking out, unless it was the rainy season. We'd come to think of it as second nature. A couple of days without light were torturous for us. Finally, on the third morning, we awoke to a dim disk of sun pushing its way through the dark residue in the sky. By day's end, the blackness had been replaced by sunlight. The air still reeked of the burning oil, though, assaulting our senses every time we inhaled.

The following week found us adjusting back to life at the Kretzers'. We took up our pastimes again, our interest renewed after not being able to pursue them in darkness. Peggy tinkled a whimsical tune on the piano, a fairy song of high notes dancing their way through the air. Mammy read a book with Justin, who was fidgeting more than ever now that the sun had returned from its exile. He was clearly itching to be outside. George looked lost in thought as he petted Mrs. Kretzer's cat and idly gazed out the window.

I was just finishing a scarf, knitting a final row on the bright red border. I was wondering wryly if I should send it off to our troops in Holland, where they could actually get some use out of it, when Mari, Mrs. Kretzer's maid, rushed into the room, pouring through the door like water through a dam. Her face was flushed and excited, a strand of dark hair escaping her French twist. Her words tumbled out, not clear enough at first for us to decipher.

"Mari, slow down, dear. What is it you are trying to say? *Who* did you say is here?" questioned Mammy in Malay.

"Mr. Londt-Schultz, madam. He's returned. He's here, in the foyer . . . and he's asking for his wife and children. Come! Come!"

We were up and out of the room before Mari had finished her last sentence, sprinting through the house with Mammy in the lead. We had just rounded the corner leading to the front door when we spotted him. I stopped short at the sight. *What had happened to our father?*

In the doorway, framed by the sunlight, stood a man. Thin, sunburned, unshaven, and disheveled. He was an emaciated shadow of the man I had watched walk away a mere two months before. If his face had not been so infinitely dear to me, I wouldn't have recognized him. He leaned against the wall, not trusting his own strength to hold his weight.

It took a minute for us children to recover from the shock but not our mother. She ran to him immediately, not hesitating for a second. She stroked his hair. She touched his swollen face, her eyes searching his, taking in every part of him. Her strong and capable arms wrapped around him tightly, a sob escaping her lips. Relief, mingled with concern, covered her face.

"Thank God. Thank God, you're alive," she whispered into his neck.

We ran to him then too. I could feel his shoulder blades, sharp and prominent triangles, as I hugged his thin frame. His eyes held a familiar twinkle, and a smile, weak though it was, lit his face. Tears pricked behind my eyes, quickly escaping and streaming steadily down my cheeks. Our father had returned to us. Granted, something horrible had happened, but he was alive. He was with us again. My heart nearly beat out of my chest with joy and gratitude.

We helped him into the sitting room, Peggy plumping the cushions behind him, my mother never letting go of his hand. I sat at his feet, holding his leg, resting my head on his knee. He smelled like dust and perspiration, like he'd been journeying forever. Questions floated in the air unasked as we simply basked in the warmth of our father's being. Justin and George stared at him in awe.

"Pappy, you look like a native or a mountain man or something. What's happened to you?" Justin exclaimed in wonder. We all laughed at his innocent assessment, most of us through tears, but that simple moment of humor relieved some of the tension. Mammy patted Justin's shoulder.

"Let him rest now, darling. We'll learn all about his adventure tomorrow, okay? It'll keep one more day."

I studied my father. His eyes were almost swollen shut. His arms and face were dotted with pink bumps, indicating insect bites. His clothes were ripped and were the cool, rough cotton of a local's traditional clothing. His feet were swollen, and I detected blisters the size of coins through his worn and dusty sandals. Whatever my father had been through, it had been some ordeal. Mammy was right. Our first priority was to get Pappy well and rested.

We shuffled him off to bed after a warm, soothing bath. I watched my mother care for him, gently smoothing the bedclothes over his shoulders, kissing him tenderly, her soft, round cheek lingering next to his.

It reminded me of how she used to nurse me as a child when I had any number of childhood illnesses. During those fitful times, all I had wanted was my mother's capable touch and soothing voice. She had always known just what to do to comfort me. As my father nestled into the pillow, his body relaxing into sleep, I knew my mother had done it once more. Her touch was the perfect balm for what ailed him.

4

Pappy's Adventure

THE DAY DAWNED SUNNY AND radiant, a feeling that reflected in our hearts as we woke to find Pappy reading a newspaper on the sofa. What a familiar sight that was. He looked forward to reading his paper each morning, a ritual never broken once the war had broken out in Europe. And he was even more diligent about poring over the news once Holland was invaded in May 1940.

Pappy's face was still swollen, and the insect bites stood out like chicken pox across his arms and face. His body was quiet, exhausted from its recent ordeal, but he looked restful enough, reclining on the cushions. Mammy, ever present, was hovering nearby, a needle in hand as she hemmed a dress of creamy white material. Pappy's face brightened as he saw us watching him from the doorway.

"Come in, children. Don't be shy. I've missed you all so much. Just wait until you hear the story I have to tell you," Pappy said in a weak, scratchy voice. We inched closer, and each found a comfortable space at his feet, anticipating the tale with eagerness. Justin was wrapped tightly in his blue and white quilt, and though he was yawning, his eyes were alert and eagerly waiting for my father to begin. Lounging next to him, George leaned his tired head against the settee, his black hair unruly and wild from his night's sleep.

Once he saw that we were situated, Pappy began the story of his journey. As he spoke, his eyes had a far-off, dreamy look, like he was reliving his experiences all over again.

"It all seems so long ago. Let's see. After saying good-bye to you that afternoon in January, I arrived in town to find most of the other miners awaiting orders from the military as well. They were milling around the marketplace with their travel bags in hand, discussing the war with friends. Kretzer and I recognized many of them as well as other men from the surrounding area.

"Mr. Beers instructed us to travel to Palembang so we could join a larger regiment that was forming there. As the mine boss, he was asked to stay behind and keep watch over the town while we were gone. I remember he had a kind of wistful look as we shook hands good-bye. I think he wished he could join up too.

"We took the afternoon train and pulled into the Palembang station at dusk. A man in uniform directed us to report to the temporary military headquarters near the town square. Once there, we were quickly introduced to the officer in charge, a colonel from up north. He was a tall man, with a very commanding presence. After recording our names and other information into a ledger, he separated us into different groups according to our abilities.

"When he learned that Kretzer and I were geologists who worked for the coal mines, we were quickly shuffled into the colonel's own tent, where we had a very covert meeting with him and his first officer. The colonel asked us some technical questions about our work and our knowledge of fossil fuels. When he was satisfied we were capable, he lost his formality and seemed relieved. He kept twirling his wedding ring over and over. A nervous gesture, I suppose.

"He told us he had been searching for men with just our skills for quite some time. Apparently, his first officer had heard rumors that two geologists from the mines might have the knowledge to accomplish a significant mission for the army. He said he was relieved to finally meet us. Without going into too much detail, as a lot of it is classified, we were asked to 'take care' of the mines and oil fields, to render them inoperable so the Japanese wouldn't have access to our resources when they invaded Sumatra."

"It's just as you suspected, Pappy. So, was there anyone else assigned to work with you, or was it just you and Mr. Kretzer?" Peggy asked excitedly.

At Peggy's interjection, I glanced at my brothers. Both were watching my father, spellbound as they stared into his face. Mammy was looking down at her sewing, but her brows were knit together in concentration; I knew she was listening intently to every word my father was saying.

"Only the two of us were asked to go," Pappy answered. "I think the idea was that a pair of us sneaking into some of these areas would be harder to detect than a whole squad of men. We were given a map with different locations starred in red. Each of the stars represented a mine or an oil field we would need to disable. We were issued knapsacks with a few provisions, a compass, and the chemicals and tools necessary to complete our task. After we'd finished our assignment, Kretzer and I were to make our way down to the southernmost tip of Sumatra, near Lampoeng Bandar, and connect with the rest of our regiment at a rendezvous point in a small harbor nearby. After that, we were to sail to Java to help the Royal Netherlands East Indies Army secure the island against the Japanese.

"We bunked with the other men in the regiment that first night. Then at dawn we were up and out of the camp right after breakfast. An unmarked truck dropped us near our first site. We spent the next several hours watching the mining facility from the jungle. That was one of the worst parts of our assignment. It was tedious sitting still, but we had to so we wouldn't be detected. And we were like a free gourmet lunch for every insect in the surrounding area. That's where I started collecting my beautiful pink polka dots."

We laughed. I was amazed my father could keep his sense of humor after all he had been through, but maybe humor was the perfect response to this craziness. Maybe it had helped him stay sane.

"Hiding in the jungle was a surveillance of sorts, to make sure no one was there at the mining facilities. The last thing we wanted to do was have someone injured because of what we were doing. We also needed to be sure the Japanese weren't watching the area.

"After our surveillance, we had to prepare our solutions and let them set up. It was a full moon that first night, I remember. At first, we were pleased, thinking it would enable us to see what we were doing. Soon, though, self-preservation set in. We realized that if *we* could see clearly by night, so could any lurking Japanese soldiers who might be on the lookout. We were scared we'd get caught before we finished our directive. We used the trees as cover as well as boulders, underbrush, anything that might keep us from being seen.

"Once we were inside the facility, things went smoothly. Kretzer and I have worked together long enough to anticipate each other's needs without a word. We completed our task quickly and quietly. We snuck back out and were safely in the cover of the forest again in no time."

I realized I'd been holding my breath the whole time my father had been talking. My lungs burned as I exhaled. I caught Peggy's eye. She raised her eyebrows in disbelief. This was our father? He sounded like a spy or a highly trained soldier, not the pleasant, easy-mannered man we'd grown up with our whole lives.

My father started coughing then, a weak hack that rattled his body. My mother immediately pushed aside her sewing and knelt by his side. She ran her hand across his forehead and laid her head on his chest listening to him breathe. As she stood, she had the same steely expression on her face that I recognized from her previous nursing experiences.

"Your father needs his rest now, children. He really shouldn't be talking this much." She put up her hand to squash the argument about to spew forth from my brothers' lips. They stopped and looked down as she continued in a gentler tone, "He's still not well. Let's give him a rest. If he feels up to it, you can talk to him some more this afternoon. In the meantime, pack your things. Now that Pappy is home, we shouldn't impose on Mrs. Kretzer's hospitality any longer. We can go home now."

There was a whoop of excitement from the boys as they jumped up and flew down the hall to collect their books and clothes and other belongings that lay scattered in the room they shared.

Peggy and I looked at Pappy, worried we had overexerted him on his first day back. Mammy put her arms around us.

"He'll be okay, girls. He just needs a rest."

I leaned over my father's swollen, sunbaked face, freckled with insect bites, and softly kissed his cheek. His tired eyes fluttered open and a weak smile lit up his face.

"All's well, love. I'll see you both in a bit," he said sleepily. Peggy and I quietly closed the door behind us, our imaginations running rampant as we mulled over all our father had seen and done during the time he had been away from us.

Peggy let out a huge sigh as she exclaimed, "What an adventure he's had. No wonder he needs a nap."

I laughed as we raced to pack our things too. I couldn't wait to sleep in my own bed.

***

We arrived home at dusk. The yellow roses in Mammy's garden looked like dim lamps as the car stopped at our front gate. Mammy had arranged for Mr. Beers, the mine boss, to drive us from the Kretzers' to our home a few streets away. I saw Mr. Beers's worried look as he glanced in the mirror to peer at Pappy, his watery blue eyes darting back and forth every few seconds. He was silent, though I am sure he had some of the same questions we all had.

Mammy gratefully shook Mr. Beers's hand in parting, assuring him that Pappy would contact him in a few days when he felt better. We were already hurrying down the front walk to the door. Mammy's hand trembled as she tried to get the key in the lock. Peggy and I were holding Pappy's arms as he leaned against the porch and looked out over the front lawn. It was as if he were seeing everything for the first time.

I felt different as I walked inside. The clock on the mantel, Pappy's comfortable chair, Mammy's settee, the colorful Persian rug under the coffee table—they were like old friends greeting me after a long time away. I was happy to see them, stopping briefly in the hallway to breathe in the comfortable peace of being home.

Before we had even finished unpacking, there was a soft knock at the front door. A shadow of worry immediately covered Pappy's face. He was cautious as he approached the entryway, but Mammy flew past him and yanked open the door.

There stood Kokie on the front step, with Ape climbing on her shoulder and Knorrie chasing circles around her feet, grunting all the while. George shoved past us all, hugging Kokie as he gently extracted her from Ape's long arms and wiry legs. Our hairy chimp friend seemed as delighted to see George as George was to see him. They did some kind of monkey dance together in the doorway before Mammy shuffled us all inside, with the exception of Knorrie, who was perfectly happy rooting his merry way around Mammy's garden, sniffing for who-knows-what in the shrubbery.

"Oh, Kokie, when I sent a message to your village telling you we were coming back home, I expected you tomorrow at the very earliest. You must have flown here," exclaimed Mammy as she took one of the bags out of our cook's arms and hugged her.

Kokie seemed choked up as she set down another worn suitcase and replied, "Miss Tina, I must admit, I had been hoping for word from you for weeks. These children feel like my own, and my little cottage seems quiet after the hustle and bustle of life here. Thank goodness I had Ape and Knorrie for company. How is Mr. Alex, though? He doesn't look well."

We all glanced into the sitting room where Pappy was resting in his favorite chair, already half asleep. I thought he looked improved, his insect bites less apparent on his face and his cheeks not so burned and swollen.

"I'm fine, Kokie, just fine. Thought I'd put my feet up for a minute, that's all," Pappy said jovially, his eyes still shut.

"He's been through something horrible, Kokie. We haven't gotten many details from him yet, and we haven't wanted to push him. I'm hoping he'll start feeling better tomorrow," Mammy confided in a whisper, still looking at her husband with a hint of worry marring her forehead.

"Well, I'll go boil him some of my chamomile tea. It works wonders. For dinner, I thought I'd cook up some of his favorite seafood bisque. I bought a loaf of bread and some milk on my way into town, so I'll get started right away." She picked up her suitcase and turned to go. As she passed Pappy, I saw the fleeting look of compassion on her face.

"It's good to have you home with us, Kokie," I said, giving her a quick hug. Her shoulders were so petite that she reminded me of a little bird, but her smallness belied her inner strength. I saw the swift flash of her smile as she continued down the hall to the kitchen, her silk sari swishing softly back and forth as she walked.

After dinner, Pappy felt better. He assured Mammy he felt well enough to continue his story. We all gathered in the sitting room once more, excited to hear the rest of Pappy's tale. I glanced at Mammy. She was threading her needle, poised to begin sewing again as she listened. I wondered what she thought so far of Pappy's adventure. Her husband had put himself in harm's way to serve his country. Was she proud, angry, or maybe just relieved that he was safe? It was difficult to tell. My attention was drawn back to Pappy as he cleared his throat.

"Let me think. I believe I was telling you about that first day on our mission. Well, after Kretzer and I returned to the jungle, we knew we couldn't be found near the area when the mines were discovered to be disabled, so we journeyed the rest of that night to our next target. We figured that it would be safer to travel under the cover of darkness and sleep while it was light. We found a nice secluded place in the jungle and slept in shifts that following day. Not the most comfortable digs, with the heat and the mosquitoes, but at least we were safe from curious eyes. We saw no one that day as we stayed away from the beaten path.

"At dusk, we continued on. Geographically, we were closest to a remote oil field, so we arrived and hit that before dawn broke. I remember feeling sad that we were destroying such a useful substance. As the wreaths of smoke rose into the sky, I wished it didn't have to be so . . . that we didn't have to waste this fuel that had been brewing and percolating underground for millions of years. I guess that was the geologist in me talking. It just seemed like such an awful waste.

"Looking back, that night was one of my hardest, morally speaking. Always the voice of reason, Kretzer brought me back to reality, though, reminding me of the damage the enemy could wreak on us and others with all of the coal and oil we have stored here in Sumatra. It was our duty to aid our country—plain and simple. I clung to that thought every night after that.

"During the next couple of weeks, we visited all of the facilities on our map. We felt an urgency to keep pushing forward because in all of the villages we'd skirted on our trip, we'd heard rumors of the Japanese invading Sumatra from the north. We knew it was only a matter of time before the enemy made their way down to us in the south.

"Once, we were so close to Tandjoengenim that we could have snuck back here for a few hours. It was very tempting because we missed our families so much, but it would have put us and our mission in grave danger, not to mention our loved ones. We couldn't risk it," Pappy said apologetically.

"Was that the night the oil fields outside of town burned? It was dark for almost three days, and we wondered if you had done it," Peggy said from her perch on the arm of Pappy's chair.

"Yes, that was us, I'm afraid. I'm sorry the effects of the oil burning were so long-lived. I had no idea," answered Pappy softly, looking troubled.

"Keep going, Pappy. Tell us why it took you so long to come home. We looked for you every day," Justin said with a hint of impatience in his voice.

"Well," Pappy said thoughtfully. "Sometimes we had to travel several days, walking at night and sleeping during the day before we reached our next destination. Kretzer and I were exhausted by the time we had crossed off the last coal mine from our map. We had to finish our assignment within a certain allotted time frame because we had agreed to meet the rest of our unit on the southernmost shore of Sumatra, near Lampoeng Bandar, on a given date. We pushed ourselves to finish and still have travel time to meet the rest of the troops.

"We walked at a brisk pace, not sleeping much those last few nights. But on the final morning, we noticed that the rich brown soil under our feet had become a little grainy. Before long, the jungle canopy began to thin, and by midday we saw the blue of the ocean through the last few trees. What a sight to behold. The waves were gentle and the water calm. I remember it was the most beautiful shade of turquoise. Kretzer and I stood and marveled at it for the longest time. We walked along the shore until we found the little harbor that was to be our rendezvous point the following morning. We discovered a secluded spot near the jungle entrance to set up camp, and then we went swimming," Pappy said. His eyes grew dreamy as he remembered the ocean.

"I can't tell you how soothing the water felt after the heat of the jungle. We glided and floated in the cool depths. Swimming never felt so good, let me tell you. After awhile, though, we were both so fatigued from our assignment of the last few weeks that we crawled onto the beach and fell asleep. I don't know how long I was out, but when I awoke it was to the delicious smell of dinner sizzling on an open fire. Kretzer had caught a couple of nice-sized fish and some crab and was cooking them. I was nervous that someone might see the smoke, so we put the campfire out quickly. The whole time we were gone, I felt a little like we were fugitives. I guess we were in a way. Did we ever enjoy that meal, though. I'll never forget how sweet and succulent that crab tasted.

"Afterward, we watched the sun set over the water, changing it from blue to a beautiful amber. We called it a night soon after that and slept on the beach, high up and away from the tide. The waves lapping onto the sand were relaxing, and we fell asleep in no time. I think that afternoon at the beach with Kretzer was my best memory of the whole trip," Pappy said nostalgically.

"It sounds amazing, Pappy. I'm glad you had that time to relax a little after all you'd been through," I said, hugging his leg.

He patted my head and then continued. "Well, Kretzer and I awoke early the next morning feeling pretty rested, all things considered. We broke camp and then sat near the harbor and waited. We waited and waited for the rest of the unit to arrive. We had no idea if they were coming by land or sea, so we just waited and watched, confident that they would soon arrive. By noon, we were starting to wonder what was keeping them. Maybe the group had been held up by something unforeseen. They had no way of contacting us to let us know if they had been delayed. We hadn't been issued a radio or anything like that.

"We even checked our compass bearings to make sure we had made it to the correct harbor. Kretzer had been keeping track of the days since we had left, so we knew our timing was accurate. As near as we could tell, we were in the right place at the right time. It was the regiment that was late, not us.

"We waited all afternoon, enjoying our scenic view of the ocean. We even slipped in a quick swim before dinner to get rid of the sticky heat of the day. Just like before, we felt refreshed and alive as we played and swam in the waves. We didn't chance a fire that evening, but we ate some raw fish and coconuts for dinner.

"We figured something unexpected had delayed the troops. Surely they would arrive sometime that evening or the following morning. We took turns keeping watch that night, but nothing happened. All the next day, we waited and watched. No one came. Over dinner we discussed our options. We could continue waiting, but it had been more than forty-eight hours since our meeting time had come and gone. We figured something had happened and the officers' plans had changed. Maybe they had to take a different route to Java, or worse, maybe the Japanese had thwarted their plans somehow. It was our understanding that a ship would be there to meet us. Maybe they had gone ahead out of necessity.

"We decided to explore the coast a little the following morning. We had to be somewhat secretive because we didn't know what the situation was like with the Japanese. We'd been out of the loop for the last few weeks, not having talked to anyone during our mission.

"As we were walking, I noticed a red-tiled roof not far down the shore, kind of tucked away in the jungle. We got as close as we could to the building to do a little reconnaissance. Before long, we saw several men walking through the gardens behind the building. We could easily see their plain brown robes. They were monks. The building we had found was a Catholic monastery, and we were excited. We knew we would be safe within those walls until we could figure out what to do next," Pappy said. He was beginning to look a little haggard after his time in the family spotlight.

I looked around. We'd been glued to Pappy's story for almost an hour. The sun had set, and it was getting dark outside. Mammy had long since stopped sewing, her attention captured by the thrilling story my father told. Our eyes met, and, once again, her mama-bear protectiveness surfaced.

"Alex, dear. It's getting late. Aren't you tired out after all you've been through? Why not wrap it up until tomorrow morning? We can wait to hear the rest until then, can't we, children? I'll have Kokie draw you a hot bath, and you can soak for as long as you like. It will help those insect bites and your blistered feet," Mammy persuaded, her voice gentle but with a firm edge.

"Well, a warm bath *does* sound relaxing, and I think I might like a little more of Kokie's shellfish soup, too. Do you mind if we finish this up in the morning, children?"

"Of course not, Pappy. You enjoy your bath," I said quickly, giving my two younger brothers "the eye" before they got any ideas. Peggy followed my lead.

"Yes, good night, Pappy. I need to get a little practice time in anyway, and I heard Hanny say she would love to play a game of Snap with George and Justin before bed. Isn't that right, boys?"

Surprisingly, the boys got the hint and reluctantly waved good night to Pappy as Mammy led him down the hall, arm in arm, to the bathing room.

5
Journey Home

PAPPY LOOKED MUCH STRONGER THE following morning. The insect bites were fading quickly, and some had already disappeared. His eyes were no longer swollen, and yesterday's sunburn was transforming into a healthier looking tan. He was quick to smile when we met him and Mammy on the back patio.

They were just finishing their traditional cup of tea and eating hot, flaky biscuits that Kokie had baked earlier that morning. We joined them around the table and dug in ourselves, buttering biscuits and helping ourselves to fresh *durian*, which would soon be at its ripest. It was my favorite Sumatran fruit; I loved to squeeze each succulent section between my teeth, always surprised by the little burst of sweet juice it produced. Justin, complete with a milk mustache and crumbs on his collar, pleaded with Pappy to continue his story where he'd left off the night before.

"Remember, Pappy. You'd just discovered the monastery hidden on the edge of the jungle. What happened next?" Pappy laughed at Justin's earnest expression.

"Yes, thank goodness we noticed that roof nestled in the trees. Kretzer and I watched the monks come and go for a good half hour before we felt safe enough to approach their complex. After observing them, we were convinced they were the peaceful, religious men you'd expect. We watched some of them gather herbs and plants from their beautifully manicured garden. Others sat silently reading from their Bibles and other books. Some of the monks just walked along the shady paths—quietly pondering life, I imagine.

"Kretzer and I approached the garden slowly, with our hands in the air to show the residents we meant them no harm. After nearly a month in the jungle, we were looking very disheveled. Kretzer had a scraggly, salt-

and-pepper-colored beard, and we were both sunburned and in dire need of a hot shower. Our clothes, issued by the military, had seen better days as well. We were well aware of how frightening we must have appeared to strangers.

"To the monks' credit, though, they were kind to us right from the start. We explained our situation: that we had been waiting to meet a larger group of soldiers farther along the shore two days before but had apparently been stranded. Brother Tomás and Brother Matteo kindly took us to the head of the monastery, Father Jean-Paul.

"He was an unassuming little man who radiated sincerity. He was slightly built, with a bald dome that glistened in the sun. After greeting us warmly, Father Jean-Paul ushered us into his own personal suite of rooms and hurried off to make us some herbal tea. Oh, how good that hot drink tasted as we rested comfortably in his sitting area. Looking around, we saw the sparseness one would expect from a monk who had made vows of poverty and sacrifice, yet his rooms emanated the kind of quiet you cannot manufacture anywhere else. It was the stillness of a man at peace with God, himself, and his world.

"We repeated our story to Father Jean-Paul of having somehow missed the rendezvous with our regiment two mornings before. He didn't seem surprised. In fact, the little harbor down the coast was very familiar to him as a covert meeting place for soldiers who were arriving on the island or leaving Sumatra for other destinations. We learned that in recent days, he and his brothers had, on occasion, even hidden soldiers in the monastery when they had been in danger of being captured by the Japanese.

"The kind father also told us that there had indeed been a ship in the harbor earlier that week. However, he'd learned from the captain that the regiment needed to leave abruptly as news of Japanese in the area had come to their attention. The captain had asked that the monks relay to any men who came later that they should try to make their way to Java if they could.

"My heart sank to think that I had missed the boat, literally. What were we to do? How were we to proceed? I think Father Jean-Paul recognized our indecision because he quickly came to our rescue with an offer of a hot shower and a delicious breakfast—an offer we couldn't refuse.

"'Come, gentlemen. No need to make any big decisions now. We offer you a place to bathe and a breakfast of porridge and fruit that Brother Patrick has so kindly cooked for us this morning. Right this way. We'll provide you with clean clothes while we launder your old ones,' Father Jean-Paul said as he directed us toward the bathing room at the back of the monastery.

"Once we were clean, shaven, and dressed in the simple linens of native Sumatran men, we rejoined Father Jean-Paul in the dining room. Although he had already eaten, he kept us company as we nearly devoured the pot of porridge on the table. We savored the fresh berries and sugar covered with cream. Our stomachs had been only half full for most of our mission. Now they were filled with hearty homemade food, and it felt wonderful.

"'My, what healthy appetites you two gentlemen have. Here, Mr. Londt-Schultz, some more porridge? Have another mug of milk, won't you, Mr. Kretzer?' Father Jean-Paul asked, his chin resting on his hands. He was clearly delighted that we were such enthusiastic eaters.

"'This really hit the spot, Father. Thank you so much for your hospitality,' I told him after the meal.

"'Don't thank me, my son. Thank our Father above, who provides us with all we have,' he said piously, his hands clasped together in the attitude of prayer. 'You are welcome to attend our morning devotional if you would like. But I imagine a midmorning nap might be more appreciated. From the looks of it, you men haven't seen a bed in a while, have you?' he said, smiling. His wrinkles were permanently pressed into laugh lines, and I suspect he was a happy soul, quick to see humor in life's oddities.

"'Thank you, Father. A nap sounds lovely,' Kretzer replied gratefully.

"'I think I would like a little wander through your garden, if that's all right, Father. Perhaps, I will nap later,' I added.

"Father Jean-Paul nodded his approval. He then quietly walked away in the direction of the muffled singing somewhere on the other side of the monastery.

"We enjoyed our time at the monastery, feeling welcomed by the brethren in residence. Time creeps by very strangely there; a minute melts into an hour, an hour into a day. The monks did not ask us questions about our journey or what had brought us there, although I am sure their vows didn't include stamping out natural curiosity. We felt no pressure to disclose to them anything personal or confidential, though. We were allowed to roam at will, eating with the monks at lunch and dinner and then having time to ourselves to rest or think or look over a book from the library.

"When nighttime fell and evening devotional had ended on the second day of our stay, we met again with Father Jean-Paul, who kissed us on both cheeks as if we were long-lost friends.

"'My sons, you are welcome to stay here for as long as you wish. We consider this place a sanctuary from the world. It's God's sanctuary and free from worldly cares. May I offer a word of counsel? I would advise that you not consider following the troops to Java, as your captain suggested. My associates tell me that the waters between here and there are no longer safe. The Japanese have eyes everywhere now. Stay with us until things settle down, won't you? You are certainly welcome,' he said warmly. Kretzer and I looked at each other, each trying to gauge what the other was thinking.

"'May we sleep on it, Father? These past couple of days have been very restful for us, and while we can't divulge too much of our travels, may we say how much we appreciate your kind hospitality? You and your brethren have made us feel very welcome.' I shook his hand warmly.

"'Of course. May you both rest peacefully. We will talk again in the morning,' he said, simply.

"Kretzer and I whispered long into the night. Our options were limited. We agreed with the father that going to Java after our regiment would likely end in our capture, which would benefit no one. We could also accept Father Jean-Paul's offer to stay at the monastery for a while, until the danger subsided. But who knew when that would be? We finally resolved that we needed to go where our hearts were. We missed our families, and our first obligation and our greatest wish was to be with them again."

I glanced to my left when I heard a distinct sniff coming from my mother's direction. She was weeping silently, and judging from her blotchy cheeks, she had been for a while. My father also realized then that she had been crying. He put his arm around her shoulders and wiped her eyes with a clean handkerchief from his pocket. Looking at her, he said softly, "Tina, you know if it had been up to me, I would never have left in the first place. I felt it a duty to help our cause in any way I could, but I can honestly say I missed you every hour of every day I was gone."

Still crying, Mammy laid her dark head on his shoulder and whispered, "I missed you too, Alex—we all did."

For a second, it didn't seem as if my parents even remembered that we children were there with them. My brother, George, discreetly cleared his throat, embarrassed by the exchange of affection he'd just witnessed. Apparently, it was too mushy for his young adolescent years to take. Peggy caught my attention, rolling her eyes at our brother's blatant attempt to change the subject. We both smiled.

"Uh, so Pappy, wasn't it dangerous to come back after all you'd done for the military? What was your plan?" George asked. Pappy kept his arm around my mother's shoulder, gently soothing her while he continued.

"We spent a great deal of time trying to figure out how we should travel home. When we told Father Jean-Paul of our decision to head back to Tandjoengenim the next morning, he was very helpful. We asked his advice, as we both suspected he was more connected to what was happening with the war on our island than he let on. I think he was glad we consulted him. We certainly were.

"He advised us to travel separately, suggesting we would be less conspicuous to the Japanese if we traveled alone. At first this was hard for us to swallow, since we had come to rely on each other so much during the last few weeks. We had never once considered going back without the other's company, but after chewing on it for a few minutes, we agreed it was the right decision.

"Father Jean-Paul also brought us fresh linen clothing, clean but worn. He gave us each a pair of sandals, a straw hat, and a woven bag similar to those carried by locals in the area. We would blend in much better wearing native clothing than using our old military-issue uniforms. Having Asian features, we would have a much better chance of passing as locals than if we looked completely European. The good father supplied us with fruit, crackers, and bread as well as water pouches. When he learned that we had only one map and one compass, he gave us duplicates of those as well. All we had left were good-byes, and they were harder than we had imagined. Father Jean-Paul had been a savior to us over the last few days, providing us with rest, food, and a plan to return home.

"'Father, thank you so much for all you've done for us. Where would we be without you?' Kretzer said with tears in his eyes.

"I grasped the father's hand tightly, my throat constricting as I tried to bid him farewell. He put his arms around me and held me tightly. Looking into my eyes, wet with tears, he whispered, 'Thank the Lord, my son, not me. I am only a simple tool in His hands. May God be with you both as you travel home, and may you find your loved ones safe and out of harm's way upon your return.'"

***

"For the first leg of the trip, we hid in a farm wagon full of hay that Father Jean-Paul had arranged. After an hour or two of traveling together, we separated. The farm wagon was continuing northwest. That was Kretzer's route. We had decided that I would travel northeast, so I continued on foot alone after a heartfelt good-bye. For the last several weeks, he'd been my only companion. We'd literally kept one another alive during some perilous times. I felt I was leaving my left arm in that cart with my friend; that's how close we had become.

"The path I walked was long and hot. I was pestered the whole time by irksome little mosquitoes nipping at me day and night with no relief. The first day turned into the second, which turned into the third. I kept checking my compass to ensure I was making my way north. I ate fruit and drank water sparingly, refilling my water pouch as often as I could. I tried to reserve the crackers and bread for the lean times I knew would happen before I made it home.

"I disciplined myself to speak only Malay, never reverting to Dutch when I encountered the locals. I knew that while some of the natives were loyal to the Dutch crown, others had allied themselves with the Japanese, who had promised them freedom from Holland's watchful eye. I would not be able to tell who was loyal to whom at first glance, so I stayed in character the whole time.

"I did run across some Japanese from time to time in the villages I had to walk through. I spotted the soldiers' uniforms from a distance, which gave me time to blend in with a crowd or change direction if need be. Each time I saw them, my heart would jump into my throat, and I'd break out into a cold sweat. If they only knew what I had done!"

"How scary," I said, a shaky hand over my mouth. "To realize you came that close to the enemy and went undetected."

"You must have a very powerful guardian angel sitting on your shoulder, Alex," Mammy said, shaking her head. She smiled tremulously, and I knew she was trying to let him know she was all right again. I saw him squeeze her shoulder.

"Well, certainly an overworked one, that's for sure," Peggy said under her breath. Pappy laughed out loud at her wry comment.

"About a week into my trip, I started getting the chills. I knew it was a sultry hot day, but I was shaking from some glacier in my inner core. By the next morning, I ached all over. It even felt like the strands of hair on my head hurt. I knew I would not be able to get very far feeling as I did. The symptoms I had could mean only one thing: malaria. I peeled a little bark from a quinine tree like I'd seen my mother do when I was a child. Then I brewed the peel with water to make a little tea. I drained the cup, bitter though it tasted, and peeled off more to save for later. Then I went in search of a hiding spot.

"I was near a small village, where it seemed many of the locals scraped together a meager existence foraging and selling fruit they picked from the jungle trees. I didn't see any sign of enemy troops in the vicinity, so I looked for a place to wait out the wave of malaria I could feel rushing through me.

"I ended up finding an old, abandoned lean-to near the edge of town. It was on its last leg, but it would be a roof over my head. I also had to be careful of tigers and other predators that prowl near the jungle. Kretzer and I had heard several of them roaring at night in the trees while we were on our mission for the army. I figured the lean-to was close enough to the sounds of the village and its occupants that beasts of prey would not venture too close. I hoped they wouldn't anyway.

"The next day or two were a blur. I forced myself to make the quinine tea again and managed to drink it, but the rest of the time the world seemed a hazy place to me. By what I believe was the third morning, I felt shaky and weak but better. I gathered my few supplies, downed another cup of the tea, and then cautiously slipped back into the jungle. Before long, I realized that the malaria had taken a toll. I was tired and weak. I knew I wouldn't be able to travel far that day either. I did the only thing I knew to do. I prayed. I needed help from a power greater than myself.

"I continued along the little dirt path for another hour or so, stopping frequently to rest, when I suddenly heard a far-off whistle. I couldn't believe it. Was my mind playing tricks on me? It sounded like a train. I mustered my strength and went northwest, the direction in which I had heard the sound. I pulled out my map, and sure enough, there was a train line near my location. I soon saw the tracks coming through the jungle like a twisting black snake. I hid in the trees, hoping against hope that the train would be heading in my direction. I didn't quite know what I would do once it happened upon me, but I felt that if somehow I could stow away on it, it would be an answer to my desperate prayer.

"A short while later, I heard the train chugging down its jungle path, click-clacking along. The black steam from its engine was a telltale sign of its exact location. The ground began to tremble as it approached, and soon the train was rumbling past me. I looked to see how long it was. I couldn't locate the caboose, but I figured it was a fairly good size since it had several reserve coal cars linked to it.

"I had to think fast, not wanting to miss a golden opportunity for a ride. There were four or five livestock cars coming closer. I was frantically trying to devise a plan to board, when, lo and behold, the train began to slow down until it came to a complete stop. I was so shocked I couldn't move at first. Then, quick as a cat, I jumped aboard.

"I slid into a car inhabited by a flock of chickens. They were all caged, but what a commotion they made, clucking and cackling like a bunch of old women. And the smell. Ugh. It makes me want to gag just thinking about it. There's nothing worse than chicken manure, but at the time I couldn't complain. It was a ride when I desperately needed one, and I thanked God for it. Some things just can't be explained away by coincidence. I pulled out my map once more and through a small ray of light learned that the train would be heading north for a while. I anticipated that I would safely be traveling in the right direction until well after lunchtime.

"Though I had every intention of staying awake and alert during my ride, once the train began moving again, the rhythmic sound of the cars clicking along the track lulled me to sleep. It was a restful sleep in an unlikely setting, but for the first time since the monastery, I felt safe. I awoke hours later to the sound of the train slowing down. I searched through the slats of the car I was in to try and figure out where I was. What I saw as we slowed to a stop sent the hair on the backs of my arms straight on end. There was a group of six or so Japanese soldiers congregating right outside my car.

"If they were planning on boarding the train to perform a search, I could be in serious danger. I literally held my breath, my heart beating out of my chest, until mercifully the train started moving again several minutes later. Apparently they were just supervising the unloading of a car farther down, because I saw the soldiers stacking bags of grain about fifty yards away.

"I decided to leave the train as soon as I safely could. Judging by the sun's height in the sky, I estimated the time to be around two or three in the afternoon. The train would be changing direction soon, so it was no longer useful for me to stay on board, and after my close scare with the Japanese, I suddenly longed for the cover of the jungle trees.

"About twenty minutes later, I felt the train slow again. It looked like we were about to go over a bridge. I opened the door to my car very slowly, and then, right before the train eased onto the bridge, I jumped off, rolling as I hit the ground. I quickly crawled into the jungle, crossing my fingers that no enemy soldiers had been aboard that train, looking in my direction at precisely that moment.

"It took a few minutes for me to catch my breath and stop myself from shaking. After looking at the map, I found the bridge we had been about to cross and realized I could locate the path that would take me northeast just a couple of miles away."

I looked around at my brothers and sister. They were sitting on the edge of their seats, the flaky biscuits forgotten. Mammy was no different. She sat riveted by what she was hearing. Pappy's story had us spellbound.

"Mercifully, my bout with malaria was short-lived," he continued. "The age-old remedy of quinine tea that my mother had passed down to me saved me from a debilitating illness. Although I tired more quickly than usual over the next few days, I had enough strength to travel quite far. A couple of times I was even able to catch a ride on the back of a farm wagon for a while. The locals were generally very good-natured when I passed them. A handful insisted on giving me fruit or bread, assuming correctly that I was traveling a long distance. I was grateful for their generosity but still cautious. I maintained my cover as an Indonesian local all the way home, and they seemed to buy it.

"Each night I would find a safe place to sleep for a few hours, sometimes near a village or in the brush. Once, I even slept in the hollow of a huge tree. I was nervous that a tiger or snake would happen upon me while I was sleeping. It was during the nighttime that I missed Kretzer the most. When we were together, we had taken turns keeping watch while the other slept. With him, I never had the sensation of sleeping with one eye open like I did while traveling back home.

"I missed you all the most at night too. I went to sleep listening to Peggy's piano music in my head, imagining my Tina next to me, and you children gathered in the parlor singing together. Then I would realize I was alone in the jungle, and I would look up at the stars and think to myself that my loved ones were not so far away. We shared the same stars, and I hung on to that thought. My darling children might be looking up at the same twinkling lights in the sky as I was. That thought kept me focused on my goal of reaching home as soon as possible.

"Clearly, nature had its way with my body, what with the sunburn, the bug bites, and the effects of the malaria. But my spirit, tired though I was, remained strong and determined. I am so grateful to be home." He finished his story by winking at Mammy and smiling at each one of us.

"Wow, Pappy. What an adventure you had. It's like you're a hero or something," Justin said, staring in awe at our father.

"Or something, son. I'm no hero. Just grateful I could do my duty and make it home safely to my family."

"Still, what an amazing story, Pappy. You were like Robinson Crusoe out there, braving the wild and living to tell about it. I wish I had been right there with you," George exclaimed.

"You mentioned tigers. Did you see any tigers or poisonous snakes on your mission?" Peggy asked curiously.

"I did see some snakes, but I was never in any danger of being bitten by one—at least not that I'm aware of. And, thankfully, I never saw a tiger the whole time I was gone."

"Pappy, I can't believe all you've been through. Were you scared?" I asked.

"I think the better question would be, when was I *not* scared, my dear. Fear was a constant presence during my time in the jungle. I feared for my life. I feared the work I was assigned wouldn't get done. I feared detection. I feared nature's elements. I feared for my family.

"As anxious as I was, though, I think fear gave me an edge. I felt more alert, more conscious of my surroundings and the people I encountered. Fear fostered in me a need to be prepared for whatever circumstances we came up against. I was definitely afraid; but in a way, I am grateful for my fear. It may have helped keep me alive and free from the enemy," Pappy said, getting up to stretch his legs. We all looked at one another in wonder, still marveling at the story we had just heard.

***

Later in the day, after playing a rousing game of European football in the backyard with us, Pappy looked happy and refreshed as we sat down and drank tall icy glasses of lemonade. Lemonade is such an intriguing drink—a perfect mix of tart and sweet.

Mammy laughed at Ape, who was making himself dizzy running in circles. He was chasing a playful butterfly that flitted just out of his reach. My mother seemed more relaxed sitting there in the shade with a hand resting on Pappy's shoulder than I had seen her look in weeks. As always, she looked cool and crisp in an apricot linen shift dress, while we looked tousled and out of breath from our afternoon exercise.

George was sporting blades of grass in his hair, souvenirs from some superhuman soccer moves he'd managed in our game. Peggy's braid was unraveling, leaving wisps of hair flying in every direction, and Justin was collapsed on the grass, panting heavily. What a sight we must have made.

Later, after another game, Pappy looked more serious sitting in his chair under the awning. Peggy and the boys were hunting for butterflies with their nets, and I was plucking weeds out of the flower beds when I heard Pappy talking to Mammy in low tones. "Tina, I didn't want to alarm the children, but I believe our days of independence are numbered. The Japanese are routinely rounding up Europeans in other areas of Sumatra, especially the Dutch, and dumping them in prison camps. As remote as Tandjoengenim is, they will find us eventually. Sooner or later, they *will* come."

I heard my mother gasp. Glancing up, I saw her shaky hand cover her mouth in an attempt to hide her emotion. I echoed her sentiment as I felt cold sweat bead on my brow. Prison camps? The thought sent shivers down my spine.

Pappy cleared his throat. "Once it begins, we may be separated. From what I gather, the camps are typically segregated by sex. But even if they aren't, I have a feeling I am being watched. The Japanese have to realize that the mines and oil fields were sabotaged by someone who knew what he was doing. There are only a few of us in the area who fall into that category. Once someone lets it slip that I've been gone for almost two months and that I just arrived back, the Japanese will be quick to follow the facts to a certain conclusion. There will be consequences once that happens.

"I'm telling you this not to scare you, my love, but to prepare you. If you are picked up by the Japanese, do not forget that old brown suitcase. Try to carry it with you wherever you are taken. The papers hidden in the bottom are our best hope of regaining our lives after all this madness ends. No matter how rattled you are, you mustn't forget that case, Tina."

Mammy was rattled. Even from my crouched position among the flowers, I could see the way her hand trembled as she tried to lift her drinking glass. It was evident in the pale face that she turned toward my father's. Seeing her afraid squeezed any trace of courage I had right out of me, like juice being squeezed from a lemon. I listened intently, but

Pappy changed the topic to ask how my uncle and aunt were doing. I think he realized then that we children were in listening distance of their conversation. Little did we know that it wouldn't be long before Pappy's prediction became our reality.

6

Seizure

WE SPENT THE NEXT DAY packing our suitcases. Mammy's ominous brown case was already filled and conspicuously placed next to her side of the bed. Every time I saw it, I realized that we might be living on borrowed time here in our quiet home nestled in the heart of rural Sumatra. It was early April 1942, and the Japanese army was already picking up other European citizens in our country. Pappy insisted we children also pack travel bags in case the Japanese allowed us to keep them. As usual, he was thinking ahead, anticipating what might come.

"I can't stand the thought of doing this, Hanny," my sister said sullenly as she shoved her blue and white linen sundress into a small suitcase.

"I know. It's incredible to think we may need to use these someday soon. I feel a little like a sitting duck," I said, arranging my dresses and slips for the third time. We glanced around when we heard a gentle knock on our bedroom door.

"Here, girls. Your Mammy wants you to pack a couple of cans of food in your cases. Who knows what the Japanese prison camps are like or what the food situation will be there. It's all a big mystery, isn't it?" Kokie asked, trying to keep her tone light. She handed us each some canned fruits and vegetables.

"I was never one for mysteries," Peggy said under her breath. "What will you do, Kokie? They are only picking up European citizens. Will you stay here?"

"If you are gone for only a couple of days, yes. If it's any longer than that, then no. I'll head back to my village. But I will keep an eye on the place. Your mother entrusted me with her jewelry, all the good pieces anyway. When I know you all are back, I'll come quickly." Kokie must have seen the worry on our faces.

"I'll be fine. Things will be a bit lonely around here—quieter, mind you—but lonely without you children racing up and down the halls and outside. It will be just me and old Ape and Knorrie, of course. They'll keep me company."

"We'll miss you, Kokie. The whole situation is so unthinkable," I said, tears welling as I adjusted my case to make room for the food.

"War *is* unthinkable, Hanny. To disrupt a peaceful existence so far away from the uproar in Europe . . . it's hard to understand, even for grown-ups," Kokie replied as she squeezed my shoulder.

"Well, *I'm* going to take some of my music. I've just decided. I can't stand to think of it gathering dust in my piano bench or, worse yet, in the hands of some Japanese soldier. I'll bring my new music book, *Piano Pieces the Whole World Plays*. It's one of my favorites, and it won't take much room. Maybe by some weird twist of fate there will be a piano wherever they send us," Peggy said, her face brightening at the thought. I watched her run to the parlor to fetch it.

Peggy's passion for her music got me thinking. What things would I find irreplaceable if by some horrible circumstance we couldn't come back for a while? I scanned my room until my eyes lighted on a couple of photos. They were pictures of my grandparents that had been hanging in our room since we moved here. Sometimes I would talk to those pictures as if the likenesses of my grandparents were alive and breathing. I would be so sad if I didn't have them with me. On a whim, I took the photos down and packed them in my suitcase, cushioning them in clothing to protect against breakage.

Just as I was finishing, I heard Mammy's light step reach our door. She looked so polished standing there by my bed, her dark hair coiled elegantly on her head. Only the dark circles under her eyes let me know that sleep had not come easily for her last night, a sure sign that she was troubled.

She glanced into my case and said, "I see you've already packed away the fruit Kokie brought you. We may not even need it. Still, it's better to be prepared, I guess." Her voice trailed off as she neatly refolded a crumpled dress from Peggy's bag.

"I'm almost done here. Just a few last-minute things, like my hairbrush. How are the boys getting along?" I asked.

"Well, George tried to tuck away his ant farm under a towel, but I caught him just in time, and Justin wants to pack all of his toys and none of his clothes. It's been an interesting morning." She sighed. "I brought both you and Peggy new dresses I just finished this morning. These are special ones, like my case with the secret compartments."

I looked at her curiously.

"In the hems of these white dresses, I've sewn some of our best gold chains and rings. See? Pappy isn't the only inventive one in our family," she said playfully as she pointed out the raised surfaces under each hem. They were virtually invisible. Only someone who was searching for the jewelry would ever notice them sewn into the hems. My mother, the mistress of intrigue? Who would have thought it? I was impressed.

"Mammy, that is brilliant. Do you have chains sewn into your dresses too?" I asked.

"No. I think the soldiers would be more likely to search a grown woman than two young girls. And if the jewelry was detected, I bet the Japanese would be more lenient with you and Peggy than with me."

"You're probably right. I hope I won't feel nervous wearing this dress. It really is beautiful, Mammy," I said, fingering the silky white sleeves and the scarlet satin sash.

"Thanks. I have been working on these since your father left with the army. Just try not to think of the gold sewn into the bottoms. Then it'll be easier to act natural," she replied, looking down.

Suddenly, something caught her attention. She swept away a pair of stockings to uncover the gilded corner of a photo frame in my suitcase.

"Hanny, why are these photos in here? You can't be lugging these all over Sumatra. They could easily be broken. We need to keep them here," she said. She gently lifted the photos of my grandparents out of the corner of the bag and hung them back on the wall.

"But I don't want them lost if we are forced to leave. These photos are important to me," I pleaded, trying to appeal to her sense of extended family. I looked longingly at the photos on the wall.

"That's very thoughtful of you, dear, but they'll make your suitcase too heavy. Besides, if your bag gets confiscated, they'll be lost forever. We can't have that, can we?" she reasoned sensibly. As practical as her words appeared on the surface, I could sense a tender note to her voice as she turned to wipe a speck of dust from my grandmother's frame. She was touched.

Before I could respond, Peggy rounded the corner with her piano book in hand. She slid it deftly into her case. Then Mammy showed her the new white dress she had made. Peggy's dress had an emerald green sash that would complement her dark wavy hair perfectly. When she tried it on, her dress was a little long, so Mammy ushered her down the hall to alter it.

I finished my packing, but before I fastened my suitcase, I paused. I looked over at the smiling faces I dearly loved and quietly took down the photos and placed them back in my suitcase. Right or wrong, I felt strongly that those pictures needed to stay with us if we were captured.

***

Bang! Bang! Bang!

"Interrogation. Interrogation. Open the door. Open now!" My foggy brain registered that people were knocking insistently at the door, yelling at us in broken Dutch. It was a moonlit night, so I glanced at the clock. Once my eyes focused, I saw that it was 3:00 AM. Peggy was already out of bed, listening at the door. My father was walking quickly down the hall, whispering loudly for us to wake up.

My brothers' door opened, and George and Justin ran swiftly into our room.

"It's the Japanese, Hanny! There's a whole group of them. What'll we do?" George was frantic. My heart raced as my mind tried to grip the reality of what my brother was saying.

"We need to stay calm. We've got to do as Pappy taught us. Throw your cases out the window, and hopefully we'll be able to pick them up again when we leave. Go. Quickly. We haven't got a lot of time." I tried to keep my voice steady, belying the anxiety I felt inside. My brothers darted back to their room, and I heard their window slide open quietly. Peggy had already chucked her suitcase out and was just grabbing mine from me when we heard loud footsteps stomping quickly down the hall. Peggy pushed the bag out and then ran to my side, slipping her hand in mine.

Our bedroom door opened, and there stood Mammy, her eyes large brown pools, filled with terror, like a doe that has seen her hunter. Behind her were two Japanese soldiers in full uniform.

"Girls, we must go now. Are you ready?" she asked in a small, shaky voice. I looked down at my clothing. I was still in my soft cotton pajamas. I slid on sandals and a robe and nodded to my mother. She led us down the hall to the foyer, where I saw my father flanked by two Japanese officers. Kokie was there too, with her arms around my two brothers.

"Gone only for short time. Weekend only. Then you come back," one of the Japanese soldiers said to my mother, who had tears streaming down her face now. She nodded but was unable to speak, her emotions so close to the surface that she didn't trust her voice.

The soldiers led us outside. "Wait, by tree," one said gruffly, while they made room for us in the Japanese military truck parked on the street. As we walked along the path by our house, we each discreetly picked up our discarded travel bags, Mammy gripping the old brown case tightly. Even in the moonlight, I could tell her knuckles were white from holding on so tight. The soldier accompanying us did not seem to notice, or maybe he just didn't care this late at night.

The other soldiers returned as we approached the tree by our front walk. I did not dare meet their eyes, as a healthy distrust of these new captors filled me with fear. I obediently followed Peggy into the big truck they motioned for us to board and then sat on the floor, scrunched next to my mother and sister.

I kept looking out the back of the truck, knowing that any minute they would close the tailgate in an act of finality. I tried to soak in everything my eyes lighted on in those last few seconds—the familiar tree outside the front gate, the cheerful flowers in Mammy's garden, and especially our home, the warm lamplight still shining in the front window, beckoning us to come back. I couldn't tear my eyes away. Tears threatened as the soldiers swung the door closed and my oasis of safety was gone from my sight. I huddled next to Peggy, needing to feel her warmth, her familiarity. George and Justin leaned against my father who sat across from us, their heads bowed in grief.

***

The truck was already nearly filled with Europeans from our area, people I recognized from town and the mines. There were others there too who I had never seen. No one spoke or even smiled, so thick was the fear that permeated the air. It was like a tangible blanket that covered us from head to foot, smothering us and making us slick with perspiration. The only sounds in the truck were that of a young child sniffling and a mother soothing him with a soft "Shh! Shh!"

The motor from the truck's engine started, and we were off. We bumped along down the road, and in my mind's eye, I could picture our house moving farther and farther away, along with the tree, the garden, Kokie, and our pets. It was at that moment that I shed my first tear.

Our ride in the truck was short-lived. We stopped at the train station and were quickly thrust onto a train. The guards gestured for us to sit on the floor of a cattle car. An older gentleman grumbled to my father that only the Japanese and Germans were allowed the luxury of sitting in the passenger cars farther up.

Our car was packed with people—captives like us, prisoners of the Japanese. There were children clinging to their mothers' skirts, teenagers trying to act brave with their chins held high, and older people balancing on unsteady legs as the train departed. We were a school of sardines shoved into a tin can, with no thought of comfort, only the convenience of our captors.

I glanced around and saw a curious group sitting together nearby. They were sunburned and sea worn, with bleached hair and peeling noses. I later learned they had been shipwrecked while on a Dutch freighter called the *Poelau Bras,* trying to escape to Australia. It had been hit by a Japanese air raid. Many of those trying to flee on the outgoing vessel had died. A lucky few had made it to the lifeboats and after several days at sea had washed ashore off the southern tip of Sumatra. After barely surviving their trauma, most had been easy targets for the Japanese to capture. Some had clearly been injured. One man I saw had a festering wound on his leg that was still bloody and unwashed. I cringed to look at it.

Tearing my eyes away, I looked to my left and saw the telltale habits of nuns clustered together in the corner. Some of the sisters had children bouncing on their laps in an obvious attempt to comfort them and laugh away the fear they must have felt. I wondered if the nuns I had grown to care for at the boarding school had been captured as well. Almost all had been European. Perhaps the Japanese had spared these kind women because of their higher calling. I banished that thought as quickly as it had come. The Japanese had no love for Christianity, at least not that I had seen.

As the train rumbled on, people began to speak in low tones to their neighbors.

"Where are you from?"

"When did they come for you?"

"Do you know if my cousin, Edmund such-and-such, from your town was picked up?

"Where do you think we're headed?"

"How will we live?"

These questions were asked tentatively, in hushed voices so as not to attract notice from the Japanese soldiers standing watch over us with raised bayonets. They stood as still as if they had been set in stone, no emotion lighting their faces. Still, their presence was a constant reminder of our situation. This was no joy ride.

"I've got to go to the bathroom," Justin said suddenly.

"There are no restrooms in this car, my boy," Pappy said, squeezing his shoulder.

"But I've really got to go!" my brother said emphatically, squirming as he sat on his case. His crossed legs and bouncy movements were further proof that time was of the essence.

"Son, you are going to have to hold it for a few more minutes. I don't think we'll be on the train much longer," assured my father, looking at Justin anxiously.

"Okay, but I've been holding it since about two minutes after we left the station. My bladder is about to burst," Justin whispered in obvious discomfort. I felt for my brother.

"Others of us have been in this train car for hours and hours. The soldiers have stopped to relieve themselves, but they have not given us the chance. I'd just let your son go over there behind those crates," suggested the older man seated next to Pappy.

"Thanks, but we'll see if he can wait a few more minutes," Pappy said with a smile.

Pappy's prediction was right; the trip was drawing to an end. The thump-thump of the train racing across the tracks began to slow its rhythm until it finally hissed to a stop. A tension settled in among the car's passengers. Once those doors opened, we would face an unknown we had only dreamed about in our nightmares and heard hints of in hushed whispers. Peggy and I held hands tightly as we waited to see what would happen next.

The car doors flung open, and several Japanese soldiers boarded. They began barking out a list of names. Those they called needed to leave the train immediately. Pappy looked startled. I saw him study the landscape behind the soldiers. Clearly, we were not where he thought we would be. Then our names rang out—my father's, my mother's, and finally ours. I broke into a cold sweat. I felt others on the train watching us curiously, but I kept my eyes firmly planted on the floor. We gathered our bags and belongings and stepped out.

"We're not in Palembang," Pappy said, almost to himself.

The woman in front of us whispered over her shoulder, "Moeara-enim. My mother's family is from this area."

I looked to Mammy for guidance as I always had when I was unsure of what to do next. Her head hung down, and the back of her hand wiped tears from her cheeks. She had become emotionally unraveled since our capture, her control popping like the threads of one of her dresses that needed mending. I touched her hand, trying to give her some sort of reassurance. She held it and squeezed. We fell into line behind George and Peggy and continued inching forward, wondering where this path would take us.

I looked around, trying to get my bearings. Two queues were forming, one on the right and the other on the left. I immediately thought I recognized the Japanese army's goal in gathering us here. The men and women were being separated. On one side of the square, women and children were being guided onto flatbed trucks. On the other, men were being crowded onto similar vehicles.

My chest felt heavy as I saw the teary good-byes of children leaving fathers and wives kissing their husbands good-bye. My heart sank like a lead weight as we edged forward in the line, knowing that our father would soon be taken from us for who knew how long.

"Why are they putting us in two different lines, Pappy?" Justin asked tremulously.

"It looks like they are taking the men to a different place than the women and children, son."

My mother gripped Pappy's arm, as if by doing so, they would not have to part. He stroked her silky hair.

"Investigation. Investigation. Background checks," a soldier growled as we approached.

Before we knew it, we were at the front of the line. My father held each of us children one by one. When I turned to him, he whispered so only I could hear, "Remember, Hanny. Remember what I asked of you that afternoon in the bird sanctuary. Promise me that no matter what, you will always look after your mother."

I was shocked to hear my father remind me of that now. I looked into his dark eyes, and they stared down at me, filled with an intensity that scared me. Surely we would be together in a week or so. The soldier at our house had said we'd be together again after the weekend, but Pappy was acting like we might be apart for a long time. I hugged him tightly and nodded that I remembered my promise, trying to smile and be brave. He held my mother last and for as long as he could before a soldier gruffly grabbed his arm and pushed him into a line to the right. A faint wisp of his aftershave lingered, and I breathed it in greedily.

"Lekas! Lekas!" the soldier yelled, motioning for the men to board the truck. We would become very familiar with that word. It was the Malay word for "quick, quick," and the Japanese used it often; it was one of the few Malay expressions they knew. Generally they spoke to us in Japanese, fully expecting us to understand. In the town square that day, we heard *"Lekas! Lekas!"* over and over as our captors tried to get us to move faster.

We waved to Pappy for as long as we could see him. We saw his tan hand wave back above the other men's heads. Before long, the truck's engine started, and he was gone. There was no time to dwell on our separation, though, as we too were made to climb onto a truck, its destination a mystery to us.

Peggy quietly gazed in the direction my father's truck had gone. I could picture her thoughts. I am sure they echoed my own. *Would he be safe? Where were they taking him? Would we be together again soon?*

Mercifully, our ride was short. My backside was starting to ache from the bumpity-bump of bad shocks. We were driven to a complex of abandoned buildings somewhere in the heart of Moeara-enim.

There we were again asked to line up so the Japanese could search our bags and our bodies—for what specifically, I didn't know, but it was apparent the soldiers were bent on taking anything of value. I swallowed back fear as I thought of the gold chains and rings Mammy had sewn into the hem of the white dresses she had given us earlier that week. Still, she had only included the most dainty of our gold chains in the hemming, so with luck they would go unnoticed.

As I drew closer to the soldiers performing the search, I noticed that any jewelry they found was immediately confiscated and tossed into a metal bucket, the pile slowly gaining height. Their beetle-black eyes showed no emotion as they stole these people's belongings, not a hint of greed or regret. Nothing. That disturbed me more than it would have if I could have glimpsed some sense of their souls. I vowed to keep my head down and stay out of their way.

My family and I were searched without incident. The soldiers rummaged through our clothes and food without paying any real attention to what they were doing. Fortunately, our jewelry was not detected, and we were waved through the gate. Peggy's eyes met mine. She winked quickly, before dropping them again. We'd gained a small victory over our enemies, just a little something to hold onto after all they had taken away.

The guard in charge was yelling *"lekas, lekas"* yet again. He grew angry when we didn't move fast enough. Women were trying to gather their bags and their children, a process that did not lend itself to speed. I watched as one young woman dropped her woven basket filled with food. She collected the cans one by one, only to have her baby get on all fours and begin to crawl away. I wasn't the only one watching. The guards began to yell at her. She rose clumsily to her feet, her baby balanced haphazardly in her arms, only to be kicked by a heavy black boot and shoved into line. Her baby cried. She desperately tried to quiet him, obviously terrified that he might incur more wrath from the guards in charge.

Two women stepped out of line and leaned down to help her. One of the good Samaritans, an older woman, grabbed her basket from the ground, while the other patted her gently on the back and gave the baby a biscuit to suck. They helped the young mother into line and continued to aid her as we crept along.

At the front of the next line, we gave our names and became part of the Japanese army's count, a number on the camp roll. After passing through this checkpoint, I glanced around just in time to see iron gates close and lock behind us. We were like the birds in Pappy's sanctuary, birds in a cage.

7

Incarceration

AFTER CHECKING IN, WE WERE herded like cattle along a row of buildings. Each building had bars on the door. They were jail cells. People inside crowded the barred doors to get a look at the newcomers as we passed, their eyes pleading for us to help them. Justin slowed to watch, dismayed at their misery, but he was shoved in the back by the butt of a bayonet. The message was clear: keep moving. The guards pushed us along until we stopped at a single cell.

They opened the door, and then the soldiers started squeezing us through the tight opening until I thought I would be smothered by the number of bodies surrounding me. Forty, no fifty, sixty or more of us in a single cell. There were no windows, and a feeling of suffocation loomed. The only light emanated from the barred door and a single, unshaded lightbulb that hung from the ceiling. The guards, confident that we were secure, clicked the lock and left.

"What's happening? Why are we here?" a single, panic-stricken voice questioned, speaking for us all.

"They said we're here to be investigated. But why us?" another woman asked in a muffled tone.

"Maybe we are under suspicion for some reason," an older woman near the door proposed.

Immediately I thought of my father's mission to destroy the mines. If the Japanese army had been tipped off about him by one of the natives, then we too might be suspect. Heaven knew where they had taken him.

I looked at Peggy, alarmed at my thoughts. "Pappy," I mouthed silently. She looked at me intently, nodding imperceptibly. I felt her hand reach for mine in the dimness of the cell.

"I suggest we get organized. How many of us did they cram into this chamber anyway?" asked a tall blond woman standing erect in the corner.

After quite a bit of maneuvering, we discovered that we numbered seventy-two, all shoved away in this prison cell.

The heat was oppressive. The Sumatran sun baked the roof of the cell in which we were packed, making us feel like we were bread in an oven. It was hot and humid, more so because of the close quarters we were forced to endure. Not so much as a few inches of room separated one person from the next. Time inched by over the following hours as people quietly endured these new living conditions. Most people didn't speak, as if conserving their energy during this, the hottest part of the day. Flies buzzed around our heads, pestering us and teasing us with their very presence. Babies, not understanding their discomfort, cried pathetically, adding to the oppression.

Suddenly, we could hear footsteps outside our cell. The children perked up and slipped their hands outside of the bars in greeting.

"Let us out. Please, we want to go home," they begged.

The soldiers ignored them, their faces smooth and untroubled as if they hadn't heard the children's pleas, or maybe they had heard them so often they were immune. They opened the door just wide enough to shove a couple of buckets full of food and water inside, their eyes expressionless. Then they locked the door once more and marched away.

"Good. Food. I could eat a whole chicken—feathers and all," George said enthusiastically.

He crept forward, gingerly sidestepping bodies, to take a look. Many of the cell's tenants encircled the buckets, curious to see what we would be having for dinner that evening. But one peek inside was enough to bring groans of displeasure or shouts of disgust.

"*Kasave*! And it's all rotten," yelled a Eurasian woman near the front of the cell. To prove her point, she lifted a sample of the popular root above her head, using only her thumb and forefinger. It looked slimy and purple, a sure sign that it was past its prime. Many women shook their heads disapprovingly; others turned away, hands up as if to push away the offensive food. While a few practical women tried to eat the fare, knowing it was all we were getting that evening, most couldn't stomach the mess. My stomach did flip-flops as I envisioned myself trying to swallow the rotting food.

We ended up throwing most of the *kasave* out of the cell. We were utterly surprised to hear a stampede of footsteps run up to the discarded food and grab it.

The children near the door peeked out of the bars, exclaiming in awe, "It's some of the other prisoners. They're eating that mess like it's chocolate ice cream or something. They're licking it off of the ground with their tongues."

Mammy looked intently in the direction of the door. "I pray with all I am that we are out of here before we too get that hungry."

I felt chills run down my spine, despite the oppressive heat, at the thought that we might be brought so low as to eat rotten vegetables off the dirt floor. My heart suddenly echoed Mammy's simple prayer.

Night fell, and the dilemma of what to do about sleeping arrangements became a topic of discussion. With seventy-two of us packed in such tight quarters, how were we ever to sleep?

"Perhaps we just sleep sitting up," one woman suggested.

"We've been in this cramped sitting position all afternoon. We need to at least be able to stretch our legs," her neighbor replied, shaking her head.

"Yes, and surely the children need a place to lie down and sleep," a grandmotherly woman agreed, kindly stroking the long silky hair of a young girl next to her.

"What if we sleep in shifts?" suggested the same blond woman in the corner who had earlier offered the suggestion that we get organized.

"What do you mean?"

"Well, half of us could sleep for three or four hours, stretched out and lying down, while the others sit up. After the first group has rested, those sitting up will then take their turn to lie down and sleep."

Murmurs of approval ascended through the cell.

"That's a fine idea; let's try it" was the general feeling.

Again, the blond woman took the lead and organized the shifts into rows. Those who had been assigned to be in the first shift, my family included, lay down as comfortably as possible on the hard floor, while the others continued sitting. Peggy laid her head on my thighs, and Justin nestled into my side. Quiet fell over the group as sleep visited many of those who sought it. Others never seemed to settle down, tossing and turning in their tight spaces.

Later that night, my family and I were awakened from our restless slumber so our neighbors could try their best to stretch and sleep. They weren't ideal circumstances for resting, but this became our routine each night when darkness fell. I kept reminding myself that it was better than sleeping sitting up.

The cries of babies and little children were endless in that crowded prison cell. We could hear mothers quietly soothing and singing lullabies to their little ones but with limited success. The children were uncomfortable, as we all were, and they were expressing that. I, for one, didn't blame them for crying. As old as I was, I felt like crawling into a little ball and weeping many times as I sat on the dirt floor of that hellhole.

The living circumstances were horrible and so unlike what we were used to. Gone was our comfortable home with its genteel furnishings and plentiful food. Here the rotten *kasave* we had the first night was the food we were given every night. If we were lucky there was a bucket of gritty rice to go with it. We choked it down, and that is what sustained us, along with a few crackers Mammy had packed in her case. The cans we had packed at home were of little use without a can opener, a fact we woefully discovered the second day in the cell. Besides, quarters in the cell were so tight that we could only get to our bags with great difficulty. Most of the time they served as our pillows and chairs as we tried every position imaginable to get comfortable in the jail cell.

The muggy heat continued, but we were only given murky river water to drink. My mother warned us to drink the water only when we were desperately thirsty, as it probably contained bacteria that could make us sick. Several of the tenants in the cell with us suffered from dysentery while we were there. We knew because there was no hiding our bathroom visits. We tried to go as discreetly as possible, but we counted the Japanese's disregard for our privacy as one of their most serious offenses.

One of the worst parts of living in a crowded jail cell for me was the bugs. I dreaded lying down each night, despite feeling tired and achy from sitting all day. I knew I would be eaten alive by the bedbugs running rampant on the cell floor. We could feel them viciously sink their little vampire teeth into our flesh as we lay in the dark. In the morning, we routinely checked our skin for bite marks, many of which still had traces of blood on them. Those littlest of predators were so small you could barely see them, but there was no doubt they packed a powerful punch. I hated the little vermin.

Mammy continually tried to keep our spirits up during our time in that hot little box. I know she was anxious about Pappy, though. In quiet moments, I watched her face turn toward the bars, searching past them into the night, wondering and worrying about our father, her forehead pinched. In this world turned upside down, what was happening to the man we loved so well, the same man who had injured the Japanese's best chance of obtaining the resources they so desperately needed? Surely if the Japanese learned of his bold deeds against them, there would be hell to pay.

In the situation we were in, the only things we had in abundance were time and each other. We had far too much thinking time to dwell on what was happening to our Pappy.

"Maybe he is close by—even in one of these other cells," Justin said quietly, breaking the silence that hung over us like a wet blanket during the heat of one particularly stifling afternoon.

"Justin, that doesn't make sense. They drove him away in a different direction. We all saw it." Peggy sighed impatiently as she wiped a grimy hand across her brow.

"Yes, but maybe they've moved him back since then. You never know," he suggested wistfully, his voice trailing off as he finished.

Mammy shot Peggy a warning look and shook her head slightly as my sister opened her mouth to speak.

"Darling, I'm sure he is safe. God is watching over him wherever he is," Mammy reassured Justin kindly. She smoothed his tousled hair and kissed his cheek. He melted into her, smiling as she rubbed his back softly.

"I don't blame Justin for wondering. I spend hours speculating about where he is myself," I said to Peggy under my breath.

"I know. I just don't want him to get carried away with false hopes that Pappy is here somewhere," Peggy explained softly. Her face reddened, and I knew she was near to tears.

"I know what you mean, but we're all entitled to hope, Peg. And Justin is still so young. All children should have a little stardust in their eyes, don't you think?" I whispered, squeezing her hand.

She shrugged her shoulders and nodded, looking away. Silence again fell over our little group as we got lost in our own thoughts once more.

***

Our time in prison ended abruptly but not a second too soon. After we'd spent two weeks in that cramped cell, completely isolated from the world, the guards strode up and unlocked the barred doors. They promptly read off a list of about forty names, ours included. We looked around at one another, wondering what our fate was to be.

"You, line up here. Investigation is over. You will ride to your new camp," a young guard said with no expression on his face.

Investigation over—what relief those words brought. Whatever they were searching for, they must have either found it or given up looking. No Japanese had asked us a single question about Pappy or anything else the entire two weeks we had been incarcerated.

We gathered our belongings and stumbled through the crowd to the door. The bright morning sun blinded us. We had to shade our eyes in order to focus after living with so little light for all that time.

"So much for 'You'll be home in two days,' huh?" Peggy said, mimicking the Japanese guards who had picked us up and brought us here. She nudged me with her elbow.

I nodded and smiled at my sister. *We made it*, I thought. Feelings of gratitude coursed through my veins. *Thank you, Lord. Thank you.*

We heard well-wishes of good-bye and good luck whispered through the cell. Tears welled to the surface, and I cried for those left behind in that evil place. I cried too with relief that we were finally leaving. *May we never lay eyes on that dark, dank cell as long as we live,* was my earnest prayer.

8

Palembang Houses

OUR TRAIN RIDE WAS UNEVENTFUL. I think we were all a little shell-shocked after the last two weeks in the prison cell and our abrupt reprieve from that awful place. The rhythmic clicking of wheels hitting the tracks quieted my nerves and helped me relax. I felt the strain of the last month slowly slough away as we traveled mile after mile away from Moeara-enim and our jail experience. I guess I should have been more worried about what was coming next for us, but to be honest, at that point, I couldn't imagine anything worse than what we had just been through.

We traveled in a cattle car of some sort, similar to our last train ride, so there was no way to discover our new destination by looking out the window. Our trip wasn't a long one though, and when the train slowed and the doors opened, I realized we were at the Palembang train station. I had been there many times before, traveling into the city for errands with Mammy.

No sooner had we disembarked than we were quickly loaded onto a truck and taken to a place in the heart of the city. As we journeyed, I noticed the Japanese presence everywhere. Soldiers smoking cigarettes on street corners. Officers strutting along the marketplace like arrogant roosters. Guards in uniform restricting the locals' access to certain buildings and roads, their faces expressionless and bayonets always close at hand.

I was used to seeing people riding their bicycles and neighbors chatting together over a common fence as they examined one another's flower gardens. You could normally hear the sound of children running and laughing and the boot of a soccer ball from dawn to sunset on Sumatran streets. But none of that was anywhere to be seen or heard on our truck ride through town. Palembang would have been a ghost town were it not for a few brave merchants doing business, the locals running their daily errands with bowed heads, and, of course, the soldiers keeping never-ending watch. The sadness of the situation touched me as we bumped along the road. What had our peaceful life become? I looked around dazed and confused, searching for an answer that wasn't there.

The truck jolted to an unexpected stop, and my mind returned to the situation at hand. Curiosity and nerves began easing like an elixir through my veins. The area we were in looked as if it had once been a community inhabited by European citizens, as the style of the houses was not Indonesian. From the size of the homes and their appearance, it seemed certain that these had been the quarters of some well-to-do people before the invasion.

However, barbed wire surrounded the homes in every direction, reminding me that we were still being detained. Freedom was not ours. Prison life was again on the agenda, though perhaps in a milder form. I could only hope that was the case. As we stepped down from the truck, carrying our bags and suitcases, we tried to get our bearings.

"They didn't take George and Justin," my mother said in a low voice, barely above a whisper. I looked around the truck and the courtyard in front of us and discovered that my brothers were some of the oldest boys in the group now. When we were in Moeara-enim, many of the teenage boys had been separated from their mothers and forced to go with the men. It seemed to be the same situation here in Palembang. At eleven and twelve, my brothers must have barely missed the cut.

"You're right, Mammy. I hadn't noticed before. Thank goodness they are still with us," I said gratefully.

"God *is* watching over us, Hanny. Even in the midst of all this chaos, He is still in charge, and we can trust Him." She squeezed my hand encouragingly. She looked more at peace than I had seen her look in weeks. The fact that my brothers were allowed to stay with us was the tender mercy she needed to keep going. Mammy's strength buoyed me up as well. We were going to make it through this ordeal yet.

Escorted by a disgruntled guard, we soon found ourselves in front of a European-style house with chipped plaster and high windows, even a chimney on top. The house was whitewashed, but it looked in bad repair. Weeds riddled their way up the mailbox and throughout the garden, strangling the few flowers bold enough to push their way through the hard, cracked soil. I had a bad feeling about this place. Before I had time to consider why I felt such a strong sense of foreboding, George prodded me forward.

I opened the door to a rotten, pungent smell I couldn't put my finger on. Assaulted by the odor, I backed away, letting Justin and George go in first. My mother followed closely behind. Peggy and I brought up the rear, plugging our noses and screwing up our faces at the stench.

"Find a corner to sleep. Others here already, but you find place in this house to stay," the guard grumbled in broken Dutch. Without another word, he did an about-face, shutting the door behind him as he left.

Alone now, we turned to see where we would be living. Our jaws dropped as we surveyed the room. The floor was tiled but in need of a good mopping. There was no furniture anywhere in sight. But what glued our attention most were the walls. No pictures were hung. In their place, brown smear marks scarred the white walls from ceiling to floor. I looked at them curiously. Who would wipe mud all over the walls, unless in a fit of childish rage?

"Feces," Mammy said, correcting my assumption as if she had read my mind.

"But . . . but why? Who would do such a thing?" Peggy asked incredulously. This was so out of our realm of experience that we could not understand such a vile act.

"I don't know for sure, children, but I suspect the European citizens who owned these homes were forced out. Maybe they are being held prisoner just as we are. It's my guess that they couldn't bear the thought of the Japanese living in their houses, so they smeared feces over them to dissuade the soldiers from setting up camp. I'm sure they didn't expect that people like us would be forced to live here."

Looking around the forlorn rooms, she continued, "Perhaps they destroyed all the furniture too, or maybe the Japanese just stole it like they did the jewelry in Moeara-enim."

There was no furniture in any of the rooms we walked through. Only the suitcases and belongings of other prisoners forced to camp here by the Japanese lay scattered on the floors. There was no one to greet us or to explain what we were to do. We assumed they were out working in the camp.

"Whoever dirtied the walls was angry, that's for sure. Maybe that was their way of lashing out at those who had pushed them out of their homes," I said, looking from wall to wall in awe.

"Thanks for the psychoanalysis, Sigmund Freud," Peggy retorted, rolling her eyes. "I guess we'll never know what exactly drove them to do this, but whatever it was, they definitely weren't happy," she continued.

That was an understatement.

"I guess that explains the smell. Ugh. This house reeks. How are we going to stand it here?" George asked loudly, his whole face contorting at the foul odor.

"Well, we're going to start by washing the walls," said Mammy matter-of-factly.

"What?"

"No way, Mammy!"

"And the floors," she continued.

"That's disgusting," shouted the boys in unison.

"It would be more disgusting to live here in this filth and do nothing about it. Who knows how long we will be here, but until they tell us otherwise, *this* is home. It's not much, I admit," she sighed, "but we'll do what we can to make it livable. Agreed?" Mammy asked, looking at each of us solemnly.

"Agreed," we said without any enthusiasm.

Peggy found a dented tin can in another room and went in search of water to fill it. Mammy found some old rags and used a bar of soap she had brought in her suitcase. Before long, we rolled up our sleeves and went to work, scrubbing and rescrubbing until the walls began to resemble their white color again.

Funny thing. Once we got cracking on our task, we forgot how disgusted we were. By the time we started to get hungry for dinner, the place looked somewhat presentable. The floor was free of dust and the walls were clean again. We placed our cases neatly in a small corner of the room that didn't look inhabited, and we waited. For what, we didn't know—perhaps for someone to come and help us make sense of all that had happened in the last month. It still seemed like a dream if I dwelt on it for too long, so I tried not to. I tried desperately to live in the present.

Soon we heard the give and take of women's voices approaching the house. We guessed they were the women who bunked here, coming home from their chores. Their pleasant exchange dissipated some of my fear of meeting new people, always an unwanted companion at the mere thought of introductions. Mammy greeted the women with an easy smile.

"Hello. I am Tina Londt-Schultz. These are my daughters, Hanny and Peggy. Over there are my sons, George and Justin. We just arrived on the morning train."

"Oh, hello there," one of the women said with a big smile. She was older, with wiry blond hair and a friendly face. "You came in with the big group earlier. We were out near the back of the camp working the garden when we heard the truck pull up. Where are you from?"

"We're from Tandjoengenim, a small mining town to the south," Mammy answered.

"Oh, uh-huh. I know of the place. We're all from right here in Palembang. We were brought to the camp almost a month ago when the Japanese picked up all of the Dutch in the city. I suppose now they are working their way out to the rural areas."

"Yes, we saw a number of people from the outlying areas on the train. Plantation owners, field workers, and, of course, the mining families from our town. We were separated from most of them about two weeks ago, though. Is it just the Dutch here, or were all the Europeans picked up?" Mammy asked.

"The soldiers collected all the Europeans and many of the Eurasians. There are no Germans, of course. They got a free pass because of their alliance with the Japanese in the war. My German neighbor, Bridgette, was allowed to stay in her home. I don't know, though," she said speculatively. "She's free, obviously, but I don't know how safe I would feel with all of those Japanese soldiers lurking around all high and mighty. From what I've seen, they're no lovers of women. I hear they treat their own wives like second-class citizens."

Peggy looked at me. We were remembering Pappy's warning about how the Japanese treated the women they found. This woman's opinion seemed to confirm what our father had told us.

The woman who greeted us was named Marta. She was middle-aged and freckled from her work in the camps. Her eyes were a blinding green that almost hurt to look at.

She kindly went around and introduced us to the other tenants of this house and their children. There were more residents than I had initially thought. I counted at least twenty to twenty-five. Some seemed warm, while others looked sullen as they murmured their welcome. Clearly, more people meant less space in this already overcrowded house. I tried to shake off the sour reception and smile my hello, timid though it was. I had always struggled with self-confidence, but I tried not to take their lukewarm greeting personally. These women would be our neighbors for the foreseeable future. Best to try and be friendly.

A thin hand landed on my mother's shoulder. The tan face it belonged to broke into a shy grin. The woman who had touched my mother spoke in French-accented Dutch.

"Thank you for cleaning the walls. The guards just moved us into this house a couple of days ago, and we've been so tired and overworked that our best intentions to clean up didn't amount to much, as you can tell."

There were a couple of other mumbled comments of appreciation from our roommates, who were clearly exhausted from their labors in the hot Sumatran sun. It felt good to know we had both helped them and made the place a little more habitable for ourselves.

While the other women rested and chatted, debriefing each other on their chores and whom they had seen throughout their day in the camp, my family and I unpacked our meager belongings. A few changes of clothes, an extra pair of sandals each, and our canned food. It made me feel good to know we had a small reserve.

Suddenly, it occurred to me that something was missing. I sifted through the cans and shuffled once more through my small stack of clothes. Where were my pictures? The ones of my grandparents that I had smuggled back into my case? My heart dropped. They weren't there. Sometime between packing them and our departure, Mammy must have given our suitcases a once-over to make sure we were all set in case of capture. Of course she would have run across the photos she had specifically asked that I return to the wall. Those pictures had been an anchor for me as I had packed, keeping me from feeling cut adrift from the life I was leaving behind. While I understood my mother's position, discovering I was without those photos left me feeling bereft. I finished unpacking my few belongings with a heavy heart.

Before we knew it, it was time for dinner.

"Not a moment too soon. I'm starving," announced George, who was always looking for his next meal. "I could eat a horse."

"Well, son, dinner here is not very exciting. A cup of rice and some old veggies seem to be the menu for every meal. I hope they've thought ahead and rationed us more food, seeing as our numbers have just increased," Marta said matter-of-factly as she led us to the common area in the center of the camp.

"Ugh. Not more rotten *kasave*. I'll die of starvation," George exclaimed under his breath.

"It's a good thing Mammy thought ahead and packed a little extra food. I wonder how many of the other women here did the same," Peggy said in a low tone.

Looking around, I wondered at the women I saw as we crossed the compound. Some were standing alone, but most were talking quietly among themselves. All had a guarded look in their eyes, as if they could never truly be comfortable in these restricted surroundings.

I wondered at the families that had been torn apart and the lives that had been left behind. Each woman had her own story, her own history; yet, here we were all shoved together and forced to live the same lives, at least for a time.

I saw the nuns and the sunburned castaways I had noticed on the first train milling around, talking. They hadn't been called off to go to the prison cell like we had, so they must have just come straight here. Glancing around camp, I saw several other houses like the one we were staying in. I guessed the women who looked familiar to me from the train had been assigned to other residences. I also recognized several other women and children from our village and smiled to them as we lined up to eat.

I noticed right away that the interns were helping one another, even in these dire circumstances.

"Here, I'll hold your baby for a moment while you get situated."

"I saw that you arrived without a bag. You must be hungry. Here, have a couple of my crackers."

"Would your daughter like a turn playing with my son's rattle? It might keep her occupied for a while so you can eat."

I felt a connection forming with these women and children. They were living the same nightmare we were and, though guarded, were still trying to stay positive. They reminded me a lot of Mammy. I vowed to try to be less fearful and more helpful in the future, but for now, we were occupied with the business of eating.

A truck backed up to the courtyard. The Japanese guards were divvying out rice to the women who were catching it in old cans. They were then tossed a few bruised vegetables before shuffling away. On our way back to the house barracks, we pumped water from the well near the truck's cab to cook with. Mammy was given so little rice to feed the five of us that I had to keep reminding myself that rice swells when you cook it. But after the rotten *kasave* in Moeara-enim, the vegetables, old as they were, were at least edible, and the well water was much cleaner and fresher than the brown river water we'd been given in the cell. Things were looking up.

***

Ironically, I thought about my optimism of the night before as I stood baking in the scorching sun during roll call the next day. Roll call was something we would grow to dread. The whistle calling us each morning became more and more shrill over time. Every morning we gathered in the center of the compound in front of the Japanese soldiers and were forced to bow to the captain. He represented the emperor of Japan, Emperor Hirohito, we later learned. We bowed not just at the waist but nearly in half so that we could almost touch our toes—this to show the proper respect to a man we had never seen nor had any wish to see in any of our lifetimes.

I glanced at Peggy on the first day of roll call as she stood next to me, bent as a hairpin, with sweat rolling down her flushed face, and wondered how long it would last. I was in the same position, perspiration trickling toward my neck as we stood minute after minute in the sticky Sumatran heat. When each woman and child was accounted for and all had bowed accordingly, we were dismissed. Roll call that morning took about twenty minutes. Other times, we learned, it took hours.

During roll call we all lined up with our housemates in rows, and the Japanese counted us by house. If someone was missing, which happened occasionally, the guards marched to the house of the absent woman to discover where she was. More often than not, they found the woman lying prostrate on the floor, sick from malaria or dysentery. Most times the guards forced her to join the group, but in extreme cases, the sick woman was granted a reprieve for the day.

A few days after our arrival, a fellow prisoner refused to bow during morning roll call. We stared at her in awe as she firmly shook her head and folded her arms in defiance. Tall and Australian, she was one of the nurses who had been trying to flee the island before the invasion. She had a nice open face with piercing blue eyes that held your gaze when you looked at her. She refused to bow, claiming it was uncomfortable for someone of her height to be in that position. She towered over the Japanese guards who tended to be quite small in stature. Perhaps they were intimidated by her height or humiliated by her insubordination, but they slapped her abruptly several times in the face and kicked her until she fell. When she dropped to her knees, the guards dragged her away to beat her, her head lolling from side to side in semiconsciousness.

Never before had I witnessed such violence. I looked at Peggy, her eyes as big as saucers and mirroring my own dismay at such behavior—especially to a woman. I trembled at the poor woman's plight but secretly admired her pluck. The scene that morning burned itself into my memory.

After that experience, roll call became a necessary evil. No one wanted to be punished like that poor Australian nurse had been.

Over the course of my time in the camps, I would watch weakened women, skinny with starvation, fall like flies during roll call. The sun became a cruel accomplice to the Japanese war tactics. As they dropped limp to the ground, the Japanese would often kick these poor women or hit them with their sticks until they rose again. Sometimes they were simply too ill to stand, so after a sound beating they would be hauled off to the house the nurses had transformed into a makeshift hospital to recover.

Although on most days roll call was limited to sunup and sundown, at times the Japanese used roll call as a punishment for defiance. If one of the interns broke a rule, was insubordinate to a guard, or simply failed to bow, the guards might call a midday roll call and we would all stand as a penalty for that woman's disobedience. We came to hate the whistle blow that called us to line up.

Our lives in Palembang consisted of chores—and lots of them. We teenagers chopped firewood and gathered water each morning. George and Justin were often assigned these chores because they were among the oldest boys in camp. In just a short time, their young muscles began to grow strong and supple. Women in the camp often complimented Mammy on how hard her boys worked.

"Mrs. Londt-Schultz, what good workers your boys are. They're a godsend to us, hauling in those heavy buckets of water each morning. Thank them, will you?" an older woman shouted amiably across the compound one afternoon. Mammy simply nodded, smiling her appreciation.

But later that day as she was undressing for bed, she said, "I'm proud of you, George and Justin . . . and you girls too. You pull your weight around camp. I know it's not easy to see others laze around, claiming it's too hot to work, but trust me, you'll do better here and be more content if you stay busy."

We thought Mammy was just trying to lift our spirits, but as the weeks and months went on, we saw the truth in what she had said. Those women whose days were empty had too much time to dwell on their disappointments. They turned dull and listless, many succumbing to debilitating illness. Those interns who kept their bodies strong and their minds sharp through daily work, in general, seemed to fare better.

Peggy and I sometimes hauled water from the well too, but our main job early on was to tend the children whose mothers were working, playing with them and trying to keep them occupied. It was no small task when there were no toys in camp, and the few picture books to be had were at a premium. Still, we grew to love the little ones in camp who found inventive ways, as only children can, to have fun in these sparse circumstances.

Once, Peggy and I were enjoying an evening stroll after dinner when we heard the distinctive sound of muffled giggling around the corner of the soldiers' barracks. Drawn by the infectious sound of children's laughter, we followed to see what was so funny. Peering through the slats of the fence surrounding the soldiers' building, eight or nine children were immensely enjoying what they saw, slapping their knees and trying to silence their laughs with hands over their mouths. Afraid they would be reprimanded, we called to them quietly.

"What's going on here, kids? Is there a circus in town?" Peggy asked with a twinkle in her eye. They pulled their eyes away from the fence, still laughing.

"We come here all the time after dinner. It's the soldiers' time to bathe." The oldest girl in the bunch giggled. She was a thin child, maybe six or seven, with long dark hair twisted in a braid down her back. She quickly turned back to the peep show.

"I'm not sure you should be watching them bathe, kids. You might see something that'll give you nightmares," I said jokingly.

"We think it's hilarious! The guards bring out this big tub and fill it with clean water. The colonel is the first to take his dip. After he's done, the captain hops in and cleans up. When he's finished, it's the lieutenant's turn, then the sergeant's, then the corporal's, right down to the lowliest of them all. The private ends up bathing in old, dirty, brown water left over from the rest. What really makes us laugh is when they leave the tub, they salute each other with just their towel wrapped around them to signal it's the next person's turn," the girl with the braid explained. The others were giggling softly as they watched the peep show.

Peggy warily placed her eye next to the hole in the fence and then laughed out loud.

"It's true, Hanny! All they need is a rubber ducky and a bottle of bubbles, and they might as well be relaxing in their own tub at home," she whispered under her breath, her eyes wild with laughter.

"Whew. What I wouldn't give for some quality time in a tub full of clean, piping hot water and a brand new bar of soap. Doesn't that sound heavenly?" I asked dreamily, turning away from the fence and the giggling children.

"Someday, Hanny. Someday we'll have that again," Peggy said wistfully as we continued our walk in the late afternoon shadows.

***

We were also assigned to care for the garden in the back of the camp and clean the bathrooms in our house, two of the most challenging jobs we had been given to date.

"What is this stuff we're dumping on the garden, Hanny? I know what it smells like, but what is it really?" Peggy grunted as she heaved a bucket of manure from the pile to fertilize the garden.

"I'm afraid to ask," I replied, hoeing and spreading the manure around the plants. I stopped to wipe the sweat from my eyes.

"It's human manure," our friend Anna, a young rural girl from outside Palembang, informed us. Anna often joined in our chores and was the voice of experience about camp life. She and her mother had been interned here since the beginning.

"I don't believe it. You're trying to pull one over on us," Peggy said, shaking her head. She was leaning on her hoe now, her full attention on Anna.

"No, really. I heard some of the ladies talking. They empty the camp latrines a couple of times a week and then reuse it on the garden as fertilizer," Anna replied, shoveling as she talked.

"It definitely smells bad enough! That's just not sanitary, though. Even the Japanese have to know that," Peggy said, throwing another bucketful on the garden plot.

"They may know it, but do you think they care?" our blond friend retorted. Nobody replied since we could all guess the answer to that question.

***

Mammy began to collect seeds from the rotten vegetables we were given. Before we cooked them over a fire outside our house, she would slice them open with her fingers and extract the seeds. She dried them out for a day or two in the sun and then planted them in a small garden patch of her own on the side of the house. Gardening was so ingrained in Mammy's nature that I wasn't surprised to see tender young shoots sprouting up out of the earth before a week had passed. I was admiring Mammy's handiwork in the garden one evening when I heard her voice behind me.

"My little plants are doing well, aren't they? Your grandfather used to always tell me when I was a girl, 'Tina, in Sumatra you can grow anything. Just shove an old stick in the ground and it will start to grow.'" She smiled at the memory.

"I learned how to garden from watching him. He taught me which vegetables and flowers to plant at certain times of year." She pointed lovingly to her small plants. "These are pepper plants. They'll give us vitamin C, which will keep us from getting scurvy and other sicknesses. The few vegetables we get at dinner just aren't enough to keep us going, and who knows how long we'll even get those? Best to try and supplement with ones we can grow ourselves."

Night had fallen, so after pulling a few weeds, we headed inside to get some rest. There wasn't a lot to entertain us at night, and after a hard day's work, our meager bedding called to us. We were so tired that most nights we even forgot the hard floor beneath us. We were happy to just lay our heads down and let sleep take over.

***

After living in the Palembang houses for several months, we awoke one morning to a strange phenomenon. Snails. They had invaded the camp overnight, infiltrating our houses—the ceilings, the floors, everywhere. They glided up and down the walls, trailing their strange slime behind. We literally had to brush snails off of our bed linens and clothes and out of our shoes each morning. Everywhere you stepped, you'd feel the crunch of tiny snail shells. They were in every nook and cranny, reminding us of the strange science fiction stories we'd heard on the radio at home from time to time. They were never my favorite.

The snails' arrival provided a new topic of conversation for those women who gossiped and chatted with one another all day long. No one recalled having ever seen such an infestation of snails in all their years. Even the grandmas and older women in camp shook their heads at such a sight.

"My goodness, these snails are a nuisance. I had to rewash my bowl and cup three times yesterday because they were slick with snail slime," Marta told Mammy one morning, a disgusted look on her face.

"It's just so strange. I wonder what brought them all here. I had to shake out our sheets twice because they were covered from top to bottom with snails. Poor George won't admit it, but he twitched and turned all night. I think he's a little afraid of them," Mammy said, grinning.

"Well, George isn't the only one. They're disturbing to me too. There are just so darn many of them. It's like they are going to take over the world or something." Marta shuddered at the thought. Two of the other house residents joined her, and she waved as she walked out the door to start her day.

The snails lived among us for two or three days and then slowly disappeared. We weren't hungry enough yet to see that the snail epidemic could have been a godsend, sort of like manna from heaven in the story of Moses' people. At the time, we only saw them as an annoyance, a little unexplainable plague sent to stir things up a bit.

***

"Mammy, what is this collection of cans you have in the corner? We are starting to be overrun," Peggy asked playfully one evening as we were getting ready for bed.

"We can't throw anything away now, dear. We don't know how long we are going to be here, and I'm of the opinion everything can be reused for something. These cans can be used for containers or as a pot. You've seen me cook rice in them, haven't you?" Mammy reminded Peggy, as she continued mending a tear in one of George's shirts. She'd bartered for a can opener, which solved our earlier problem of not being able to get into the food we had brought. We rationed it very carefully, though, because we didn't know how long we would be here.

"Well, yeah. But do you need so many of them?" Peggy asked.

"I think Mammy is right. We keep everything. Maybe down the road we can trade them for some necessities too," I said in defense of Mammy's collection.

"That's true, I guess. The other day I saw Marta swap an old pair of sandals for two cans of peas. Since money doesn't matter much here, trading might be the way to go," Peggy said thoughtfully.

"Exactly my point, dear. If those cans are bothering you there, just find them another home—under our bags or something. But don't throw them away." Mammy lay down on the floor, shifting her body to try to get comfortable. Strangely enough, Mammy's can collection and her own personal garden plot were two of the things that helped me settle down to sleep most nights. I felt safe. I knew that with Mammy we were in capable hands, ones that were strong enough to weather the storm we'd been thrown into. Little did I know the storm was about to change directions yet again.

9

Reprieve

THE HEAT OF THE DAY was slowly ebbing. Dinner had been the same affair it had been every evening for the last few months in the Palembang camp: rice and vegetables. Mammy had often supplemented, though, with some of her own *kasave* and peppers she had grown in her garden.

Justin and George were playing some speed game with their hands to see who would flinch first. Peggy and I were lounging after having cleaned the lavatories for most of the afternoon—a job we truly hated—and Mammy was using the last of the natural light to work on her mending, which was a service that seemed never ending the longer we were here.

"Girls, did Anna help you today on bathroom duty?" Mammy asked conversationally as she rethreaded her needle.

"Yes, she was there holding her nose like the rest of us." Peggy sighed. "It's getting worse and worse, Mammy. The dysentery in this place is sending people running for the toilets, and sadly, they are *not* always making it in time."

"Poor people," she replied, clicking her tongue in concern.

"Poor us," I retorted. "I could hardly get through our chores today without dry heaving from the stench." Peggy laughed out loud, and it was a good sound, an infectious sound. Laughter still existed in the camp, but not as often, or as genuinely, as it had before the invasion. The boys joined in too, giggling away at our malodorous servitude. Mammy couldn't resist either, and we all enjoyed a moment of pure fun. What a healing elixir! Our laughter stopped abruptly, though, as three loud knocks reverberated on our door.

Just as we were rising to answer, a lieutenant dressed in his khaki uniform strode through the house. Other women rose from their corners and bedrolls to see what was happening, each bowing abjectly as the soldier passed. It was customary—no, it was required—to show deference to officers by bowing low in their presence. To not follow this protocol would lead to punishment, swift and sure.

Ignoring the bows and the silence that followed in his wake, the lieutenant strode to the center of the house and, without further ado, called out loudly, "Londt-Schultz family. Justine. Hanny. Peggy. George. Justin." We instinctively jumped up like little jack-in-the-boxes as our names were called. My heart felt like it was going to beat through my chest. What could he want with us? We weren't rule breakers. We worked hard, day after day, doing what we were asked. Why single us out now?

"Gather your things and report to the front gate. You will be leaving the camp shortly." The lieutenant's black-beetle eyes never lighted on us once as he spoke. He gave no further explanation before he turned abruptly and marched out again.

I vaguely registered the gasps of surprise from our housemates as I turned to collect my few belongings. I herded my wrinkled clothes back into the small bag I had brought here almost six months ago. My hands shook as I tried to work, slowing me down and rendering me almost useless. I could feel Peggy glance at me several times as she folded our bed linens and stacked them in a neat pile. For once, I didn't meet her gaze. I was simply floored.

Mammy mechanically organized her case, trying to fit in her cans and other sundry items she had collected while at camp. Her forehead knotted together over her eyes, and I saw the heel of her hand fly to massage it out more than once. She was worried too.

The boys were done with their packing quickly and, for once, sat quietly on their cases as they watched us finish our tasks. I looked through my lashes to see if they were upset. Their eyes were cast down, and Justin's lip looked as if it might be trembling. I finished next and squeezed in between my brothers, putting an arm around each of their shoulders and holding them reassuringly as we waited for Mammy and Peggy.

"Where do you think you'll be going?" one of the housemates from another room asked as she peered around the corner. Her eyes shifted warily and were calculating, as if we had turned enemy all of a sudden.

"I have no idea," my mother replied simply, meeting her eyes. She stretched to stand upright, clutching her brown battered suitcase in hand. The woman threw us a cautious look before shuffling back to her floor space in the next room.

"Well, darling, God be with you, wherever you go," Marta said kindly as she walked over and squeezed my mother's arm. She smiled at each one of us children and patted Justin on the head. Several of the other women waved their farewells as we walked to the door. Mammy smiled a tremulous good-bye to our friends, and then we left, conscious of the many curious eyes following our departure.

We wound our way around the other prison houses, looking at the camp and the people there, not knowing if this would be the last time we would ever see them. Strangely, I registered a sadness that I didn't expect to feel. Maybe it was the question of what our future held, the sense that a known evil was better than one not yet known. I pondered that thought as I walked by the guard tower.

At the gate, we boarded a truck and were transported through town. It was the same route I remembered traveling months before, but, if possible, the streets were even less inhabited than I recalled. They reminded me of the ghost towns I had heard about on the radio while sitting at Pappy's feet after dinner. The silent Japanese officers standing rigidly on what seemed like every street corner were the only sign of life we saw.

Before long, we found ourselves on a train, this time in a passenger car. I ran my hand along the smooth mahogany seats and admired the furnishings. After our cattle-car experiences, I felt we were traveling in luxury. The fleeting thought that my grimy clothes and hair might stain the velvet cushions made me feel a twinge of nervousness. There was a question forming in the back of my mind. Treating us as human beings did not match my idea of how the Japanese operated.

George and Justin looked out the window, mesmerized by the country-side as it flew by. Mammy's forehead still had a pinched look, but she closed her eyes as if resting.

Peggy whispered quietly in my ear, so as not to disturb her, "We're going south . . . the direction of Tandjoengenim. Could it be we're going home?"

"I don't know, Peggy. Maybe we're just being hauled off to a new camp somewhere. I can't get my hopes up just to have them shot down again," I replied quietly.

She nodded in agreement, her drooping head on my shoulder now. Nobody spoke again as the train ate up miles and miles of track toward who knew where.

I must have dozed off because it was dark when we slowed down. Peggy started awake at the sound of the train's brakes squealing to a stop.

"Where are we?" she questioned, curiosity dripping from her voice as she tried to look out the dark window.

"We're at Tanjoengenim Station," Mammy breathed quietly.

"*What?* And you didn't wake us?" she exclaimed, clearly astonished.

"We're *home?*" George asked incredulously. He stretched himself awake, cracking his joints as he reached forward and upward to his full height. We all looked at Mammy expectantly.

"I didn't wake you all because I wasn't sure if this was our final destination or just a pit stop. I didn't want you to get excited for no reason," she explained, patting Peggy on the leg.

We sat on eggshells as the doors slid open. I looked up and down the aisle, anxiously searching for a guard to inform us as to what would happen next. Nothing happened. Nobody came.

After several minutes, my heart stopped racing and instead thudded to the pit of my stomach as disappointment set in. Obviously, we must have only stopped to pick up more passengers before continuing. I looked out the window now, trying to absorb anything familiar I could see, but the scene was simply a train station, like any other. I did get a glimpse of the path I had taken to walk home almost a year ago, which caused a little knot to form in my throat. I could feel tears pricking my eyes, threatening to fall. I blinked hard to stop them. We were so close.

Just as we expected the doors to shut, a Japanese soldier leaned through the opening, looking frustrated. His eyes questioned Mammy's.

"Londt-Schultz family?" he asked swiftly.

He didn't need to call us twice. We quickly grabbed our suitcases and bags and stumbled after him, hardly able to rein in our enthusiasm. We clamored down the steps, trying to keep up as he strode along a path to the road where a shiny black car was parked and idling.

I could see the admiration in Justin's face as his eyes lighted on the sleek automobile.

The soldier escorting us was already opening the doors and popping the trunk to put our bags inside. Even after much maneuvering, the cases didn't all fit, just as we hardly fit in the car. We were used to tight spaces by now though, so we made it work.

He ducked his head in as we were trying to adjust and said, gesturing to the cases lined up behind the car, "I will bring the rest later. They don't fit."

My mother, just sitting down, jumped up quickly and turned to the rear of the car. I heard her reply courteously but firmly that she would carry the old, brown suitcase in the car with her. I winced slightly, thinking the soldier would suspect there was something of value inside, but he just shrugged his shoulders before closing the trunk.

Mammy sat in the back with us, Justin perched on her lap, while George sat in the front seat with the officer. I could tell from the look on my brother's face that, while he was somewhat repelled by the soldier's closeness, he still felt a twinge of pleasure at being able to sit in the front where all the gadgets and controls were located.

The shiny car made easy miles of our trip home. We were at the corner of our street in no time. I could see the big tree in front of our house as we rounded the bend, its thick branches waving a welcome. We passed the country club on the way and soon saw a few hearty flowers from our garden hanging haphazardly over the fence as if to see who was coming to visit.

My heart beat so hard as we parked that I was certain the soldier attending us must have heard it. He quickly unloaded us and our luggage and then marched down the path. We followed right behind him like overly anxious puppies nipping at their master's heels. He opened the door, and we slid quickly by him into the house. He nodded his head briefly before turning to leave, never breathing a word of explanation as to why we were all here.

My heart was not going to survive this day because no sooner had we set our bags down than who should appear around the corner but our father. My heart stopped beating entirely at the very sight of him standing there. He had his hands in his pockets and a book nestled under his arm, leaning against the door frame, feigning relaxation.

We all ran to our Pappy, arms wrapping around his waist as tears of joy streamed down our faces. We were together at last. And we were home. There was nothing else to ask for.

***

"How are we here? How did this all happen?" Mammy asked Pappy, looking bewildered but glowing with happiness after our initial rejoicing had died down a bit. I noticed she couldn't stop touching him. Her hands were nestled in his hands, then rubbing his arm, then touching his face.

We were sitting around his chair, with the radio in its usual place and Pappy resting comfortably with us at his feet. Everything felt so familiar. It could have been a scene from a year ago, but inside I knew that we were different people than we'd been before. We were the same but different. The war had changed us, matured us.

I looked at Pappy, analyzing his face for changes too. He looked tired, haggard almost, and he looked weathered, as if he had been in the sun each day since we had parted. His face was thin as well. He'd always had a slight build, but he looked very small sitting there in his chair.

His eyes were the same, though. There was that twinkle that I remembered so clearly. And the way they crinkled in the corners when he smiled, that was still there too. We all looked up at our father, like sunflowers seeking their source, waiting for his reply.

"Well, I was approached last week in my prison camp in Muntok. That is where they took me when I was separated from you all those months ago.

"I was trying desperately to fall asleep on my mat, surrounded by a chorus of snores on all sides, when I was tapped firmly on the shoulder by a prison guard who was summoning me to the camp headquarters. I bowed instinctively. A colonel was waiting for me in his office. He smiled and greeted me courteously. I immediately started to suspect that the Japanese needed something from me, as no one in camp had been treated well by the soldiers since we'd arrived. My mind was working overtime, trying to figure out what they might want so I could use it to my advantage.

"After the initial pleasantries were over, the colonel got right down to business. He crossed his arms on his desk and leaned toward me, his calculating eyes never leaving my face. I sensed this was a test of some sort, so I made my face as blank and unreadable as I could, a poker face if you will.

"He explained that he was going to share something confidential with me—something very few people knew. He told me that the mines and the oil fields up and down the island of Sumatra had been disabled. Knowing I was a geologist, he asked if I was aware of that.

"Though my heart plummeted to the soles of my feet and I could feel cold sweat dripping down my back, I looked him right in the eye and said, 'No, I wasn't aware of that.' I forced my hands to stay quiet in my lap, although I felt compelled to wring them like crazy. He stared in my eyes for a long time, searching. I held his gaze, trying my best to look slightly confused but not sure if my ruse was working.

"He must have been convinced of my innocence because he continued to explain that these resources were very vital to the Japanese, and they would be willing to compromise a great deal in order to have them restored.

"Again trying to act as puzzled as I could, I asked how the mines had been disabled and if they could be returned to working order. He replied that he didn't know but he was hopeful. Then, rising from his chair and leaning close, he put all his cards on the table.

"'We need you, Londt-Schultz,' he said intently. 'Your name was brought up as someone who might be capable of fixing the mines. Will you look at them?'

"I must have hesitated before answering. I knew in my mind that I could have any number of concessions if I agreed to do what he asked. He must have read my mind because, before I could reply, he continued, 'Of course, we will make allowances for you. We will give you your freedom . . . money if you want. Name the price.' His eyes shone as he knew the game was on. I weighed my options. They wanted my expertise badly. If not, the colonel wouldn't have been this straightforward with me. I thought about what I could possibly get, what they would give me, if I fixed their mine situation. The only thing I wanted, the only priority I had, was my family. I wanted us together again and safely back in our home.

"Looking the colonel boldly in the eye, I gave him my demands. My family and my home and time together before I performed my duty. He looked at me hard, desperately trying to gauge my intentions. He must have realized I wasn't bluffing because he heaved a great sigh and closed his eyes. 'Done, but it *is* going to take some time to locate your family. A few days.'

"I nodded, not trusting myself to speak. Silence filled the room as I waited for him to dismiss me. As if on cue, a sergeant appeared at the door to escort me back to my barracks. Before leaving, I turned to the colonel. 'I don't know if the mines *can* be fixed. I will have to examine the situation first.' He acknowledged that he had heard me by a brief incline of his head before turning away and staring out the window into the black night.

"Before sunup, I was put on the next train home. I was glad of that because I didn't want to have to explain anything to the others in my barracks. I knew they would have been curious, and if they had caught wind of what I was doing, my well-being might have been in jeopardy."

We were quiet as Pappy finished his story. The clock ticking softly on the mantel was the only sound that could be heard. He had paid a hefty price to bring us all together again. Was it treason for him to agree to fix the very facilities he had been ordered to destroy by the Dutch Indonesian Army only months before? Morally, wasn't it more important to protect his family at all costs? I knelt there weighing these questions in my mind when George spoke up.

"Pappy, you can't do that. You can't help the Japanese like that. That's not right," he said, shaking his head from side to side. He looked completely disillusioned by my father's admission.

"I think I'd rather go back to the prison camp than know that you are going to help them. They're the *enemy*, Pappy," Justin whispered accusingly, his face turning a pale shade of green. Our heads shot up when Pappy laughed out loud. We all stared at him in disbelief. What was so funny?

"You don't honestly think I am going to fix the mines, do you? Why should I honor an agreement with our enemy? I only agreed to the colonel's request to buy the Allied troops more time. You see, if *I* didn't acquiesce, then someone else surely would have. The longer I hold out, the longer the Japanese are short the resources they so desperately need and the more time the Allies have to prepare to fight.

"Frankly, I was shocked that they believed the mine facilities were at all salvageable after Kretzer and I had had our go at them—we were pretty thorough. I want a chance to inspect them again and render them completely useless . . . forever. Of course, being home with you all for a short time before I go is an added perk I'm glad I negotiated."

Peggy and I looked at one another, both feeling relief. Our father was still the bravest, smartest, most loyal man we knew. Mammy looked disturbed though. Her worried eyes never left my father's face. The look I saw in them stayed with me as we all departed to unpack our cases. Our father had been granted three weeks leave to be with his family before he was to embark on his pseudo-mission for the Japanese.

My first item of business was to bathe. I still remembered the conversation Peggy and I'd had outside the soldiers' barracks a few weeks ago. I dragged the old metal tub out of the laundry area and into the bathroom and began filling it with water. I was new at this, as Nanny had always drawn our baths for us before the invasion, but Kokie and Nanny had both sent word that they were not able to come and be with us until after the war was resolved. They were fearful of the Japanese presence in our town now and felt it was safer for them to stay in their own villages. Pappy and Mammy agreed. They didn't want our dear friends to put themselves at greater risk for our sakes either.

After heating the water and filling it with bath salts, I took off my ragged, old clothes and slid into the bathtub. Never had a bath felt so divine. The hot water wrapped around me like a blanket, soothing my aching muscles one by one. The smell of lavender from the salts I had used filled my nostrils and relaxed me until I was totally inert and at ease. The only sound to be heard was the quiet lapping of the water from time to time as it touched the side of the tub. This bath was even better than I'd dreamed it would be in all my days in camp—and I'd had some very vivid dreams. I don't know how long I lay there, but every minute was worth it.

At first I forced my mind to be blank, not wanting my thoughts to add any tension to the moment. But eventually, like insects scurrying on the floor at night, they crept in: thoughts about the horrors we had experienced in Moeara-enim's prison, the deprivation in the Palembang houses, and the exhilaration of being home again raced through my head. It all seemed a little surreal to me, lying here in this bathtub in the quiet of the bathhouse.

Then Mammy's face came to my mind. Why had she been so silent and looked so worried by my father's story earlier? Once we had learned that Pappy was still a true patriot, the rest of us had breathed a sigh of relief but not her. If anything her worry lines had increased, and her forehead had become more puckered than before. My mind wandered through the possibilities and then lighted on the most obvious explanation.

She was worried about the outcome of my father's latest venture for the Japanese. There was more danger in this than he had ever faced the first time.

Before, he was an anonymous face to them. The Japanese knew that there was a saboteur, but they had no name to put to the crime. How would Pappy ever permanently disable the mines now without them recognizing that this had been his true intention? He would have to make it look like an accident or like they had been beyond repair all along. That would be very difficult.

My own forehead wrinkled at the thought of the danger Pappy was placing himself in, but if anyone was up to the task, it was my father. Resourcefulness was second nature to him. I trusted that he would find a way to accomplish his task without bringing the anger and censure of the Japanese army down on his head . . . on all of ours.

Bang! Bang! Bang! I started out of my reverie at the sound of the door reverberating from the beating it was taking.

"Hanny, we're all waiting. If you don't get a move on, I am going to break down this door and join you," Peggy shouted in mock anger. I heard her muffled giggle.

"I'm just getting the water good and dirty for you, Pegs. Then you'll have the same experience those lowly privates had back at camp. Nothing like a little sweat and caked-on mud to season the water just right," I retorted, stepping reluctantly out of the water and wrapping a thick, fluffy towel around my body. I sighed as I shrugged on clean clothes. My personal spa experience was officially over. I saluted Peggy as I passed her on the way out the door. Time to unpack.

***

The next few weeks were heavenly. Knowing our time might be limited, we made the most of it. Peggy was at the piano for hours each day, her fingers hungrily eating up the keys, playing piece after challenging piece. The boys were outside in the backyard all afternoon, kicking their soccer ball or racing around, playing like their lives depended on it. My father was often outside with them, enjoying their youthful games, even joining in occasionally. Mammy took on the lion's share of the cooking with Kokie away, so I pitched in to help her. In the evenings, we sewed, lengthening dresses and shorts and wrapping ourselves up in the beautiful piano music, sometimes accompanied by Pappy's violin. This reprieve we had been given was a peaceful time. We breathed easy and simply enjoyed being together those first few weeks.

It was not all sunshine, though; there were shadows as well that threatened us, waiting to block the light. For example, on strict orders from my father, Peggy and I were not to leave the confines of our home, except to sit in the backyard. At first we balked at such a restrictive rule.

"Pappy, we've already *been* to prison. It feels like you're locking us up all over again. We want our freedom," Peggy groaned, her eyes pleading as she looked into my father's implacable face.

"No, Peggy. There are dangers I don't even want to discuss with you girls. It would give you nightmares if I told you the stories I've heard," Pappy said firmly, shaking his head, his arms folded as they faced off.

"We're not babies. You could at least tell us why we're being punished," Peggy grumbled, still looking defiant. His eyes softened noticeably at her choice of words.

"You girls are not being punished. I can't have you leave because . . . I'm trying to protect you. You are two of my most priceless treasures. It's like I told you before; there have been rumors, from very reliable sources I might add, that some of the Japanese soldiers have lured women and young girls, like yourselves, into their quarters and made them . . . concubines," he said, exerting great effort to say that last word.

"Pappy, don't those kind of women do that sort of . . . thing by choice?" I asked awkwardly.

"Sometimes, dear. It's like . . . they feel they have no power, or something, so they agree to live that kind of life in hopes that they can regain some control. It's not wise, and it usually ends tragically. In other situations, the women have no choice." He sighed as he continued, "I don't want that kind of life for my girls. I want to keep you out of their line of vision at all costs. That's why I am imposing this rule once again."

"Listen to your father, girls," Mammy said, glancing up from her book. Her eyes were unreadable, but her forehead was puckered with worry lines.

"I don't mind if you go out in the backyard but not the garden out front. It's too close to the road. The boys or I will do all the shopping for food and whatever else you need," he said matter-of-factly.

At the crestfallen look on our faces, he added gently, "It won't be so bad, girls. You have each other, your mammy—we're all together. Let's be grateful for that. I'm sorry it has to be this way. Truly, I am."

Peggy and I bobbed our heads in acknowledgement. In my heart, I knew my father wouldn't restrict us unless he believed it was absolutely necessary.

***

One evening near the close of our first three weeks at home, after a light dinner of fruit and fish cooked in banana leaves, we sat down for a comfortable couple of hours by the radio. After listening for the first twenty minutes or so, we realized that, for once, there was nothing noteworthy on the news that night. Pappy leaned over and clicked off the radio. He cleared his throat and announced, "I'd like to talk to you all for a few minutes. My three weeks of R&R are up on Thursday. That's only two days from now, and I expect that the Japanese will be very prompt in their request for me to leave and fulfill my end of the bargain.

"I just wanted to sit you all down and remind you of a couple of things. The first is that the rule about you girls not leaving the yard still applies . . . *especially* applies when I am gone," he said, looking Peggy directly in the eye but winking at her in the end. She couldn't help but smile, her resistance all used up.

"Secondly, you need to repack your cases and keep them by your beds again. I don't know how this mission will play out. It may end . . . badly, and we want to stay prepared. I'm not trying to frighten you; I just want you ready for whatever happens."

Peggy and I glanced at each other, fearful despite his plea that we not be.

"Along with that, if you *are* recaptured, stay within your camps. If you are ever given a choice to leave, which some Eurasians may be, I'm asking you to stay in the prison camps. It's a hard life as you well know, but you are under the protection of international treaties when you are prisoners of war. If the Japanese honor those, as they have said they will, then it would be an extreme breech of those agreements to violate you in any way while you are in their custody. No such protection applies outside of the camps."

We nodded that we understood.

"Last, remember that I love you dearly, each one of you." His voice broke as he continued, "During those months away . . . every day I kept thinking I should have told you more how much you mean to me. I don't want to make that same mistake again. I love you." His eyes glistened with emotion.

"We love you too, Pappy," we murmured in reply. It felt like "good-bye." *Please just let it be "until we meet again,"* I thought.

The next day proved that my father's vigilance with us girls was well founded. My aunt and cousins lived only a few streets away. Days after we were released, they were released too, maybe because of their Eurasian status. I never really knew why for certain. My uncle Alfred had been one of the first to enlist in the Dutch Indonesian Army after Pearl Harbor, and he had been one of the first to be captured. Last we heard, he had been forced to work in the Japanese mines for the enemy. Pappy took my *tante* Mien and her daughters under his wing after my uncle's capture.

Shortly after their arrival to Tandjoengenim from the camps, they received the same spiel we had from Pappy about not leaving home without an escort. Uncle Alfred's older daughters were roughly the same age as Peggy and me and had been our playmates since childhood. I could tell by the look in their eyes at the time that everything my father said about safety went in one ear and out the other. They had always been boisterous and fun loving. Words of caution to them were fleeting and ethereal.

I wasn't nearly as surprised as I should have been when, on the morning before the three-week mark, my cousins came flying through our backyard, their eyes bulging with fear. Their hair was dripping wet, and they had their swimming suits on, white towels whipping out behind them as they ran. They had clearly just come from swimming at the country club.

"Alex! Uncle Alex!" they yelled as they stumbled up our back steps, banging on the patio door with all their might. I was refilling the feeders in the bird sanctuary when I heard the commotion. I dropped what I was doing and ran to see if they were all right.

"Renie, Aldi, Herra! What's going on? You look like you've seen a ghost."

"Oh, Hanny! We've just been swimming down the street, and who should drive by but a huge truck of Japanese soldiers, leering, hanging off the sides, and catcalling to us," Aldi explained, her voice shaking with emotion and disgust. Renie was crying into her towel now, and I put my arm around her to comfort her.

"But why were you over at the country club? Don't you remember Pappy telling us it wasn't safe?" I questioned.

"We were bored, Hanny—tired of being shut away in our house. We thought it would be an adventure to go swimming. We were sure we could avoid seeing any soldiers. That was part of the fun of it," Herra explained offhandedly.

"We were wrong," Renie wailed into my shoulder.

I started patting her back in hopes that it would calm her down. I glanced up as I heard the back door squeak open. Mammy and Pappy were standing there, watching the scene before them but looking a little bewildered.

"Girls, what is going on here?" Mammy asked kindly, noticing the tears and my cousins' pale cheeks.

"What are you three doing in your swimming costumes? And you're soaking wet," Pappy said, observing critical details Mammy had missed.

"Uncle, we're so frightened. We know it was horrible of us, but we were bored, so we decided to go for a swim over at the . . . country . . . club," my cousin explained, her words getting softer and more tentative as she noticed the thunderous expression on Pappy's face.

"Get in here this instant. What were you thinking?" he stormed at them as he herded them inside the back door.

"We were just so tired of being restricted. We couldn't take it for another second, Uncle, so we slipped out while Mum was napping. We . . . we realize now it was a mistake, what with those Japanese soldiers driving by and ogling us. Who knows what they would have done if we hadn't jumped the fence and run through the backyards to your house," Aldi said.

"Japanese soldiers? You saw Japanese soldiers dressed like that? You are so . . . *so* fortunate they didn't stop and pull you aboard their truck. How could you *do* this? Didn't you think of your poor mother? She's already lost her husband to the Japanese. She would be heartbroken if something happened to you three on top of that," Pappy thundered, his eyes like flint.

My cousin Aldi finally looked abashed at what she had done, while Renie and Herra just continued crying at an even higher octave than before. I shuddered at my father's anger. It was so uncharacteristic of him. I sensed the fear beneath his bravado. Clearly he was shaken by the possibility of what could have happened to my careless cousins. Mammy stepped in now, bringing them dry clothes and shuffling them down to the kitchen for some hot chocolate. Pappy would escort them home after their snack.

I looked thoughtfully down the hallway after them. I didn't think they would risk disobeying Pappy's requests again. I trembled as I remembered his anger. I knew *I* wouldn't chance it, anyway.

***

Just as Pappy had predicted, breakfast wasn't even over on Thursday morning, the day of the three-week mark, when two Japanese soldiers tapped quietly on the door. They had come to accompany Pappy to a rendezvous point where he would collect any supplies he needed for his faux mission to fix the mines in the area.

Our good-byes were tender, and they pulled at me. My heart ached, and my mind balked against another separation. My father stared hungrily at Mammy's face for more than a minute, his eyes smoldering as he leaned in to kiss her good-bye. He held each of us children close too.

When it was my turn, he breathed one word into my ear so low I wasn't sure I had heard it correctly.

"Remember."

Then he was gone.

The next seven or eight weeks were nondescript, bland, vanilla. Our father was gone, and that took the joy out of everything we did. We got up in the morning. We dressed, ate, and went about our various activities but only in a halfhearted way. The other half of our hearts and minds lay nestled away with Pappy, wherever he was, doing whatever he could to help our country. Mammy just kept saying over and over, almost as if to convince herself, "Just leave it to the Lord, children. Leave it to the Lord."

Life became monotonous to me. I sewed and cooked and was truly grateful to be in my own home. But I worried constantly about my father. We all did.

After almost two months, the soldiers came again. We heard them rolling down the street, and I knew instinctively the truck was coming for us. A thought came to me, an impulse I couldn't shake. I flew as fast as I could out in the backyard, to the bird sanctuary. I wrenched open the doors. Freedom. I felt compelled to grant those birds their freedom, though in my heart I knew they were quite content in the little world my father had manufactured for them. Yet, it was theirs if they wanted it. *Fly away, little ones.* I raced back into the house just in time to hear the banging on the door.

10

Request

Driving through Palembang on a bumpy military truck felt like déjà vu. Apparently, we were headed back to the camp we'd left a short two months ago.

"Same song, second verse," I heard Peggy whisper under her breath to no one in particular.

We traveled back to Palembang on the train again, in the cattle car this time. No plush accommodations for the family of someone who presumably had failed in his duty to restore the mines. We had received no information about Pappy since his departure, but based on the Japanese soldiers' treatment of us, things hadn't gone well.

Pappy was featured in my thoughts so often that I sometimes imagined he would just show up, turn a corner or something, and be with us again. Where was he? Where had they taken him? I prayed he wasn't dead.

Mrs. Kretzer had come to visit Mammy when we had been home for a couple of weeks. She had looked frail, her skin papery thin. The gleam was gone in her dead eyes. Mr. Kretzer had never returned from his mission with my father. She had gotten word several weeks later that her husband had been captured by the Japanese. He was never afforded a trial. They had assumed his guilt right then and there. His sentence—to be tied to the back of a truck and dragged to death. We were devastated to hear the fate of Pappy's loyal friend. I was secretly glad my father had left unaware of his friend's death. I knew he would have been truly affected by it.

Thinking of that awful punishment was enough to produce that golf-ball-sized lump in the back of my mouth again. I tried to swallow it back, but it just made my throat ache. Tears threatened as I squeezed my eyes shut. Poor Mr. Kretzer—and poor Pappy.

I started remembering all of the good times we'd had together, the outings into the jungle, the soccer games, the violin music. Pappy was like a little kid when it came to kite flying when the wind was just right. And, of course, his beloved birds. Those recollections warmed me, but it was one particular memory my mind lighted on that truly summed up the feelings of love I had for my father.

I was younger, eleven maybe, and my mouth hurt. Hurt was an understatement. I had a terrible toothache. The pain radiated from my rotten tooth throughout my mouth and down into my jaw and neck. I had woken in the middle of the night, crying out in pain. Mammy had given me an ice pack, but nothing seemed to help. I needed to see a dentist.

Unfortunately, Tandjoengenim was just a remote town surrounded by miles and miles of jungle. There was only one country doctor who resided there but no dentist. Pappy had promised to take me to see the doctor the following morning. I'd held onto that promise with all I had, but still, the pain was excruciating. I could get no relief. I just remember crying pitiful tears into my pillow because of my poor mouth.

The next thing I knew, Pappy had lifted me out of bed and onto his lap and was holding me close, humming one of my favorite lullabies softly in my ear. The faint smell of his aftershave wafted near me, and slowly my sobs quieted to a soft whimper. He wrapped my quilt around me and rocked me like that all night long. The pain in my mouth was still there, but somehow his love for me that night helped soothe it until I was able to see the doctor the next morning.

Who was caring for him now? Who was quieting his fears as he lay in some dark, dank prison cell, for all we knew? The not knowing was my undoing. I didn't know how to picture him: in a Japanese work camp, in a prison cell, or . . . worse. I didn't want to think about that, so I made my thoughts return to the present.

***

I looked around. Somehow the streets we were driving through in Palembang looked different, not familiar. I vividly remembered a barbershop on the corner before we turned right down one of the main streets, but today we passed the barbershop and continued going straight. Maybe we were just taking a more circuitous route to the camp. After a few minutes though, I realized we were going too far. It seemed our old camp had been more to the west before.

I looked at Mammy for her opinion, but she was worlds away, twisting a strand of dark hair absentmindedly as she looked beyond the

Palembang streets to her own private vistas. Peggy was resting her head against George's shoulder, and Justin was lying on her lap. Not wanting to disturb them, I just kept watching and waiting. Before long, we turned onto a dirt road. Again, it looked unfamiliar. The brakes squealed to an abrupt halt outside iron gates. Barbed wire snaked around them and the fence they were attached to for as far as I could see.

My family awoke with the jolt of the truck stopping. We gathered our few possessions, the old brown case being one of them, and jumped down off the truck. The guards motioned for us to follow them through the gates, and before we knew it, we were locked up again.

It was at that point that we looked around, trying to gauge our new surroundings. Gone were the quaint little houses I remembered from our first camp. This new camp had long wooden barracks instead. We were directed toward one of them. As I entered, my eyes needed a minute to adjust to the new lighting, or the lack thereof. It was dark inside, with just a single unshaded lightbulb hanging from the ceiling. There were racks consisting of thin sticks tied together side by side, ramrod straight, forming stripes throughout the barracks. This was where we were to sleep.

The guard motioned to us to take a section of the wooden rack near the door. It was so small, only four feet wide and about six feet long. We learned later that day that it was called a *balai-balai*. Mammy looked up at him in confusion. He gestured toward the area again. "Here. It is yours. This is where you sleep."

"But . . . but, my children. Where will they sleep? Can't we stay together?"

The guard looked at her in frustration. "This is where you *all* sleep. No more room."

My mother's mouth turned into a little *O* shape, but she just nodded. Peggy and I looked at each other and shrugged. As small and cramped as the quarters were, we had experienced worse in Moeara-enim's prison cell. We would make it work.

We met the other women we would be living with later in the afternoon as they trudged in from their various work details. They looked hot and tired as they fell onto their racks. The barracks was stifling, with only the two doors on either end to allow airflow in and out. It offered the exhausted women very little relief.

After a few minutes, an older woman wandered over to meet us. She had a welcoming smile on her face. Her skin was crisscrossed with laugh lines.

"Hello, darlings. Just arrived, have you? I'm Mrs. Hoop; I'm right over here, not twenty feet from you."

"Hello, Mrs. Hoop. I'm Tina Londt-Schultz, and these are my children. There's Hanny, Peggy, George, and Justin."

"Very nice. Where are you from then, love?"

"We're from a mining town south of here. Tandjoengenim? Have you ever heard of it?"

"I think so. I'm from a plantation northwest of Palembang. What good luck that they let your boys stay with you. The Japanese just separated the older lads like them last week and sent them off to the men's camp. The poor mammies. I felt for them so," she explained, shaking her silver head with concern.

"How do meals work here, Mrs. Hoop? Do we each collect our ration and cook it on our own, or what?" George asked inquisitively. I rolled my eyes. He was always most concerned about the food situation.

"No, dear. There are several women who cook it in a community kitchen and dish it out to everyone. That's their job here in the camp. They work hard. I'm sure it can't be very exciting, cooking the same old rice and spinach day after day."

Turning to look at us, she said, "There now. You can come along with me, if you like. It's almost that time now. I'll show you how it's done. Do you have plates to take along with you? Oh, good. I see your mammy's got it all," she said, smiling as she shuffled out of the barracks.

As we walked across camp to the kitchen facility, we noticed some of the same people we had seen in the Palembang house camp. We saw some of the nurses milling around together, laughing over a private joke. We also saw a couple of the Catholic sisters in their traditional garb and some of the women who had been shipwrecked, as well as familiar faces we knew from around Tandjoengenim. It felt reassuring to see people we recognized from before; it made things feel more familiar.

"Mrs. Hoop, were you in the Palembang house camp first, or did they bring you directly here from your plantation?" I asked.

"Oh, you know about the houses?" she asked. She seemed surprised.

"Yes, we were there for more than six months, but we were . . . transferred for a while. Some confusion, I guess. Now we're back here," Mammy explained, skimming lightly over the details. She shot a telling glance our way, as if to warn us not to go into specifics with our new friend.

"I was brought here to this camp straight from my plantation just a few weeks ago. I kept expecting the Japanese troops to arrive and take me away after my husband joined up. But our rubber plantation is well off the beaten track. I guess they simply didn't realize we were there for all those months."

"You were fortunate to be able to stay in your home for that time," Mammy said, smiling at her warmly.

"Yes, dear, I was. I've no complaints. This camp though . . . they say it used to be a men's camp. The interned men built it from the ground up on the enemy's orders. They were only here for a month or two after it was finished. Then they were shipped off to a new place, somewhere far away," she explained to us.

By this time, we were in line, inching along to get our evening meal. One or two people nodded in welcome or exclaimed in surprise at seeing us again.

I thought about Mammy's reluctance to share our history with Mrs. Hoop. She was right. It was best to be cautious; we needed time to learn whom we could trust and who was acting as a spy for the Japanese. It sounded very cloak-and-dagger, even in my thoughts. But in the Palembang house camp there had been those prison interns who tattled to the enemy for favors—they were called "lovers of the Japanese" behind closed doors. Everyone knew to avoid them because they could make your life very difficult if you butted heads with them. In my opinion, though, sweet Mrs. Hoop seemed innocent enough.

As the days slipped by, it became apparent that not much had changed since our time in the Palembang houses. The food was the same; the chores were very similar. Again, my mother was praised for her hardworking sons. They took on the strenuous chores and did them quickly and efficiently, without complaint. I was proud of George and Justin. They were slowly growing into responsible young men, trading their baby fat for calluses. Justin especially pushed himself, taking on tasks that most twelve-year-olds wouldn't. In just one short year, he'd grown from a naive boy to a promising young man.

Soon after our return, my *tante* Mien and her daughters also arrived back at the camps. It was too difficult and terrifying to be alone in the townships now with the Japanese presence so strong. My aunt had taken Pappy's advice to stay in the camps, and we felt fortunate to be together again. Our cousins were such good friends to us. Peggy and I would often team up with Renie and Aldi for chores, which made the work seem lighter and the time slip by faster.

***

One afternoon not long after we had arrived, just as we were finishing our dinner, a tall, regal woman swept through the crowd of women, looking as if she were seeking someone out. She wore the white habit and long robes of a nun, and I recognized her at once. It was Mother Laurentia from the boarding school I had attended in Lahat. There, she had been the mother superior, and all the students had loved her. She had such a serene, capable look about her. She exuded quiet confidence. I watched the way the women here fell away to let her by. Clearly, she was still highly respected.

Mother Laurentia continued scanning the faces of those she passed until she lighted on my mother's. Her face broke into a beaming smile as she came over and put her arm tenderly around my mother's shoulders.

"Ahhh. Mrs. Londt-Schultz. Hanny dear, how are you? I had heard you and your family were back in the camps. I hope all is well with you and your children, madam?" she asked warmly, nodding to Peggy and the boys.

"Yes, Mother. We are well. And you and your sisters?" Mammy questioned politely.

"God is in charge, Mrs. Londt-Schultz. We are content with our lot." The nun shrugged with a slight smile.

"How funny. Mammy always says that too, Mother. One of her favorite sayings is that God is in charge," I reflected, smiling up at my old teacher.

"Does she now? Faith in God is definitely needed here in these circumstances. Your mother is a very wise woman, Hanny. Capable too, if I remember right. Wasn't it you, Mrs. Londt-Schultz, who baked cake enough for the whole school and transported it yourself to Lahat?" Mother Laurentia asked, a smile on her face. Her eyes were unreadable, though, and I sensed there was more to her question than just polite interest.

I had not thought about that day, my thirteenth birthday, for a long time. I had just arrived at the boarding school and was incredibly homesick. When I awoke, I didn't think anyone would realize my birthday was that day, so I'd kept it to myself. Frankly, the only people I wanted to celebrate with were my family, and they were miles away in Tandjoengenim.

Little did I know that my mother had arranged to bring cake to the school that day for all my classmates to help me celebrate. Mammy had contacted Mother Laurentia to ask her permission. It was granted. So for dessert that night, we all enjoyed delicious homemade chocolate cake. The cakes had been beautifully decorated with pink swirling roses and green vines. Of course, my favorite part of the day was simply seeing Mammy again.

I remember Mother Laurentia raising her eyebrows in surprise when she learned that Mammy had not ordered the cakes but had baked them herself. I guess I had never realized what a feat it was to make all that cake, decorate it, and transport it by train to the school. My mother never ceased to amaze me. I was surprised that my old teacher had remembered that specific occasion, though.

"Why yes, Mother. I did do that for Hanny's birthday one year. Funny you should remember that," my mother mused, smiling to herself.

"Hmm. I have a proposition for you, Mrs. Londt-Schultz. I'd like to talk with you more about it but in private. Would you mind coming by my barracks tomorrow morning early? Say directly after roll call? I live in the building closest to the north fence. Bring Hanny along too. This will affect her and your other children as well. I know she will be discreet," Mother Laurentia remarked in a low voice.

"Of course, Mother. I'll be there as soon as roll call is over," Mammy replied, looking at her quizzically. Mother Laurentia then turned and floated back through the crowd of women, nodding to some and smiling to others along her path.

My mother turned in surprise as she felt a gentle tap on her shoulder. Mrs. Hoop had left her gaggle of friends and was standing next to us.

"Oooh, Mrs. Londt-Schultz. You know Mother Laurentia, do you? Why, she's one of the liaisons for the camp, her and the good doctor lady. They're the go-betweens for us with the Japanese. What was she wanting from you, then?" Mrs. Hoop asked, her voice dripping with curiosity.

"I'm not sure. I honestly don't know," my mother answered, shaking her head, sincerity evident in her every word.

***

We rose just after dawn, as we did every morning. Early in the day was the best time to get our chores done, before the oppressive heat set in. We dressed and attended roll call. Not much had changed in that respect. We still had to bow to our ankles and wait in the sun to be counted. After that, the boys ran off quickly to haul well water for the kitchen staff. It was a strenuous job but one they were especially dutiful about because often they would get a little something for their effort from the camp cooks, an extra handful of rice or leftovers from the night before.

One of the women in our barracks had enlisted Peggy's help to watch her two small children so that she could fulfill her chore of hoeing the camp garden that morning. Mammy and I left her playing patty-cake and other singsong games with an anxious look on her face. We promised we would come back directly and relay all we had learned from our meeting with Mother Laurentia.

Mammy and I walked quickly across the compound, past the latrines and their heavy odor, past the bustling kitchen and the central square area where women congregated in the early evenings before bed. Finally, we arrived at the barracks to which Mother Laurentia had directed us last night. She was waiting out front, watching some children play tag nearby. Again, I was struck by her stately air. She could be royalty.

"Good morning, Mrs. Londt-Schultz. Hello, Hanny. Thank you for meeting with me." She paused with an animated look on her face as she continued to watch the little ones in their game.

"Good morning, Mother," we both responded politely, Mammy with her arm around my shoulder.

"I try to make a little time to watch the young ones in their play most mornings. The children here have taught me a thing or two about hope. See? Their spirits are very rarely down or dejected, unlike many of their mammies. I love to watch their buoyancy. It's a small pleasure I afford myself when I can," she said, shrugging her shoulders and greeting us with a smile. "Come. Let's sit over here. There is a little shade by the fence we might find comfortable," she said, leading us to a small patch of grass. "I'm sure you're curious as to why I wanted to speak with you. I wanted to save our conversation for a place devoid of prying ears."

My mother simply nodded that she understood, but her eyes burned with interest.

"I'm not sure if you are aware, but it is my lot here to help relations between the camp interns and the Japanese soldiers move along without any wrinkles, to be an intermediary if you will." She sighed. "At times my job can be a challenge, but I accepted the duty in order to help the women here as much as I can. The soldiers also make requests of me, and I try to accommodate those requests as best as I can. It seems that if they are happy, they are not quite so irritable with us," she explained with a smile.

Looking off to the right through the fence, Mother Laurentia got to the point, "The captain requires a cook. Apparently the guards are growing tired of eating burnt rice and nondescript vegetables for dinner. They have asked me to arrange for one of the women here to cook for them on a daily basis."

My mother looked slightly confused as she listened to the nun's explanation. I, on the other hand, intuitively knew what was coming next. Only my mother's innate modesty kept her from seeing it too.

Mother Laurentia looked Mammy directly in the eye. "I am asking you to be their cook, Tina."

My mother looked as if she had been slapped in the face, so great was her astonishment. She inclined her head, as if reviewing the conversation to make sure she had heard correctly.

"Mrs. Londt-Schultz? Tell me what you are thinking," Mother Laurentia pressed.

"I—I don't understand. Why me?" Mammy questioned.

"I know the kind of person you are, Tina, and the kind of family you are raising. You are strong and responsible, and furthermore, I know you are a good cook. If I remember right, Hanny's birthday cake was delectable," she said, finishing on a light note.

"Mother Laurentia, I already feel stretched so thin with my chores here and the four children to care for. Surely there must be someone else . . . No, I am sorry. I am going to have to decline," Mammy said, trying to justify her decision. She nervously straightened out a wrinkle in her blue cotton dress before meeting the nun's gaze.

"*You* are my choice, Mrs. Londt-Schultz. I feel as if you will be able to do a lot of good for the interns here at camp if you accept this assignment. *You* are the one. I can't explain it, but I feel in my heart you will have opportunities to help. Will you at least think about my offer, please?" Mother Laurentia asked, her liquid eyes looking into my mother's persuasively.

Several seconds ticked by before my mother simply nodded, but I could tell she wasn't at all convinced by the good sister's line of reasoning. Mother Laurentia patted her hand good-naturedly and then turned to me.

"Hanny, this is also a chance for you and your brothers and sister to help as well. If your Mammy decides to cook for the Japanese, it will mean long hours away from her. Will you and your sister step in to help with the boys?" she asked me.

"My sister, brothers, and I will gladly support our mother . . . whatever she decides," I answered quietly, looking at my worn sandals. I could feel my face flush as I spoke. Mammy squeezed my hand at my response.

"Very well then. I must be off. There are some sick ones that need my help across camp. Even with the nurses here, there are still so many that feel poorly.

"I will visit you in a couple of days to hear your final answer. Just know, my dear, that sometimes opportunities crop up that are unexpected and even unappreciated, but very often they are God's way of intervening on our behalf. Answers to a prayer, if you will. As strange as it may sound, I truly think this may be one of those times. I will be in touch soon, ladies," she said as she strolled off in the opposite direction. Her eyes paused briefly on the children at play as she passed.

Mammy spent a lot of time out in her garden that evening. As soon as we'd transferred here, she had started drying her seeds and planting them just like before. I went to check on her at twilight and found her leaning against the sturdy stick she had dubbed her hoe. She looked up at the stars that were barely beginning to twinkle in the darkening sky. Gazing up, I felt a familiar ache in my chest. Whenever I saw the stars at night, I thought about Pappy and wondered if he were looking up into the night sky too. I looked toward my mother.

"What are you thinking about, Mammy?" I asked, fairly certain I knew. I kicked a clod of dirt out of her carefully weeded garden patch while I waited for her answer.

"Just weighing all the options, Hanny," she replied enigmatically.

"Coming to any conclusions?" I pushed, not letting the topic drop. She sighed.

"Let me ask you something, Hanny. What do you think your father would do if he were here in my place?" she questioned, still gazing into the sky.

Her question stumped me. I had to think for a couple of minutes before responding. I heard the frogs in the surrounding jungle sing their nighttime lullaby.

"I don't know. My gut says he'd do what he could to help the women here. Then again, if there were any risk at all to the family . . ." I stopped, not knowing how to end that thought.

"I think he'd do it too. As opposed to the idea as I was this morning, I have to admit that Mother Laurentia's proposition is starting to grow on me. I mean, maybe she's right. Maybe this *is* God's way of answering the pleas of the women here in camp. I can't see all the particulars yet, but isn't part of faith stepping into darkness and believing the light will come?" she asked philosophically.

"Everything I've learned about faith has come from you, Mammy. I guess if you feel it's God's will, you should accept Mother Laurentia's offer to be the soldiers' cook." I shrugged. She looked at me then, her eyes deep pools. I could see questions there but no answers. I realized she still needed time alone to hash things through, so I kissed her swiftly on the cheek and wished her a good night's sleep before returning to the barracks.

As I lay down on the hard rack, shifting from side to side in a futile attempt to get comfortable, Peggy tapped me on the shoulder.

"Hanny, what has she decided? I'm scared. I think agreeing to cook for the Japanese will put Mammy in greater danger. What do you think?" she whispered in my ear. I could sense the fear that was starting to build in the tense way she held her body next to mine.

"I don't know, Pegs. She's still trying to figure it all out. She asked me what I thought Pappy would do," I replied quietly into the darkness.

"I think he'd say, '*Forget* the Japanese.' Let them eat their burnt rice and overcooked veggies. Maybe it'd teach them a little empathy when it comes to deciding what *we* eat on a daily basis," she whispered emphatically.

I smiled to myself. That was Peggy for you, spirited and opinionated to the end.

The next morning I awoke to see Mammy bustling around noiselessly, pulling on her trusty brown sandals and folding her nightclothes.

Rolling on my side, I asked her quietly, "Did you get much sleep, Mammy?"

Sitting on the edge of the rack near my feet, she shook her head. I could see the shadows apparent under her dark eyes but also a firm resolve. She had made her decision.

"I have decided to do it, Hanny. I'm going to tell Mother Laurentia this morning that I'll cook for the Japanese. I feel it's the right thing to do, and I've got to go with that."

I nodded my head, putting her hand in mine. I knew it had not been an easy decision for her to make.

"We'll all help, Mammy. You can count on us to do whatever we can," I said, smiling up at her.

"I don't doubt that for a second, dear. You are such good children," she said, patting my hand.

Peggy must have been feigning sleep because she suddenly sat up in bed, pushing her tousled hair behind her and hugging Mammy fiercely.

"We'll be fine, Mammy. No fears. You do what you need to do," she said in support.

Mammy kissed our cheeks tenderly and then rose to leave. We watched her as she left the barracks, walking in the direction of Mother Laurentia's quarters.

"Changed your tune a little since last night, didn't you?" I needled Peggy, mussing her wild mane playfully.

"Well, you know . . . I'm always a little grumpy when I am tired," she said sheepishly as she rolled out of bed to start the day.

11

Cook

"My word, Mammy, you look exhausted. We've been so worried about you," Peggy exclaimed as our mother shuffled slowly into the barracks. Justin and George were already fast asleep after a long day of hauling firewood in for the camp kitchen staff. Peggy and I had been too worried to rest.

Mammy had left for her first day on the job as cook for the Japanese at the crack of dawn. The sun was barely peeking over the horizon when she'd kissed us good-bye that morning. Now it was close to nine o'clock at night, and we had expected her hours ago.

She collapsed on the rack next to Peggy and me, her eyes closed and the worn lines in her face telling us more than words how tired she was. I reached down and gently took off her sandals, while Peggy stroked a stray lock of hair from her face.

"It was such a long day girls, and I scarcely feel I've made a dent. I'm going to have to go back first thing tomorrow. I think I am going to take *Tante* Mien with me this time, though. I really need the help," she said groggily as she curled into a ball on her side.

"Were they . . . mean to you, Mammy?" I asked, trying to learn more about my mother's day and her exhausted condition. I gently started rubbing her swollen feet.

"No, dear. To be honest, I hardly saw a soldier the whole day. When I first arrived, one of the guards showed me their storehouse where all the food is kept, and that is where I stayed the entire time.

"What a mess. You've never seen such disorganization. There were old bananas and guavas rotting on the floor. Someone had broken a huge bag of rice, and it was strewn everywhere, so much that it felt like I was walking on sand all morning. And there was such an awful stench in that room.

I finally found the culprit though—a crate of rotten vegetables that had been there for who knows how long. Ugh. It smelled bad." She grimaced then yawned. Her voice became more mumbled as sleep began to call her. "I found a bag of sugar that had been broken. As I was trying to scrape it up, I was thinking about how much we could use that sugar. We've been saving the last of ours for ages now. What we couldn't do with all that."

Her eyes began fluttering closed. Peggy smoothed a light blanket over her and looked at me with concern in her eyes. Her brow furrowed just as I had seen my mother's do time and time again when she was worried.

"I'm going to go talk to *Tante* Mien right now and see if she'll help Mammy tomorrow. It's not curfew quite yet. It will save Mammy time in the morning," Peggy whispered, sliding gingerly off the bunk so as not to disturb our sleeping mother.

"I wish *we* could help, Peggy. I feel so helpless, but we have to show up for bathroom duty tomorrow. It's our turn, and you know no one will trade with us. Everyone dreads that heinous job," I said in a low voice.

"Mammy wouldn't let us help her in the storehouse anyway. I can tell she's still nervous about working so closely with the Japanese. I think Pappy's warnings about concubines really sunk in, you know," Peggy replied softly as she turned to go find our auntie in the next barracks.

I sank down next to Mammy, trying not to jostle the rack as I settled into my small resting space. Mammy's deep, even breathing acted as a lullaby, soothing me until I succumbed to sleep.

The next morning I awoke early but not early enough to wish Mammy good luck in finishing her task at the storehouse. Peggy said that she and *Tante* Mien were up and gone at first light.

I thought about Mammy all day. I thought about her during roll call, glad that her duty for the Japanese exempted her from standing next to us in the blazing sun as each barrack's occupants were called, slowly and methodically. I thought about her as I sloshed around the dirty bathrooms, fighting a pointless battle of trying to restore cleanliness and order to an area so far gone that it was literally impossible. It probably felt as futile as Mammy's task had seemed when she first saw the storehouse so filthy and chaotic.

I thought about her as I shepherded my brothers through the dinner line, wondering if she had taken time from her chores to eat. Probably not. Convinced she would be hungry, I saved a portion of our rice and vegetables so she could at least eat when she returned home. She wouldn't last long if she let her own health go.

Mammy was grateful for the food when she arrived home later that evening, but at least she had gotten back a little earlier than the night before and seemed to be in better spirits too. Having *Tante* Mien there to help her and talk with her had made a big difference in her day.

"We made progress girls," Mammy said as she swallowed a long drink of water. "We cleaned off the floor entirely and scrubbed it until it shone. Later, we got our first shipment of food in, and I used some old shelves I found nearby to arrange it. I think we are finally almost organized. I need to place an order for more food tomorrow, and then we'll be to a point where we can plan and cook a successful meal. I guess I need to find out more about what the Japanese like to eat, though," she mused thoughtfully.

"I know they like fish . . . and soy sauce. There were bottles and bottles of soy sauce on the truck today. I think we must be down to a two- or three-year supply of that now," she said teasingly.

"*Pray* we're not here to see it all used up if that's the case," I said emphatically but with a smile on my face. Mammy finished the last bite of her rice and then lay down on the rack.

"I hate to be the one to break up the party, but I am just so tired. I can't seem to keep my eyes open tonight. I'm meeting *Tante* Mien early again. How was your day, children?" she asked between yawns. She curled up on her side like a kitten, her head resting comfortably on her arm.

"Don't worry about us, Mammy. Same old, same old," Peggy said, grimacing as she had flashbacks of our treacherous day on bathroom duty. Peggy had slipped on some unmentionables and had nearly dived headfirst down the john. I chuckled thinking about it. She glared in my direction as if she could read my thoughts.

"You sleep, Mammy. You've earned it," George said as he and Justin finished trying to catch a pesky mouse off in the corner. They were easily amused, but then what else was there for the boys to do?

It was already dark outside, and the one lightbulb that hung farther down in the barracks didn't shed enough light for anyone to read or draw or even mend our tattered clothes. Most nights, sleep seemed very inviting, a respite for our hot, tired bodies. But sometimes we yearned for recreation, some type of pastime to get lost in for just a little while.

I know Peggy missed her music. Her fingers sometimes twitched when she thought no one noticed. I think that during those times she was playing her favorite piano pieces in her mind. She never complained, though, or even mentioned missing her piano at all. She still had her favorite music book tucked away in her case. Occasionally, she would pull it out and pore over it reverently, as if trying to memorize the notes. Then, when she got her fill, she would gently slide it back into her case for another time.

I missed home. I missed the big broad tree out in the front yard by the street, with its leafy arms protecting us from the sun. I missed the colorful flowers in Mammy's garden, their childlike heads bobbing up and down in the breeze. I missed the cool stillness of the house upon entering and the eternal tick-tick of the mantel clock in the sitting room. I missed the worn oriental rug under the coffee table that had been a fixture in our home since I was learning to walk. And I missed Pappy. No, I couldn't think about him tonight. Sometimes it just hurt too badly to think about him: his walk, his smell, his cheery expression. I pushed the memories of him away for now.

There were other things I missed that weren't quite so painful. Our pets, for one. I smiled at the memory of their antics with my brothers. I hoped Ape and Knorrie were behaving themselves. Kokie was watching them while we were gone. Dear Kokie and Nanny! I missed them too.

I shook my head to try to shake off my thoughts. It was not healthy to allow myself the luxury of thinking of home too much. Camp life was easier if I kept my thoughts on the here and now. The past was too beautiful to touch upon very often. I ended up paying for it the next day if I let myself linger on what my life had been like before the war.

***

The next evening Mammy bounded into the barracks looking triumphant. The storehouse had been tamed, her first dinner for the Japanese soldiers had been a success, and she had even earned a "thank you" for her efforts from the captain.

He had walked by the storeroom after dinner just as she was polishing the sinks and had stopped, astounded by the transformation. Mammy said he was speechless for a minute and then bowed almost imperceptibly, whispering a sincere "thank you" to my mother before moving on. I think that, more than anything else, had her flying high as she practically skipped into the barracks that evening.

***

Time seems to pass more slowly when you want it to go fast. Days in the barracks camp were obstinately long, but eventually the hot, dry months turned into the rainy season right around late December. Unfortunately, in the eight or nine months we had been in the barracks, we children had experienced a growth spurt, so much so that our sandals were now too small. Peggy and I had planned to pass ours down to our brothers, but even if they had fit George and Justin, they were so worn and broken that they probably wouldn't have benefited from them much.

At first we welcomed the rain. It cooled down the camp perceptibly. It was still hot, mind you, but a little more bearable than before. After three weeks of moisture though, the rain was unyielding. It soaked into the dry, caked ground of the camp until it eventually become a slimy, muddy mess. We squelched through the dark brown mud, the ooze squeezing through our toes and caking onto our feet. Others had to fish their clogs and sandals out of the muddy quagmire that had literally sucked them off their feet and down into the brown goo. We grew to hate the mud because it slowed us down when we walked or tried to work. It was miserable.

Mammy's garden grew because of the precipitation, though. We had plump peppers and tasty spinach to add to our rice most evenings. Lately, we had even been treated to meat in our dinners at times, thanks to the ingenuity of some of the camp members. A few of the women had bravely, or maybe desperately, taken to catching snakes to throw into the pot some evenings.

Once, we even had the luxury of a monkey that someone had caught and killed. As much as I thought eating it would remind me of our Ape, my body was so in need of protein that I didn't care in the slightest. It tasted mouthwatering to my hungry body. Like most mystery meat, it tasted like chicken.

Mammy helped the camp on the food front too. A couple of weeks after she started working for the Japanese as their cook, she got sick of throwing away all the leftovers each night. There was a lot of waste. To her, it seemed morally wrong to do that when the children in camp were getting more and more malnourished. She would pass them on her way home from camp, noticing their distended bellies and their arms and legs, skinny as toothpicks. Their eyes seemed huge and pleading in their thin faces. I remember the evening that she came home elated. It was twilight.

"George, go gather the children in the barracks around here. Don't make it very obvious, though," she requested one evening as she returned from work. Her eyes were sparkling, and she had a wide grin on her face. She looked radiant.

"Mammy, what is it? What's going on?" Peggy asked from the door as she tried to chisel the caked-on mud off of her legs.

"The best thing ever. I've been so upset about having to throw away whole pots of rice every evening after dinner. My whole body seems to rebel against doing that. It's just such a waste. I've been trying to find the right time to approach the captain about collecting the table leftovers for the children in the camp each night. See, I've discovered that children are the Japanese's weakness," she explained animatedly. "Most of them seem to melt when they talk of their own children at the dinner table, and I've seen them smile and pat the heads of the little ones in camp from time to time. I figured it was worth a try. Tonight the captain seemed to be in an exceptionally good mood after his meal, so I thought, 'This is my chance.'

"I approached the captain slowly, bowing all the while. His fellow soldiers had already left the table, laughing and chortling over some joke they had just told. He was gathering his jacket to join them when I stepped into his path. My heart was about to beat out of my chest, I was so nervous, but I kept telling myself I had to do this for the children.

"'Captain, sir, may I have a word?' I asked humbly, my voice shaking. 'The children in camp are so hungry. They cry at night, sir, because their stomachs are still empty. Might I . . . might I have the leftovers from your table each evening to take to them? The food only gets thrown away . . . no one wants it, but the children would love it.'

"I waited on eggshells for his reply. Would he get mad and blow up or would he agree? I knew it could go either way, but then he smiled a small smile and nodded to me before gathering his hat to stand up.

"'For the children? Yes, take the extra food, Cook, and give it to the young ones,' he answered.

"'Thank you, sir, thank you,' I said gratefully, bowing low as I backed out of the dining room. Tante Mien was already wrapping the extras in the kitchen. She must have heard the whole conversation through the door. Once we knew all the soldiers were gone, we did a little jig right there in the storeroom.

"Oh, girls! I'm so grateful he said yes. This will help the little ones, don't you think? Tante Mien wanted to take half the food for her girls, but I convinced her that the toddlers and those who are ill would benefit the most," she said, her excited voice jubilant.

The little ones were already following George through the barracks like he was the Pied Piper, stopping when they reached Mammy.

"I have a surprise for you, children. The captain has given you extra rice and spinach today. The best thing of all is that there are even a few bananas and some boxfruit too," she said, pulling out packages from behind her back.

The children were literally jumping up and down when they saw the little feast she had brought for them. My eyes met my mother's. She was so happy. I felt tears prick my eyes, threatening to fall. She had been right. Her decision to cook for the Japanese had made a difference. We had no idea how big of a difference until a few months later.

Every evening as Mammy was walking home from her job as cook, the children would begin to gather in the doorway of the barracks, searching for the first glance of her.

"*Tante* Tina, *Tante* Tina!" they would yell, running to her when she appeared. "What have you brought for us today?"

"Children, children. Sssh. Come along inside, and we'll see what I have for you tonight," she would reply. Sometimes there was fruit; other times there were vegetables. Nearly always there was rice. She told Peggy and me secretly once that she and *Tante* Mien would make extra rice every day, more than the soldiers could ever eat, so she would have some to take home to the children each night. They couldn't make too much extra or it would become obvious to the Japanese that she was pilfering for the children, and then there would be consequences—possibly severe consequences. She just cooked a little more than was necessary.

Once an officer slipped her a bag of candy in gratitude for a delicious meal she had made for the guards. Peggy, the boys, and I drooled over the thought of that sweet, fruit-flavored candy. Mammy handed us the bag, but just as we were about to rip it open and indulge ourselves, she put a tan hand over ours.

"Be sure to share with all of the children you can. You each may choose one piece then share the rest," she said, smiling at our looks of shock.

"Why, of course. Why didn't we think of that?" Peggy asked, chagrined.

"Absolutely. That's the right thing to do," I agreed, my mouth salivating for another piece. George just shook his head woefully, but Justin asked, "Are you sure we have to share, Mammy? Just this once, can't the candy be our little secret?"

"Justin, God has blessed us. Let's share our blessings with those less fortunate," she reminded gently. We nodded, and after we saw the joy the candy brought the little ones, we were glad we hadn't been stingy with our cache.

It wasn't just the children she gave the food to either. Sometimes women would approach her and ask for extra food to nurse loved ones back to health. I remember once Mrs. Roberts from the barracks north of us came to see Mammy. She looked so worn and tired, with worry lines creasing her face.

"Mrs. Londt-Schultz, my daughter is so sick. She has had the dysentery for two weeks now, and she gets weaker and weaker by the day. I don't know how much longer she can last. Is there anything . . . *anything* you know that can help her?" the poor woman begged quietly, her eyes like liquid pain at the thought of her daughter so ill.

"There is an old Malaysian remedy for diarrhea, Mrs. Roberts. My mammy used to cook rice until it was black, like charcoal, and then she would make a weak tea out of it. For some reason, it seemed to help with the diarrhea. Why don't you try it to see if it helps your daughter?" my mother suggested, patting Mrs. Roberts's stooped shoulders kindly.

"I—I don't have . . ." the worried woman began, but before she could finish telling my mother that she had no extra rice, Mammy deftly poured a small can of rice into the pocket of her dress.

"Take this, Mrs. Roberts, but please, *please*, don't tell anyone. I have a little store of extra rice I've been collecting for those who are sick. If the wrong person found out about it, I would be in serious trouble. Take this for your daughter, and let me know how she fares," Mammy whispered, squeezing Mrs. Roberts's shoulder as she walked her to the door.

"Thank you, Mrs. Londt-Schultz. Thank you so much," Mrs. Roberts said tremulously, emotion evident in every word.

I saw Mrs. Roberts frequently over the next few days, each time with reports that her daughter, Mary Ann, was improving . . . slowly. The burnt rice tea had helped the diarrhea. Mammy would often slip her friend a little extra rice to help her daughter regain her strength. Each time, Mrs. Roberts was heartfelt in her appreciation. We wished we could do more.

It was a wonderful day when Mrs. Roberts walked into our barracks with her daughter by her side. The thin girl looked pale and wan, her lips as white and colorless as her skin. But she had a weak smile on her face as she thanked Mammy herself for helping her get better.

The longer we were in the camp, the more people got sick from the lack of nutritious food and harsh living conditions. Dysentery had always been a frequent visitor in the Palembang barracks camp, but before long it took up permanent residence. Its ravaging diarrhea and cramping weakened many women and children. The more the women got sick, the greater responsibility Mammy felt to help them.

"Hanny and Peggy, I have a favor to ask of you," Mammy said one morning just before leaving for work.

"Sure, Mammy. What can we do?" I asked distractedly, rummaging through my bag. Where was that comb anyway?

"I want you to sew pockets in my slip for me today, about this size, one on each side," she said, showing us the dimensions she wanted.

"Tear some material from that old, tattered yellow skirt of mine. Make them as inconspicuous as you can, girls," Mammy said under her breath. Her hint at subterfuge caught our attention.

"Mammy, what do you need pockets in your slip for?" Peggy asked suspiciously, her eyes narrowing as she turned to our mother.

"The leftover rice isn't stretching far enough. I need the pockets because I'm going to . . . take . . . more." Her voice was almost a whisper as she finished. She inclined her neck but continued twisting her hair into a chignon at her neck. Peggy and I looked at her, stunned.

"Take?" I mouthed, honing in on the key word.

"Take," Mammy said, meeting our gaze with resolve in her eyes.

This shouldn't have been totally unexpected. Peggy and I knew she had a little stash of rice that seemed to magically appear when someone approached her in need. It just sounded so . . . dangerous to hear her actually say the words that could get her killed if she were caught. The Japanese wouldn't tolerate theft of any kind.

The ramifications if she were discovered almost started me hyperventilating. I could feel my breathing grow erratic, and ice-cold sweat beaded on my neck. Until that very moment, I had not had to visualize a life without my mother, but that was certainly what would happen if her ruse was uncovered by the enemy.

"No. Mammy, think about this. It's way too dangerous," Peggy implored, grabbing our mother's hand in both of hers.

"I've thought this through, girls . . . for weeks. I *have* to help. I'm one of the only prison interns here with the means to get extra food, and surprisingly . . . I'm not afraid," Mammy said serenely, looking at us both, willing us to understand.

"But, Mammy, if you were discovered, I don't know what we would do . . . I couldn't bear it if they . . . they . . ." Peggy babbled, not able to finish her last thought.

"God is in charge, girls. Period. He is in charge, and it is our job to trust in that," Mammy said, putting an arm around each of us. As she squeezed us close to her, she whispered into our hair, "The 'what if's' will kill us if we let them. We just have to keep pressing forward, and we'll be all right."

She winked at us then and turned to go. "The yellow skirt is folded in my case. I'll see you tonight," she said as she waved a good-bye in our direction.

I did as my mother asked. After my chores were finished that afternoon, I felt a little like an accomplice as I cut and sewed the alterations Mammy had asked for. As I put needle and thread to the material, I felt jumpy and skittish. I fought the urge to look over my shoulder guiltily whenever anyone approached.

The slip, with the newly sewn yellow pockets, was ready when Mammy returned from work that night. I had sewed them on as securely as I was able to, reinforcing the seams so nothing, not even one grain of rice, could leak out. I held the slip out to her that evening but refused to let it go when she tried to pick it up out of my hand.

"Be careful, Mammy. Please. We can't lose you too," I said in a low voice. We stared at each other for a long time. Clearly, both of us were thinking of the one who was lost to us now because of his bravery. It made me ache to think of him, as it always did. My arms twitched to hold him, to feel the rough hands that belied his soft touch.

"He would have wanted this, Hanny," she whispered, stroking my cheek, still looking into my frightened eyes.

"I know, but he wouldn't have wanted us to be orphans either," I said, hearing the edge in my voice. Her face blanched at my words. I knew that I had just delivered a low blow, but I hoped it would keep her vigilant about her safety in the future weeks and months. Finally, I let go of the slip, entrusting it into her open hands as I turned to get ready for bed.

***

One evening, Mammy returned home from her work as cook to find Peggy and me bustling around George. He had come back early from chopping wood, complaining of dizziness. His face and hair were wet with perspiration. We laid him down on the rack, trying to make it as comfortable as possible, lining it with the few thin, worn blankets we owned. By the time Mammy walked through the door, he was shivering and delirious with fever. Mammy took one look at his flushed face and straightened, delivering the verdict we had both suspected: "Malaria."

"What should we do, Mammy? He needs medicine," Peggy said, wiping the beads of sweat from our brother's brow.

"There is no medicine to be had here in camp, Peggy. If there were, don't you think I would have gotten it to help the other children who have come down with malaria over the past few months?" she asked gently, kneeling down to have a closer look.

"What about Pappy's remedy, making tea from the bark of the quinine tree," I suggested, grasping at straws.

"What quinine tree, dear? We'd have to leave the camp to look for one, and that would never be permitted," she responded, running her fingers through George's disheveled hair. She looked up at us with tired eyes.

"We're just going to have to wait it out, girls. What more can we do, besides try to make him as comfortable as possible?" she said quietly, covering our brother with a blanket in an effort to calm his tremors.

George spent a restless night tossing and turning without ceasing. We could hear his teeth chattering like a jackhammer. Mammy never left his side. She whispered soothing lullabies in his ear, ones I recognized from childhood. I don't know if they even registered to him, as sick as he was. He never fully regained consciousness that night, only enough to mumble a few incoherent statements about Ape and his friends from school. Seeing him like that made me glad we had shipped Justin over to our cousins' barracks to sleep for the night. Witnessing George so ill would have distressed him to no end.

When morning broke, George was no better. The blankets beneath him were drenched. His head was lolling back and forth, and his dry, cracked lips were trembling, as if he were trying to say something. His body shook uncontrollably. His eyes stayed closed, except once when, to our surprise, he snapped them open. Looking feverish, he asked for Pappy. I glanced at Peggy, suddenly wishing for him too—he would have known what to do. Mammy very soothingly stroked George's forehead and whispered reassuring nothings in his ear.

A while later, Mammy nudged Peggy and me to remind us of roll call. We were gone for a long time that morning with so many camp interns down with sickness. Each absence had to be accounted for before we were dismissed. We returned to the barracks to find that Mammy still hadn't left

George's bedside. We stayed with our mother and brother that morning, running for more water or helping her fan him when his fever rose.

We must have lost track of time. When I finally looked around me, most of the other women in our barracks had already left to do their chores, and the sun was climbing higher in the sky. It had just occurred to me that the Japanese would soon be expecting Mammy to start cooking their evening meal when we heard boots striding toward the doorway.

We turned at the sound. The captain suddenly appeared, snapping his heals to a stop as he peered into the darkened barracks. His eyes quickly found our little group huddled around George. My first thought was to scrutinize our tiny living area to make sure none of Mammy's contraband rice was anywhere in sight. I didn't see anything out of place, much to my relief. I forced my eyes to look at the captain, trying desperately to look innocent. He addressed Mammy, his tone harsh and his eyes fierce.

"Cook! Why aren't you in the kitchen? There will be no hot meal for the men this evening if you don't start preparing the food. We expected you two hours ago." We all had bowed low when he entered, as was customary when face-to-face with a Japanese officer. Mammy lifted her head a little to answer.

"Captain, I am sorry I have not been up to the kitchen to start cooking, but my young son has come down with malaria. He is very ill, sir, and I . . . I can't leave him."

"This won't do, Cook! The men need to eat. Your first duty is to us," he said brusquely, glancing hard at my sick brother. George was pallid and languid, his face looking like a wax sculpture as he turned away from the captain's voice. His eyes were still closed.

"But he is so ill, sir, and his fever hasn't broken yet. It could be days before I can leave him. My sister-in-law, Wilhelmina, who usually helps me . . . she will cook until I can return," my mother replied, her voice thick with worry.

"No, no, no! Give him some quinine pills, and he'll be feeling better by morning. We need *you* in the kitchen . . . no one else," the captain firmly said, but I noticed the harsh edge in his voice had dissipated.

"There is no medicine in camp to help him, sir. There are no quinine pills for those who are ill," my mother explained, her voice imploring him to understand.

"Then I'll have my sergeant *find* some medicine for him, if that will get you back into the kitchen more quickly," the captain replied in frustration.

"Thank you, sir. With the right medicine, he should be up in no time. I'll report back to kitchen duty when his fever breaks," my mother promised, bowing low again as he backed out of the barracks. The captain's coal-black eyes scanned each of our faces once more before he turned abruptly and left. His cold appraisal left me shivering.

The captain honored his word, sending a private back to our barracks with four quinine pills later that afternoon. Once George had taken a couple of doses, his tremors quieted and his fever broke. We all breathed a long sigh of relief as we watched him sleep restfully. What could have taken a week to run its course had been cut in half once our brother had the right medicine in his system. Because it was so short-lived, the disease did not weaken George to the point that his recovery took weeks, like many other camp interns. He was back to work with Justin before we believed possible. Fortunately, no one else in our family came down with the disease, and as Mammy had promised, she was back to work, cooking for the Japanese just two days after the captain's visit.

That first evening after she returned to work, I was outside helping weed her garden. "Weeds wait for no man," she would often say. We worked side by side in silence for a while, just listening to the tree frogs and the insects all around us. Mammy's voice pulled me out of my reverie.

"Those quinine pills were another tender mercy, Hanny. Do you see that? Few, if any, in this camp have had the luxury of medicine since we've been here. Why us? Why now?" she asked, pulling out a tenacious weed. I didn't say anything as I contemplated what she had said.

"I guess I'll never know, but I thank God," she continued, gratefully. I simply nodded that I had heard. I was thankful too, and I did see it as a blessing to have my brother's health restored.

Part of me felt a little guilty, though. My mother's words, "Why us?," resonated with me. What about all the other good women here? Why was medicine denied them and their loved ones? In my mind, I agreed with something else Mammy had said, *I guess I'll never know, but I thank God.* And I thanked Him that George was better.

12

Underground Operation

"COME ON, HANNY! WE'RE GOING to be late!" Peggy yelled, already out the barracks doorway.

"I'm coming, I'm coming. Where's the fire?" I replied under my breath as I turned to my brothers. "Mammy should be home any minute. Are you two going to be all right until she gets here?"

"Yeah, we're fine. Go have fun," George answered, intent on his game of tic-tac-toe with Justin. They used gray rocks and black rocks to distinguish teams, their grid drawn in the dirt.

Fun. I thought about George's choice of word, and a grin stole across my face. It was true. I *was* going to have fun, a bizarre concept in this godforsaken place.

"Peggy, wait up!" I yelled, chasing after her slim figure as she strode across camp. We were going to sing. Two of the interns had formulated a plan to organize a camp choir. Our attempts at singing before this had always fallen apart, as there was a language barrier that divided us like a great gulf. English, Dutch, and Malaysian women had tried to sing together, but they'd grown frustrated when they couldn't comprehend instructions or lyrics in another language. It had proven too difficult to sing the traditional way, even though our music director, Margaret Dryburgh, could speak both English and Dutch fluently.

After a couple of failed attempts, Miss Dryburgh and a fellow intern named Nora Chambers, an English woman who had studied music before the war, had devised a way of singing classical music without words. They called it a vocal orchestra. We used tones and sounds the way a normal orchestra would use musical instruments. That way we could sing together, regardless of our spoken language, and still sound united. It was wonderful to hear the women's voices rise together in harmony, altos and sopranos blended together into one song.

I walked into the barracks where we had arranged to practice. Peggy was already poring over the music, trying to memorize her part. Margaret and Nora had painstakingly copied several sets of the music on old pieces of paper. Paper of any kind was at a premium here in the camp, but somehow they had scraped it together and made their own version of sheet music.

Early on, Peggy had offered the two women her music book to use as a reference, which they gratefully accepted. As far as we knew, it was the only book of music in camp. Margaret and Nora had ingeniously translated the traditional music into something that our unique choir could sing. I considered both of them to be musical masterminds. Much of the music we sang they recalled from memory, a feat that seemed mind-boggling to a girl like me.

I looked over at Margaret Dryburgh, who was working with a couple of women on their notes. I remembered seeing her for the first time and thinking she was a plain woman. She had been a Presbyterian missionary in Sumatra before the war and was used to living without vanity. She was nondescript, wearing frumpy dresses and a bun, screwing her wavy hair back out of the way. Serviceable clogs were all she wore around camp—not the standard sandals—which added to her simple, utilitarian appearance. No, there was nothing spectacular about her . . . until she spoke.

Then she became so interesting and animated. Miss Dryburgh was the kind of woman you wanted to follow. Her enthusiasm for music bubbled over like a pot of boiling soup that can't be contained. Her face lit up as she taught us the notes. Even if we were halfhearted about the piece at first, by the end of a session with her, we were completely on board. She was a leader—our leader—and we looked forward with anticipation to seeing her most evenings for our singing sessions. It was the highlight of our day.

"Ladies, we've only got a couple of weeks before our first performance. We have to finalize the Bach piece tonight if we hope to have it ready by next Friday," Mrs. Dryburgh said, trying to round up the women who had assembled for practice.

We found our places, and Nora Chambers raised her hand to prepare us to begin. As she directed the music, the blending of our voices raised the rafters . . . and our spirits.

Peggy's excitement about the choir couldn't be stifled. So great was her enthusiasm, she talked about it nonstop, her eyes gleaming with exhilaration. I loved attending our practices too, even though my alto voice was not as strong as my sister's. Singing in the vocal orchestra filled a spot that had long been empty in both of us.

As we sang together, practicing each song meticulously time and time again, something happened to our little band of singers. During our sessions, we were no longer individuals. We were a unified group. Joined together in a common purpose, we became close. We looked forward to seeing one another each evening, not worrying as much about our language differences, but working together to accomplish a mutual goal. I think this may have been Margaret Dryburgh's ultimate goal in establishing the choir all along, to build connections among the women at camp.

As we stood together that night, practicing music by Beethoven and Brahms, I was transported back to our musical evenings at home. I could picture Peggy perched on her piano bench and my father following her lead on his violin. A familiar wisp of the warmth and security I had felt during those times entered into my heart in these, the most opposite of circumstances. It was like the music we made now was a conduit to the contentment and love I had felt then. I breathed in the nostalgia like a drug.

But the peace I felt while singing was tainted at times by my fear of the Japanese. They did not like us congregating for any reason. I think they must have feared insurrection, but why, I don't know. We were just a scrawny little band of women and children. What would we know about masterminding an uprising? In any event, the threat of retribution kept us on our toes.

"Miss Dryburgh, what will happen the night of the performance? Won't the Japanese put a stop to our singing?" a pretty young Dutch girl I recognized from my daily chores asked.

"We will stick to our plan, Elsi. A musical performance will lift the other women's spirits as well as our own. We'll trust God with the rest," she said matter-of-factly, turning to collect the music sheets.

"Good singing tonight, ladies. We finally have the Bach piece down pat. Let's meet at the same time tomorrow evening so we can keep rehearsing," Nora Chambers suggested, bidding everyone a farewell as they exited the barracks.

"Are you excited or nervous about next Friday, Hanny?" Peggy asked as we walked quickly across camp.

"Hmmm, a little of both, I guess. On the one hand, I can't wait for Mammy and the boys to hear what we've been working on. On the other, if the Japanese get involved, it could get kind of scary. You?"

"Same. More excited than scared, though. I've never been involved in anything like this choir, and I love it," she replied, her eyes gleaming in the dark. Just then, we reached our barracks. We were about to walk inside when a quick movement caught my eye.

"Peggy! Did you see that? I think someone is around the corner there," I croaked, my voice breaking with fear.

"I didn't see anything. Are you sure you're not imagining things?" she asked offhandedly, stepping inside the doorway without a second thought about what I had said. My heart constricted, and I glanced warily over my shoulder, about to follow her inside, when I caught sight of my mother's profile rounding the same corner.

"Mammy! What are you doing out here? Are you all right?" I asked nervously, my eyes large with fright.

"Oh, of course, dear. I'm just fine," she replied, but there was an unfamiliar edge to her voice, as if she was keeping something from me.

"What were you doing back there, Mammy? I thought I saw someone else with you there in the shadows," I asked again, flashing another quick look to the dark corner.

"It's nothing, dear. How was your choir practice?" she asked in a transparent attempt to change the subject.

"Uh, fine, Mammy," I answered, making a mental note to keep closer tabs on my mother and her activities. I suspected something was up, and I wanted to know what it was. It was obvious I wouldn't find out tonight, but I could be patient.

The next couple of days were uneventful. We were too busy preparing for our performance to care about much else. One night, I tossed and turned for hours, not able to ever fall into a deep sleep. I awoke early. It was still dark outside. Maybe I was just feeling a little nervous about our performance next week. I guessed it was my annoyingly shy nature giving me the jitters. My eyes still half-shut, I glanced around me and saw Justin and George curled up on the floor, dead to the world. Peggy's even breathing clued me in that she too was pleasantly unconscious. Something wasn't quite right, though. Where was Mammy?

I rubbed the sleep from my eyes and then gingerly crept off my rack as silently as I could. The moon was clear that night, so I peered outside. I instinctively looked over at the corner of the barracks where I had seen Mammy appear earlier that week. Sure enough, I saw two shadows standing side by side. I tiptoed through the doorway, drawn to the dark figures. Just before I rounded the corner, I heard two women murmuring softly, clearly trying to stay inconspicuous.

"Thank you, Mrs. Londt-Schultz. I don't know how you got this medicine. Frankly, I don't *want* to know, but I *do* thank you," mumbled an unknown voice.

"Your broach was of the highest quality, Mrs. Abbott. My connections were happy to exchange it for the quinine pills. I must be off now before my children awake. Remember, discretion is of the utmost importance," my mother whispered, turning away from her companion, who disappeared into the dark.

Mammy looked up to see me standing there in my old, threadbare pajamas, watching. Defeat registered on her face as she looked up into mine. She knew she'd been had.

"Mammy, who was that lady? Explain to me what is going on here. Are you—are you involved in something . . . illegal?" I hissed quietly, forcing the last word past my lips.

I had made it sound like a bad word. Mammy grabbed my arm firmly and escorted me back to the corner, breathing quietly in my ear words that sent chills down my spine.

"Ssh! Hanny, I didn't want you to worry. Yes, I'm involved in exactly what it sounded like . . . smuggling. I had the opportunity handed to me, and I took it . . . to help the women here in camp, of course."

My face must have registered the horror I felt in my heart because my mother stroked my hair and patted my back as I tried to absorb the information she had just disclosed to me. I couldn't bring myself to speak, so she continued in such a low tone I had to strain to hear.

"Hanny, there are things these women need that they cannot get by following the rules, and, frankly, there *are* no rules when it comes to the basic necessities of life. They need medicine for their children, clothes on their backs, and food to stay strong. I can provide that for them . . . most of the time—especially if they have things to trade. A broach or a bracelet is not going to get them very far without food to sustain them or medicine to keep them from dying. Please, think this through rationally," she pleaded, taking in the floored look on my face.

I did think about what my mother was saying. I tried to wrap my brain around her logic. At first I struggled to accept it, but then my mind went back to George, sick and feverish with malaria. I remembered how relieved we were when we got the medicine he needed to help him heal.

Could I deny other interns the same opportunity? I shook my head, trying to focus on what I wanted to say.

"I'm concerned about *you*, Mammy. You're my mother, and I love you. If you were ever caught . . ." I couldn't finish. Consequences for a smuggler caught by the Japanese were swift and painful. Death would be the end result; there was no question about it.

A couple of months before, one woman in camp who was only suspected of smuggling had been thrown into a deep hole for three or four days with no food or water. The sun had been her enemy, leaving her scorched and without shelter in the blistering heat. Surely, she would have died of dehydration had she not resourcefully dug a little hole with her hands to contain some of the rainwater that fell one afternoon. She was eventually released but had been greatly weakened by her punishment. Though they searched, the Japanese found no evidence that she had smuggled. The suspicion alone that she was involved in such things had caused them to inflict punishment. I saw Mammy turn swiftly and look over her shoulder into the darkness.

"We're going to have to continue this conversation another time, Hanny. It's almost first light, and the camp will soon be crawling with guards. We can't make them suspicious."

"But I have questions. Without answers, I'll worry even more," I grumbled.

"I'll give you the answers you want, just not now. It's not safe. When I get home tonight, let's meet in my garden. No one ventures there after dark. And don't worry about me, dear. I promise you, I take every precaution I can," she said, patting my back.

We slipped back into the barracks and lay down on our rack. We were both feigning sleep. The tension engulfing us was too great to allow for rest. My mind was a blur of images and possible outcomes. I used the quiet to organize my thoughts into questions I had for Mammy that night. Question number one, what had become of my prim, proper, perfectly groomed mother? The woman I was lying next to seemed more like some kind of motherly Robin Hood character. It was enough to send my head spinning.

We both arose as soon as we could without raising suspicion, greeting the new day with silence. She squeezed my hand and smiled before leaving. I tried to smile back, but I knew it was a halfhearted attempt. My introspective mood continued throughout the day.

"Hanny, why are you so quiet today? I thought you would be as excited as me about the performance next week," Peggy said as she pitched her shovel into the manure and transferred it to the garden plot.

"Just thinking," I replied, smoothing the manure around the sprouting pepper plants. It was our turn to weed and fertilize the camp garden. Better than cleaning the bathrooms but not by much.

"Are you nervous about performing in front of all those people? I know you don't like being the center of attention, but there are dozens of us singing. It'll be fine," she said reassuringly. My reserved nature had always been a challenge for my outgoing sister to understand.

"Oh, I'm okay. A little nervous, but . . . it's really not that," I said quietly, focusing my attention on the pepper plants to avoid her gaze.

"Then what? You're not getting sick, are you?" she asked in a worried voice, dropping her shovel to feel my forehead.

"I am not sick, Peggy. Stop it! I'm just thinking. That's all." She respected my privacy for the moment and continued to shovel in wounded silence.

After a few minutes, I peeked at her through my eyelashes and sighed. Her forehead was puckered, and her lips were pursed together. I had hurt her feelings.

"Look, I found out something that really disturbed me. I'm just trying to work it out in my head. It's okay," I said in a calm voice.

Seeing that she was not to be placated, I made a conscious decision to be honest with my sister. My words pushed out in a confusing jumble as I tried desperately not to alert our fellow workers just yards away.

"She's smuggling, Peggy. She's exchanging the prisoners' stuff for medicine and food . . . from the outside. I caught her last night. It shook me up. That's all," I said, keeping my voice as low as possible.

"*Who* is, Hanny?" Peggy asked, leaning against her shovel, her eyes large and ablaze with curiosity. She emphasized each word, as if trying to comprehend what I was saying.

"Mammy," I mouthed, no sound escaping my lips. Peggy sunk down on her haunches, the shock showing on her face. Clearly, she hadn't suspected our mother just like I hadn't.

"She promised she'd explain everything tonight when she gets home from work," I continued, seeing she was in no condition to say anything. I picked up the forgotten shovel and began working again, realizing she needed a moment to get a handle on this new information.

"I want to be there," she said in a small voice but with a firmness I recognized. She was not budging on this.

"Of course. You're her daughter too. We both have a right to know what she's doing," I whispered, continuing my job of heaving manure onto the garden patch.

Peggy reached out to pat the manure around the green shoots. Though unspoken, we both recognized that it was time to continue our chores so as not to draw any unwanted attention to ourselves. We'd revisit this later.

Dusk found us fidgeting in our barracks, anticipating Mammy's footsteps outside. We finally went out to the garden to wait, thinking we could at least be productive instead of twiddling our thumbs and worrying. When we rounded the corner of the barracks, who should we find lounging there but our brothers, George and Justin.

I shot a fiery look at Peggy, knowing she had blabbed Mammy's activities to our younger brothers sometime during the afternoon. She looked back sheepishly, shrugging her shoulders. It wasn't long before Mammy walked up. A look of surprise at seeing us all assembled together flitted across her face but was quickly replaced by a warm smile.

"Well, at least we only have to discuss this once since you are all here," she said in a chipper tone, one easily manufactured to cover her nerves. We gathered around in a circle to listen.

In a very low voice, she continued, "Children, this is extremely sensitive information. Listening ears are everywhere in camp, so I am going to keep this brief. You all act like you are being industrious while I explain so we don't look suspicious. George, you weed the spinach; Justin, those peppers need to be plucked. Hanny and Peggy, there are sticks over there. See if you can hoe around those plants there while we talk." We all obediently set to work on our assigned chores, although our efforts were halfhearted because most of our attention was focused on our mother's words.

"I work with a young Malaysian girl when I cook for the Japanese. She comes in from the outside to help me and bring me supplies. She earns a few cents for her labor each week. I like her; she's a good girl, very hardworking. I am one of the only ones who can converse with her, as she speaks only Malaysian and has a thick, rural dialect. As you know, the Japanese prefer their own language but can speak a little bit of Dutch and English, if pressed. Most can't speak a word of Malaysian.

"One morning on my way to work, I stopped to chat with Mrs. Tannenbaum. Her son and daughter had outgrown all of their clothes since the invasion, and she was lamenting about how she could possibly get new clothes here in camp. I was trying to figure out a way to help her. I could tell how upset she was when it suddenly occurred that my little Malay friend might be able to help."

"What's the girl's name, Mammy? This is the first we've heard of her," Peggy said curiously. Our mother smiled at the question.

"My young friend wants to stay as anonymous as possible. She realizes that the more people who know her name, the greater the likelihood of her being discovered. A mere slippage of her name in casual conversation could mean death for her . . . death for us both, actually. So I promised her I would not breathe it to anyone.

"Anyway, I asked my Malay friend in a very guarded, roundabout way if she might be able to find clothing for Mrs. Tannenbaum's children on the outside," Mammy said.

"'Yes,' the girl answered, nodding slowly. 'I will look for the items you need tonight after I am done here. It may take some time, and I will require payment,' she added.

"Many of the camp interns who are in need have jewelry or other things to trade. Mrs. Tannenbaum was no exception. My Malay friend and I arranged that when she agreed to look for the things I requested, she would come to the kitchen and say, 'The colonel wants his tea.' I would then give her two teapots on the tray—one filled with hot tea, the other with the jewelry she required for payment. When she located the goods I needed on the outside, she would hide them in a ratty old canvas bag in the kitchen, hanging it on a certain hook. It worked that first time, and that's the way we've done it ever since."

"How long have you been involved in this, Mammy?" I asked incredulously, racking my brain, trying to think of a time I could have detected any clandestine activity from my mother's behavior. I couldn't think of a single instance.

"Not long. A couple of months," Mammy answered evasively, gathering a handful of peppers into the pocket of her skirt.

"What kinds of things can you get for the women?" Peggy wanted to know.

"Oh, mostly food and clothing. Sometimes medicine, but that is much harder to get and costs a lot in exchange," Mammy replied, reaching down to pull an errant weed George had missed.

"Are you ever scared?" George asked quietly, forgetting his weeding assignment altogether. "I know I would be," he whispered.

"Of course, dear. I'm scared sometimes, but I also know it is the right thing to do, for me to help these women," she said with conviction. "That gives me courage to move forward. I keep remembering Mother Laurentia's words that somehow I might be able to do some good for the women here through my job as cook. Maybe this was God's mission for me all along."

She stopped and hesitated for a long minute before continuing, "I guess what really scares me is the possibility that one day I will be betrayed.

Mrs. Schwarzkopf is not trustworthy. If she ever suspected my activities, she would give me up for sure," Mammy said.

We all grimaced. Mrs. Schwarzkopf was a fellow prison intern here in the camp—one not to be trusted. She was a lover of the Japanese and openly flirted with the soldiers, flashing them her coy smile and sidling up to them for attention. She had wormed her way into their good graces and then, a few weeks ago, had insisted that she cook for the guards instead of Mammy. She wanted to be near the Japanese as much as possible, and cooking for them in their own barracks was a perfect way to fulfill her plan.

The Japanese captain wouldn't hear of Mammy leaving but instead had compromised. Mrs. Schwarzkopf would assist Mammy in the kitchen. Much to our mother's chagrin, *Tante* Mien had been ousted, and this most untrustworthy woman had succeeded her. I think knowing that Mammy was under Mrs. Schwarzkopf's watchful eye was what scared me most about all our mother had told us concerning her smuggling.

"Mammy, you have to be careful around her. Mrs. Schwarzkopf is a snipey old witch who would do anything to get a leg up on you," Peggy said, her eyes narrowed.

None of us cared for the two-faced woman who would pat us children condescendingly on the head when she saw us in camp, smiling a smile that never quite reached her cold, calculating eyes. We knew that she had no loyalties to anyone but herself. Having her in such close proximity to our mother day in and day out when Mammy was so heavily involved in this secret underground world of hers petrified us.

"Well, I, for one, am proud of you, Mammy," Justin said, his chin high and his arms folded tightly across his chest.

"We all think you are brave," Peggy agreed, "but we're scared too." We looked up into our mother's face, but it was dark out now, and we couldn't decipher her expression.

"I know. Looking back, I realize I shouldn't have kept all this from you, children. But I did have the best of intentions. In my mind, I . . . I was trying to . . . protect you. That's all. I didn't want you to worry about me any more than you already do," she whispered.

"I also never wanted you put in a position where you would have to lie for me. Still, in hindsight, I should have been honest. I won't keep anything from you again," Mammy said apologetically.

Silently, we all mulled over the things our mother had told us. I, for one, kept asking myself when my mother had changed from the peaceable, sweet woman I had known before our captivity. The answer came to me as I halfheartedly tugged on some weeds.

Mammy had always been strong. She'd always been a "doer," and she had always been someone to help others at all costs. The setting and the way she was assisting others had changed, but fundamentally, she was still the same person. I just hadn't recognized her strengths for what they were before. I continued hoeing, and only the frogs singing and an occasional parrot cawing interrupted my thoughts. Taking a short break, I looked up at the stars and immediately thought of Pappy. I knew he'd be worried about Mammy too, but secretly he'd be proud of her for helping the others.

"We need to go in now, or we'll start to arouse suspicion. I mean, who gardens in the dark, right?" Mammy finally asked flippantly. She seemed in buoyant spirits now that she'd unloaded her private burden.

We all walked the short distance back to our barracks doorway hand in hand. It felt good to be unified again, to have that unspoken solidarity that we weren't alone in this godforsaken place.

During the next few days, it was like I had a heightened awareness of anything covert. I realized that there was actually a rhyme and reason to the flickering lights we experienced from time to time in our barracks. They were a signal that the guards were on the grounds and were searching. It was a warning to beware.

Once, there was a man who had climbed through the dry sewer tunnels from the outside into the camp to deliver some smuggled goods for the camp interns. He was a local, a professional smuggler. He was just meeting his contact inside the camp when the lights started flickering. The guards were on the prowl, conducting a search. He turned around, but his escape back to the tunnel would take too long. He would be detected. Thinking fast, he darted into the barracks closest to where his transaction was taking place and dove under some blankets. His instincts proved sound; the guards came to inspect the area soon after. The women who lived in the barracks lied, saying that their children were asleep under the covers. The guards believed them and moved on. When it was safe, the smuggler made his escape. A close call. I wondered how many other close calls there were that I was never aware of. The thought sent the hairs on the back of my neck on end.

13

Close Calls

THE DAY OF THE PERFORMANCE dawned, and I was awake to greet the rising sun. Again, sleep had not come easy for me the night before. My nerves were the culprits. I had made strides in overcoming my shy nature during this past year since our capture, mostly out of necessity. Being thrown together with so many strangers day in and day out, I was forced to paste a smile on my face and put my best foot forward or life here would be even harder. There was no Mammy to buffer or protect me from awkward moments anymore because she was gone long hours each day, cooking for the Japanese. I was proud of my progress in becoming less reserved.

However, the performance tonight was something else altogether. The thought of singing in front of the whole camp was intimidating. There were some four hundred prison interns in camp, and the idea that such a large number of women would be there watching us perform made my mouth feel bone dry.

As I watched the sun rise, my thoughts turned to Pappy. I wished he could be here to watch Peggy and me sing tonight. He had always loved music so much. I knew he would have been captivated seeing the vocal orchestra perform. It was such an ingenious idea. Pappy would have been thrilled to see me and Peggy sing as a part of such a novel vocal ensemble.

I turned as I heard Peggy stir and then sit up straight on the *balai-balai*. I laughed out loud at the sight of her. She had gone to bed with wet hair after sponge bathing near the lavatories, and, after a restless night, her hair looked like a scarecrow's, with pieces flying in every direction.

"What?" she asked innocently.

"Your hair, Peggy. It's everywhere," I giggled as I shimmied out of my nightclothes and into my blue shift. I continued chuckling as I folded my blanket and set it neatly in the corner. Mammy was already gone for the day. I fleetingly wondered what time she had gotten up this morning.

"Well, it's not exactly like I have rollers or anything to control it," she said defensively. I noticed she did try to slick it down as she talked, but it wasn't cooperating. In fact, I think she was making it worse.

"Why don't you just let Mammy cut your hair? She's offered to do it at least a dozen times. I keep mine short to stave off the lice in this awful place," I said, grimacing as I pondered on the horrors of lice-infested hair.

"I don't trust Mammy with my hair. Ever since the horrific haircut she gave me a couple of summers ago, I can't seem to come to terms with Mammy and a pair of scissors. It's a nightmare waiting to happen," she replied, shuddering at the thought.

"Well, what are you going to do, Peggy? It's sort of . . . beyond help," I said, grimacing as I gingerly trapped a strand and stuck it behind her ear. She didn't say anything for a couple of seconds, and then she sighed.

"Umm, I'm waiting for Pappy to cut it," she answered in a very small voice, looking away. She busied herself, searching for her hairbrush and refusing to meet my look of astonishment.

"Pappy? What are you talking about? Who knows when we'll see him again? You can't wait that long for a haircut, or I'm going to start calling you Medusa."

"Look, I know it sounds strange, but it's kind of . . . oh, I don't know, a deal I made with myself. I'm not getting my hair cut until he can be the one to do it . . . like in the old days. After Mammy butchered my hair, Pappy was the only one I trusted to cut it. It's almost like . . . if I don't let anyone else cut it, then he has to come back, right?" she asked, looking embarrassed.

I felt tears pricking my eyes as I squeezed my sister into a tight hug.

"I don't think it's strange at all. I think it's kind of nice," I said into her shoulder. "But that is not going to help you look presentable for tonight's performance. Let me at least attempt to create *some* kind of order out of this chaos. How does a braid sound? Then at least your hair will have to *try* to conform," I said, wetting the brush with some water from our bucket.

"Thanks, Hanny. You won't tell Mammy about me not letting her cut my hair, will you? I don't want to hurt her feelings. If I keep putting her off, maybe she'll just forget about it or something."

"I won't say anything, but I hope you know that this mop is not going to get any better. You're going to have to keep it tied back or braided or it's going to take on a life of its own," I said, grunting as I tried to pull the brush through her bushy mane.

"Ouch! I think it already has." She winced as I ran the brush through some particularly tangled knots.

***

I kept clearing my throat as I stood next to Peggy in the third row of the vocal orchestra. Chores that day had been mundane, as usual. We'd helped Justin and George haul in firewood for the kitchen. I could still feel the telltale ache in my lower back from carrying all that weight through camp. Still, as "everyday" as the chores had been, there had been a new anticipation that had made the time go even slower. The sun seemed to travel at a snail's pace through the sky. Finally, though, it was dinnertime. We ate our rice and spinach, the same as we did every evening; then, out we walked to the center of camp to prepare for the performance.

We met the rest of the choir in a little wooden gazebo-like structure, called a *pendopo,* that had been erected by the men who had occupied the camp before us. It had no walls, but it did have a roof, which would suit us if it rained that evening.

After almost a year in the camps, all of our clothes, except one set, were weathered and worn. Peggy and I had each been saving a dress for the day we were freed. Many of the camp's inhabitants had a similar set that they were saving for the time when the Allies would finally liberate us, the day we all dreamed about. Some of the choir members, Peggy and I included, had worn our best clothes tonight to mark our singing debut. Seeing everyone in their bright, clean dresses added to our excitement. It was going to be a special night.

We filed in and sat in formation on little stools to conserve our strength throughout the concert. We began going methodically through our vocal exercises as the women and children started gathering to watch us perform. They stood or sat down under the shelter or on the ground in front of the *pendopo,* whispering and laughing quietly with one another. I looked at Peggy and noticed that, despite her calm face, her hands were fidgety. She was nervous too. My palms were sweaty, and my throat felt like sand as I tried to concentrate on Nora Chamber's instructions. I could hear my heart thudding its rhythmic beat so distinctly that I was surprised no one else noticed.

More and more people gathered. Finally, I saw Mammy and my brothers trailing in after a large group of the Australian nurses. Mrs. Hoop smiled and waved to Mammy, indicating that she had saved her and the boys a place near the front. How thoughtful she was! She must have realized that Mammy might be a little bit late getting to the concert because of her job cooking for the soldiers.

As Mammy sat down and smiled her confident smile at me, I knew I could overcome my nerves and perform. She believed I was up for the challenge, so how could I doubt it? I smiled back, and, drying my wet palms on my clean, new dress, I squared my shoulders and began singing like I meant it. Peggy turned to me, a look of surprise on her face. I grinned and continued my warm ups with fervor.

After we finished prepping our voices, Miss Dryburgh turned to our audience and welcomed them to this, our first concert. She explained about the unique style of singing they would encounter that night and kindly hoped they would enjoy it. She also noted some of the music we would be singing during the concert: Dvořák's "Largo" from the *New World Symphony*, Mendelssohn's "Songs without Words," and Debussy's "Reverie," to name a few. As I scanned the faces in the audience, I could sense the anticipation in them. They were almost as excited to listen as we were to sing.

Just as Miss Dryburgh was about to turn around and begin conducting, there was a little disturbance toward the back of the audience. The women had turned around and were murmuring among themselves. They seemed worried.

I strained my eyes to see what concerned them, as did Margaret Dryburgh and the rest of the orchestra. It was suddenly clear what the problem was. Japanese guards were striding toward us with bayonets in hand. From the grim looks on their faces, they were not happy.

I glanced at our leader and saw that she looked calm. Miss Dryburgh smiled at the soldiers and stepped down from the gazebo. The women seated below parted like she was Moses crossing the Red Sea. She walked briskly down the aisle to greet these uninvited guests.

"What is the meaning of this gathering? Such things are not permitted," one of the guards said in a clipped tone. His hands were on his hips, and his two comrades lined up beside him.

I would have been terrified to answer such a clearly hostile inquiry, but Miss Dryburgh bowed and then answered mildly, "We have come together to sing for these women . . . a performance, you know? There is nothing untoward here. Just a little entertainment."

"You are aware of the rules, are you not?" he asked, his eyebrows fused together and his lip jutting out in anger.

"Yes, sir. This is just a way for us to pass the time. We are going to sing a few songs for the rest of the women seated here. Perhaps you and your men would care to join us?" she asked cordially, seeming not at all perturbed by his confrontational tone.

The guard didn't look appeased. He opened his mouth to reply, but, at that point, I glanced forward and realized Nora Chambers was motioning for us to begin our first selection. She entreated us with her eyes to focus on her and to sing as we had been practicing for weeks.

As the first strains of our Dvořák piece rose into the air, the tension slipped away from me. There were about thirty of us in the choir, but our voices were as one, unified and blended together just as one would expect a real orchestra to be. We continued following Nora Chambers' lead, singing our parts as we had been trained to do. When I peeked over at the small clutch of soldiers still standing with Margaret Dryburgh a minute later, I saw that the beautiful music had arrested their attention. One sat down directly to listen. The other two appeared confused but captivated by the music we were singing.

Everyone seemed to instinctively breathe a sigh of relief. The threat of punishment had passed. The Japanese seemed to recognize our gathering for what it was—a tribute to the music of the masters. What they may have balked at, had they realized it, was the deeper purpose it held for us. Singing was a means of lifting our spirits past these earthly confines. Our singing helped us transcend the camp and the confinement of our bodies and spirits. It was a way of feeling free in spite of restrictions. It was a connection to the past and to each other. Most importantly, it was a small seed of hope for a better tomorrow.

That first concert of the vocal orchestra was held December 27, 1943. We ended it by singing "Auld Lang Syne" as a tribute to the end of the old year. I breathed a silent prayer that the new year would herald with it better tidings for us than we had experienced in the year that was ending.

***

Mammy came home from work even later than usual a few days after our first concert. Peggy and I and the boys had begun to feel concerned that maybe something had gone wrong with her "extracurricular" activities. I was just mouthing a silent prayer for her when she walked in the door. There was a mischievous gleam in her eye and a sly smile on her lips. She cleared her throat, conscious of several women chatting amiably a few racks away.

"Children, I noticed some peppers in the garden that needed picking, and perhaps that last row of *kasave* is ready. Will you help me collect it before it gets too dark?" she asked, winking at us.

"Sure, Mammy. Your wish is our command," George said gallantly, dipping into a low bow and adding an exaggerated flourish with his hand.

When we arrived in the garden, Mammy scanned the area to ensure no one was nearby. She then motioned for us to gather closer before she opened her old, worn-out canvas bag. From it, she drew a small cloth-wrapped package. She then slipped off the rag that held it to reveal the most gorgeous diamond necklace I had ever seen or even dreamed of seeing in my lifetime. It was absolutely stunning. We all gasped at it shimmering in the last light of the day as it sat coiled in Mammy's outstretched hand.

"Where . . . in the world . . . did you find *that*?" Peggy asked breathlessly, shaking her head in awe.

"Oh, I just happened to trip over it on my way to work this morning," Mammy answered lightly.

"Really?" Justin asked innocently, his eyes expanding several sizes at our mother's reply. She laughed, charmed at his gullibility.

"No, silly. Mrs. DuValle is in dire need of new shoes for her daughters, all three of them. They are playing every day in bare feet in the dirt and mud, and their mammy worries for them. She was a nurse before she married and is well aware of hookworms and other things that may lurk unsuspectingly in the soil. She is willing to trade this necklace, an heirloom from her mother, for shoes for her daughters."

"But, Mammy. Mrs. DuValle could buy shoes for the whole barracks with that necklace. It's got to be worth a pile of money," Peggy said.

"Not on the black market, and not during wartime," Mammy corrected.

"Is she sure she wants to risk getting so little for something that is clearly worth so much?" I asked incredulously.

"I have warned her several times that she won't get near its worth in trade on the black market. There is no way. It would draw too much suspicion, and the people on the outside know they have us over a barrel." We sat and stared at the necklace nestled in Mammy's palm for a minute.

"Isn't it amazing, though?" she asked in a low voice. "I wanted you all to have a look at this necklace because I am not sure you will ever see its equal again."

"May I . . . may I try it on, just for a second?" I asked.

My mother nodded and then very discreetly slipped it around my neck. It was so much heavier than I had anticipated but, at the same time, cool and smooth. I liked the feel of it. Before I had time to get used to it, though, Mammy had unclasped it and wound it around Peggy's neck. Peggy looked down and caressed it softly.

"It's gorgeous," she whispered in a reverent voice.

"Yes, it is. I certainly hope Mrs. DuValle's girls appreciate their new shoes," Mammy chuckled as she gently removed the necklace from Peggy's neck. She wrapped it carefully in the inconspicuous old rag and dropped it into her bag.

"Okay, time for bed. We've been out here for a good fifteen minutes, time enough and then some for us to pick peppers and spinach. We don't want to—"

"Draw suspicion. We know," we all chimed in, laughing.

The next day Mammy returned home from work, her face ashen and her eyes wide with fear. We knew immediately that something had happened. Most of our barracks mates were still at dinner, so we asked her in hushed tones what had happened.

"The worst thing ever," she replied weakly. "This morning before work I transferred Mrs. DuValle's necklace from my bag to my dress pocket for safekeeping while I cooked. I was waiting for my Malay friend to arrive so I could give it to her. Halfway through the morning, I slipped my hand into my pocket, and to my dismay . . . it was gone! I hadn't realized there was a hole in the pocket of this dress." Our mother's voice broke at that point. She sank onto the rack, her face as white as a corpse. Her trembling hand flew to her forehead as she absently massaged away at the worry lines. We were speechless.

"I scoured every inch of the kitchen and the supply room. The pendant was nowhere to be found. If it was still securely wrapped in the old dishcloth I had wrapped it in, I didn't think it would attract interest. My heart beating in my throat, I approached Mrs. Schwarzkopf, the only person who had been with me that morning.

"'Mrs. Schwarzkopf,' I said, 'I am missing a small package that one of my children gave to me. It's really not important . . . just my lunch for the day. I didn't realize I had a hole in my pocket, and it must have slipped out. Have you seen it by chance?' I asked, acting as casually as I could but shaking all the while.

"'Why, no, Mrs. Londt-Schultz, I haven't found anything,' she replied. I searched her face for any evidence of a lie, but I couldn't see anything suspicious there.

"I searched again, retracing all my steps, but . . . nothing. I was afraid to arouse suspicion. In fact, I was surprised Mrs. Schwarzkopf didn't question me further. She is usually such a busybody. Today though, she was silent, which makes me suspect she may know more than she is letting on. I am so fearful; that necklace would be all the evidence the Japanese need to sink me," Mammy said. She sounded so heartsick and depressed in spirit; I reached out and put my arm around her.

"I think all we can do is wait it out. Just go on, doing what we always do, and hope the Japanese aren't alerted," Peggy said, rubbing Mammy's hand comfortingly. Mammy was usually the calm one, but tonight she was a bag of nerves.

"I know you're right, but I am sick about it. What do I tell Mrs. DuValle? I lost her most valuable possession because of a hole in my dress? That sounds so thoughtless and irresponsible," Mammy said sadly.

"Is there anyone in camp whose clothes are in good repair anymore? We're all in rags after wearing them day in and day out for over a year in this hole. Mrs. DuValle's children are welcome to my old shoes. They've still got a little life in them, and they are far too small for me to wear anymore," I offered.

"Thank you, dear. But I am going to keep working on my Malay friend. I'm trying to convince her to buy the shoes anyway as cheaply as she can. I'll find a way to reimburse her, or I'll never be able to look Mrs. DuValle in the eye again," Mammy said in a determined voice.

"She has to know that trading on the black market is a tricky business," Peggy said. "I mean, anywhere along the line someone could have stolen that necklace, and what could have been done about it? There are no regulations or guarantees when it comes to smuggling."

"You're right, and I do tell all my clients that from the beginning. In this case, though, it was completely my fault. I feel horrible about it." Mammy dropped her face into her hands. She was clearly miserable. There was nothing more to be said. I only hoped Mammy's Malay friend could locate some shoes . . . cheap, and that Mrs. Schwarzkopf wasn't planning on using that necklace to betray us.

***

The next couple of weeks we watched everyone very carefully. When the lights flickered in our barracks, we waited on eggshells, thinking it might be the guards coming to search us and haul off Mammy for questioning. There was no evidence in our barracks to connect her to anything illegal. We had been very careful to remove all of it after the necklace's disappearance. There wasn't even a can full of rice to be found. Still, we were nervous.

Fortunately, time marched on, and nothing happened. It was the same routine day in and day out. We awoke every morning and went to roll call. We mechanically did our chores as we had done every day since arriving at camp. After, we sometimes rested for a while, and then it was dinner. Peggy and I would often go to our choir practice after we had eaten. We sang every Friday evening now for the women in camp, and we were continually adding new songs to our repertoire. Interestingly, the Japanese guards often attended our scheduled concerts. Now that they didn't fear an insurrection, the soldiers just came to listen to the music, and they seemed to enjoy it as much as the rest of our audience.

We started to feel comfortable again when nothing untoward happened at Mammy's job. She cooked for the guards every day, keeping a watchful eye on Mrs. Schwarzkopf. That hateful woman was there under the pretense of being helpful but really just sauntered around the kitchen, inventing any excuse to leave the room in search of a little flirtation. Mammy simply rolled her eyes and kept working. She'd grown accustomed to the woman's games.

One evening, our mother came home with a story that sent chills down our spines. We waited until we were alone before she told us what had happened to her that day at work. Mammy said that earlier that morning, she had arrived at work the same time as she did every day. She'd walked into the kitchen and was surprised to hear low voices coming from the storeroom. She could hear a woman's voice in muffled tones as well as a soldier's. Mrs. Schwarzkopf was notoriously late, always arriving in a breathless state sometime around noon. Could it be her voice she heard behind closed doors? Mammy immediately felt uneasy. Mrs. Schwarzkopf had never arrived to work this early before.

"My throat began to close, and my mouth turned dry as I strained to hear the hushed voices in the storeroom. I had commissioned my Malay friend two days before to try to find sheets for one of the shipwreck survivors who was tired of sleeping on the hard, wooden rack each night. I feared that whoever was talking in the storeroom might stumble across the old canvas bag I could envision hanging on its usual hook. What was I to do, though? Indecision racked me for a few seconds.

"Then, suddenly, I experienced the strangest sensation . . . It was like hands were literally pushing me toward the door. I found myself walking forward. The hands on my back kept pushing until I was at the door of the storeroom.

"To my horror, I heard Mrs. Schwarzkopf talking to two of the guards, trying to convince them to look into my bag. I nearly fainted, but again, I felt compelled to move forward."

"'Just look in the bag, darling. She is smuggling goods into camp. I simply know it,' Mrs. Schwarzkopf said in a husky voice, sidling up close to the guard nearest the bag.

"I could see confusion on the guards' faces. They were two with whom I've always had a good rapport. I had to think fast. I could see Mrs. Schwarzkopf gesturing toward the bag again, willing them to open it. I could picture the sheets inside that would spell my demise. I wouldn't go down without a fight. I was determined of that.

"'Why, Sergeant, just the person I wanted to see,' I said with a warm smile, trying to sound as confident as I could. I didn't spare a glance for Mrs. Schwarzkopf.

"'Remember how you told me you needed a new shirt last week but didn't have free time to go search for one in town? Well, I have always been quite a good seamstress, and although I obviously couldn't find you a shirt, I improvised. As a surprise, I was going to sew you one from these sheets the little Malay servant girl so kindly brought from home. They should do the trick very nicely,' I said in a chipper tone, smiling widely. Inside, I was praying desperately that my ruse would work. The story sounded a little forced to my ears, but it was all I could come up with on such short notice. I ventured a fleeting look at Mrs. Schwarzkopf's face, and it was completely shocked. We both waited for the guard's response.

"'Why, thank you, Cook. How did you guess that blue is my favorite color?' he added, peering into the bag. I couldn't resist flashing a wicked smile at Mrs. Schwarzkopf while the guards' eyes were averted. Her disappointment was palpable.

"'Just a lucky guess, sir. I'll have to thank my little friend when she comes in today to help with dinner. I hope this won't leave her mammy's linen cupboard any worse for the wear,' I said cheerfully. The guards chuckled, exuding goodwill.

"'Why don't you tell me your measurements, and I can get started on your shirt tonight,' I suggested. He proceeded to give me his measurements and then thanked me again before leaving the room with his companion. Assured that they were gone, I turned on Mrs. Schwarzkopf, and I must have looked as angry as I felt because she cowered in the corner.

"'You snake! How could you?' was all I could manage in Malay before brushing past her to return to the kitchen. Once there, I felt drained. I leaned against the cupboards for support and breathed a huge sigh of relief.

"It was some time before Mrs. Schwarzkopf joined me there. She was probably half afraid I would use my cleaver on her or something," Mammy said with a sigh.

"Oh . . . my . . . word," was all I could manage before putting a shaky hand over my mouth in surprise at the story Mammy had just told us.

"What a close call, Mammy. You were . . . I can't believe how close you were to being caught," Peggy said breathlessly.

"Me neither," she replied. "I am going to have to keep much closer tabs on Mrs. Schwarzkopf from now on. She's dangerous, and apparently, I am on her list."

"How could she be such a witch? I mean, doesn't she realize that we are all in this together? That we can help each other through this awful nightmare?" Peggy asked incredulously.

"No, dear. She doesn't understand that. I think it's like Pappy once said . . . some women here feel like they have to claw their way up the social ladder. They feel powerless, and they will do anything to gain what feels like a little bit of control back into their lives," Mammy said speculatively.

"But how can they do it at other people's expense? She was tossing you to the wolves, Mammy—not just tossing but instigating the whole attack. And isn't she married? How can she flirt so shamelessly with the Japanese like she does?" I asked, sickened by this traitorous behavior.

"Yes, I understand she *is* married, and I believe her husband wields some political clout as well. I don't know . . . people do strange things when they're under duress. Some people become more charitable, others' actions border on the heroic, and still others sink into behavior I fear they'll be ashamed of later. Regardless, she is someone to always be on our guard around. She's proven untrustworthy," Mammy said with a sigh.

"You can say that again," Peggy said under her breath. "A snake was the right name for her, Mammy. You never turn your back on a snake, or chances are you'll get bit. I guess now we know it's the same with Mrs. Schwarzkopf."

"Mammy, you said you felt hands pushing you toward the storeroom. What was that all about?" I asked curiously, shifting the conversation.

"I honestly don't know how to explain it, but it felt so real. It felt like if I had turned around at that precise moment, I would have seen someone right behind me, urging me forward," she responded. "I know it sounds strange, but that push felt like hands on my back."

"Whose hands?" Peggy asked skeptically.

"I honestly don't know, girls. I've thought about it all day. There was definitely no one else in that kitchen area," she said, shaking her head.

"Maybe they were . . . I don't know, otherworldly or something," I suggested, feeling chills go down my back.

"That's the conclusion I came to as well, Hanny. Angels attending, maybe? That's the only way I can explain it. I think, somehow, I was being protected this morning."

We were all silent as we pondered our conversation. Mammy had incredible faith. She had always taught us to believe in God as well. Was it such a stretch to believe that some force had stepped in to help her today in a most crucial moment? It rang true to me. I couldn't explain it and I didn't understand how, but I believed that was what had happened. It made me feel warm inside. Grateful and warm.

14

Death Camp

"Hand me those cans, Hanny, will you please?" my mother asked absentmindedly as she continued packing and repacking her case to make sure everything fit just so.

My few belongings had been packed half an hour before, as had the boys' cases. They had run over to the kitchen to see if the cooks needed help packing the pots and pans and other sundry things. Peggy was at a neighbor's section of the *balai-balai* tending a friend's young children so she could pack as well, without distractions.

We had woken early as usual to another hot Sumatran day when at roll call our lives had been turned upside down again. The guards had informed us that we would be packing up camp and moving to another location. No one knew for sure where. We were to be packed and ready to transport by noon. There had been an unusual frenzy of activity in camp, different from our usual methodical mornings.

"There! I think we're finally packed and ready to go," Mammy declared, out of breath from her exertions.

"Where do you think they will take us?" I asked thoughtfully. The idea of a new camp—who knew where—had been weighing on my mind for hours now, ever since the guards had informed us of their plans. Wondering where we would be tomorrow made me nervous. As near as we could tell, we'd been in the Palembang barracks camp a little more than a year. We knew the routine, the ins and outs of the place. The unknown loomed dark and cavernous before us.

"I don't know, dear. I know there are rumored to be prison camps like ours all over Indonesia. I think they'll probably keep us in the south somewhere. I mean, what's the point of the Japanese transporting us all the way up north," she said, sitting down on the rack beside me.

"What if . . . what if the war ends and we don't know where we are and can't get back home?" I speculated worriedly.

"I imagine it *will* take a little while to sort things out once we are liberated, but I'm sure the Allied forces will help us get back home safely," she said comfortingly. Searching my face, she must have detected my unease.

"Hanny? I can tell you have something more on your mind," Mammy continued, cocking her head to the side as she searched my face.

"What if we can't find Pappy once the war is over? They might be moving him around too," I asked quietly, not meeting Mammy's questioning eyes. My heart pounded as I realized I had just voiced one of my greatest fears.

"He'll find us. I know your father, and there's no doubt in my mind that he won't stop until we are all together again," replied Mammy confidently.

I nodded, feeling better now that she had explained away some of my fear. A series of loud whistles blew in the common area of camp. We were being summoned to assume our regular formation so we could board the trucks that would take us to our new living quarters. We looked under the rack once more to make sure no belongings had been left behind and then prepared to leave. I took one last look at this cramped little barracks space that had been my home and sighed.

I turned to my mother, who was just picking up her suitcase to go, and said sheepishly, "Do you think I'm completely crazy, Mammy, when I tell you that I actually feel a little twinge of sadness when I think of leaving this place? I know I shouldn't because it has been the means of holding me captive for the last year, but I still do," I said, somewhat appalled and amused by my reaction.

"I think it's a case of the devil we know being better than the devil we don't know. At least we were safe here, regardless of the lack of food, the sickness, the heat, and so forth. All things considered, it could have been a lot worse," Mammy said, putting her arm around me.

Little did we know how prophetic her last statement would prove to be.

We quickened our step when we heard the familiar shouts of "*Lekas! Lekas!* Hurry up! Front and center," from the guards who were trying to arrange us all into lines to board the large trucks parked by the gate. I took a quick look behind me as I was nudged forward. The awkward schoolgirl who had walked into this camp more than a year ago was gone forever. I was older now, a young woman. I said a silent good-bye to the ghost girl as I stepped up into the truck with my family.

***

Apparently, we were part of the second group leaving camp. Most of the sick and infirm had been moved the night before, although I noticed that our group had some ill interns in its ranks as well. A third group was staying behind and would travel to our new destination tomorrow.

We started our journey on a hot, sunny day well past the rainy season. My sixteenth birthday had passed quietly a few weeks before, so it must have been early fall 1944 when we were told to go and pack. I wish I knew exactly when we left Palembang, but the days had begun to blur together for me. They ran together like red paint that had started out pure but had become muddied and undefined as it swirled with its brother and sister colors.

We sat with our arms around our knees, head to head in the long cattle trucks. They were open, and there was no shelter from the hot sun, but I think I preferred that arrangement to the closed trucks in which we could have been traveling. I imagine we would have felt even more claustrophobic in those tight quarters.

"Mammy, there are a lot of new faces in these trucks. I thought I knew most of the women and children in camp, at least by face," Peggy said, looking around curiously.

"Yes, dear. I heard from the guards yesterday while I was serving them their dinner that about one hundred new women were shipped in from a camp in Bengkulen last week. That swells our numbers to between six and seven hundred," my mother said as she wrapped her arm around Justin.

"So many, Mammy?" I asked in surprise. "I would have thought there were fewer than five hundred."

"No, dear. I was talking to Mother Laurentia, and our numbers have expanded little by little over time. With this large group just added, we have reached more than six hundred interns now."

"Why do you think they're moving us, Mammy? Isn't there enough room in the barracks camp for more interns?" George asked.

"I don't know. It's puzzling me too. Maybe they think that the Allies won't be able to find us as easily wherever they are moving us. That's just a guess, though," Mammy said speculatively, her brow furrowed in thought.

"If that's the case, then maybe our side is starting to get one over on the Nazis," Justin said, punching the air with a tanned fist. We all laughed, each of us hoping that his guess would soon prove true.

After a long truck ride, we found ourselves on board a rusty steamer ship. It looked old and rickety from a distance and aged even more as we walked along the short pier. It was really too small to accommodate all of us, but somehow the Japanese soldiers found a way. The sick and infirm were packed in tightly below deck, like sardines in a can. On a day as hot as this, I could only imagine how stuffy it was for them down in the hold.

The rest of us were shepherded up a flight of stairs and onto the deck. We were shoved against one another with scarcely any room to move. I felt claustrophobia clawing at me, so I squeezed myself as close to the rail as possible in the hope that a breeze from the water would counteract my clammy, pent-up feeling.

The water was rough, and many of the women and children felt debilitating waves of seasickness as we putted along the river. Old tins were passed around for people to catch their vomit. When they were full, people along the rails emptied them overboard.

"Yet another use for the all-purpose tin can," Peggy said sarcastically as she very delicately passed a full container to her neighbor sitting near the edge. Mammy caught the humor but could only conjure up a wan smile in reply. She was starting to turn an interesting shade of green the more the waves rocked our little vessel up and down haphazardly.

I felt queasy too, but I was somehow able to resist throwing up. I didn't have anything in my stomach anyway because we hadn't been given food to eat since we'd left Palembang. I kept thinking that if I just had a cracker to eat, it might settle my stomach. What a throwback to when I was a young girl and Mammy had prompted me to nibble a little cracker or biscuit to calm an unsettled stomach.

Peggy's head began to nod after we had been on the boat for four or five hours. We were crammed together so tightly that I barely had to shift to allow her to rest her head on my shoulder. I was glad she could close her eyes for a couple minutes. The nausea I was feeling wouldn't allow me to relax for a second, and my tailbone felt as if someone had beaten it with a hammer, it was so sore from sitting on the hard deck.

Suddenly, I heard sobbing from a teenage girl sitting a few dozen yards away. She was crying into her hands, her thin body racked with sadness. As I looked on, Japanese guards were already picking their way through the mass to discover what the ruckus was all about. I worried for her. Noticing the approaching guards, her younger brother tried desperately to calm her. I saw him brush tears away from his own eyes as well.

"What is wrong with those two?" George asked, his attention caught by their grief.

"I don't know, but the guards are almost there. I'm afraid they'll be angry," I said under my breath.

"I heard their mother was very sick yesterday. One of the Australian nurses told me after roll call that they had watched over her all night long. I certainly hope she is all right," Mammy said, concern lacing her words.

The guards reached the brother and sister just then, and it was quickly discovered that their mother had, indeed, just passed away. Her children's bodies had sheltered her from our view. Besides, we were packed against one another so tightly that she was probably still propped up into a sitting position, dead as she was. Guards retrieved a thin mattress that had been stored along the rails, and I watched as they wrapped the corpse in it. They tied string around the bundle haphazardly and threw her overboard, seemingly without a second thought. The dead woman's daughter let out a pitiful wail as she watched her mother's body submerge for a moment behind the boat.

My sharp intake of air must have woken Peggy because she groggily rubbed her eyes.

"What did I miss?" she asked, trying to focus. I started to give her a brief description of what we had witnessed but was suddenly diverted from my story by a cry near me.

"The body! It's following us," yelled a young woman near the rear of the boat, a trembling hand covering her mouth. Situated close to the rails as I was, I glanced down to see what she meant. I watched in horror as the rolled-up mattress containing the dead woman seemed to be trailing us in the boat.

"Mammy! Why is it doing that?" George asked incredulously.

"Poor thing! She's been caught in the wake of the boat. The current we're kicking up is dragging her along with us," Mammy said, clicking her tongue sadly at the dead woman's plight. I couldn't say anything. I was too horrified to speak; yet, try as I might, I couldn't tear my eyes away from the corpse that seemed to be following us.

Mile after mile, the body trailed our boat. I kept thinking about the woman's son and daughter having to witness their mother's body bouncing up and down on the waves, sometimes submerged for half a minute but inevitably bobbing up to the surface again. Tears welled in my eyes as I thought of what her two children must be going through. After what seemed like hours, the body was finally pushed clear of the wake and floated slowly away. I tried not to think of what the lady next to me had whispered a few minutes earlier about these being crocodile-infested waters.

As I sat there, my eyes glued to the shapeless body drifting aimlessly in the water, my mind wandered back to a time when I was a little girl. I had been playing with one of Pappy's black work pens. The ink from the pen had smeared onto my white frock, and, try as she might, Mammy could never get the black stain off of it. This scene I was witnessing was like that indelible ink mark on my dress. I knew that no matter how hard I tried to scrub it out, the memory of that body floating behind us, following us mile after mile, would always stay with me to the end of my days—a black stain that could never be cleaned away.

We docked at a pier on the island of Bangka late in the evening. It had been a squeamishly long ride on the boat. The sick and infirm women and the nurses accompanying them were ordered off the boat first. Once they were taken on stretchers and situated in trucks, we were allowed to leave the boat. It was a long pier, and we trudged the length of it with our few blankets and suitcases in tow before we reached the trucks to take us to our next camp. I was nervous, but that feeling was secondary to the raw hunger that was waging a battle in my stomach. We hadn't eaten since breakfast, and I was starving.

I listened in on a conversation between two women seated near me in the transport trucks. It was hard to turn off my ears and not eavesdrop when people were seated in such close proximity, even though they talked in hushed tones.

"This place we're going, I think it is near the city of Muntok. My grandfather worked just across the channel there years ago, and he would come across from time to time to pick up extra jobs in Bangka," an older woman whispered to her young companion.

"I've lived all my life in Palembang and have never been this far east. What is Bangka like?" the younger woman asked curiously.

"Oh, it's dry here, very dry. It's not like the rest of Sumatra, lush and tropical. If we are going to the camp near Muntok, I hear they built it on an old Chinese burial ground," the gray-haired lady said, shuddering.

"What? That can't be! Not even the Japanese would desecrate a holy cemetery." The younger woman gasped, appalled at the thought.

"Of course they would! According to my cousin, the Japanese liked how flat it was, and, without thinking twice, they bulldozed the area, straightened it a bit to make it look presentable, threw up a few barracks for prisoners to sleep in, and called it good," the older companion retorted with a knowing expression in her eye.

"That's just hearsay. Whoever heard such an extraordinary story?" the younger companion scoffed, shaking her head.

"It's true, I tell you. We'll be sleeping atop the dead ones' coffins," the older woman muttered convincingly.

Her young friend put her palm up and turned away as if to say, "Enough!" and proceeded to close her eyes as if she were hoping to put a stop to the discussion altogether. The older woman took the hint, shrugged, and tried to strike up a conversation with the woman to her right instead.

"Did *you* ever hear that the prison camp at Muntok was built on an old Chinese burial ground?" she asked, hoping to find a pair of listening ears.

I turned away, willing myself not to hear a repeat of the conversation I had just witnessed. The younger woman might not buy her older friend's story about the burial ground, but it had been told with enough conviction to intrigue me.

A burial ground? That didn't bode well for our future at this strange new camp. There was no love lost between the Chinese and the Malaysians, but neither one would dream of desecrating the other's cemetery. The dead deserved to rest in peace.

***

We soon learned that our routine at the new camp in Bangka was very similar to the one we had followed in the Palembang barracks camp. We started bright and early with roll call, did our chores for a large part of the day, had dinner, and then bedded down early. There was no vocal orchestra in Bangka, though. No singing to look forward to after a long day of work. After the Palembang camps weakened their bodies and Bangka deprived them even more, the women's poor health and general apathy conspired to dissolve our singing group, making Peggy very sad in the process.

"I miss the music, Hanny," Peggy said one night as we were standing watch over the barracks, a job we were each enlisted to do three or four nights a week. The Japanese started the routine, but the older women in camp continued it. They felt that having someone watch over the area each night, and alerting us to any sign of trouble, was reassuring. Mercifully, to keep our senses sharp and to stave off fatigue, we were allowed to stand guard in pairs. Without a partner, the two-hour shifts would have dragged on painfully long. Peggy or one of my cousins usually watched with me, so at least I was in good company.

"I know you miss the orchestra, Peg," I said in answer to her comment, "but the women are just too tired and listless to sing anymore. The heat on this awful island drains you. By early afternoon, I'm usually daydreaming of sinking onto our *balai-balai* for a little shut-eye as well." I kept a sharp eye trained on the fence surrounding the camp as I squeezed her shoulder sympathetically.

"But the music helped motivate me so much. I got through my chores in half the time when I knew we had singing practice to look forward to," Peggy said, disgruntled.

I thought about Nora Chambers and Miss Dryburgh and the music they had helped us make as we both listened to crickets serenading us from yards away, past the barbed-wire fence, teasing us with their freedom. I could almost hear the women's voices from the vocal orchestra wafting in on the night air as I recalled our concerts in the Palembang barracks.

"I miss it too," I agreed in a small voice. "I know my feelings are nothing compared to a music person's like you, but having something fun to break the monotony helped me. We'll always have the music with us, regardless of where we are. Memories are something no one can take away."

We continued to watch into the dark night for who-knew-what menaces the Japanese feared. We were so isolated that we seriously doubted anyone even knew people were out here.

The weather in Bangka was hot, dry, and sundrenched. Cracks in the earth from the parched conditions started replicating themselves in our resolve to stay positive and well. We were living in awful conditions, much worse than Palembang. Shade was nonexistent in Bangka because it was situated in an open field with no overhanging trees nearby. We literally felt no relief from the baking sun. It had long since lost any sense of the cheerfulness we had once associated with it. The sun seemed to us a punitive overseer, omnipresent and harsh. Partnered with the Japanese guards' unyielding demands for chores to be done, many women broke under the pressure.

My feet had outgrown my shoes long ago, and I was forced to walk barefoot now. Walking barefoot in Palembang had been an inconvenience, especially during the rainy season when the mud would squish and cake onto your feet, but here in Bangka, it was painful. The ground was so scorching hot that I could scarcely walk on it without wincing and hopping in an attempt to relieve the burn.

Nothing grew in Bangka either. Even Mammy's green thumb turned brown and shriveled. Every effort she made to garden failed. There was just too much heat and not enough moisture to sustain plant life here. We were forced to make do with the small portion of rice and occasional hot pepper that we were given. Mammy feared for our health with so limited a diet.

"Where is that bone?" she asked one hot afternoon, talking to herself as she rummaged through her battered old suitcase.

"Mammy, what are you going on about over there?" Peggy asked lazily as we all rested after long hours of hauling water to the kitchen.

"I'm looking for that old hip bone I used in Palembang to make soup. You remember it, don't you?" she asked, continuing her search through my case now.

"That bear bone gave us some tasty broth, but that was months ago. Besides, it was as holey as Swiss cheese by the time we left. Don't you think it's time to let sleeping bear bones lie?" I asked. I remembered how pleased Mammy was when the Japanese guards allowed her to keep the hip bone of a bear they had hunted down near our last camp.

"Don't be ridiculous. There are still dozens of good soups left in it. We just need the marrow from the bone anyway. That's where the nutrients are, you know?" Mammy said as she started shuffling through the boys' cases.

"Ahh! Here it is. Wonderful. I'll boil this along with a few cans of water, and if we are lucky enough to get a pepper tonight, we'll throw that in too, for flavoring," she said, pleased with her discovery.

"Well, anything has to be an improvement on how the water tastes now. It's got such a strange, metallic aftertaste, doesn't it?" Peggy said, still resting on the *balai-balai*.

"I heard the water tastes bad because of all the minerals in the soil," I said offhandedly.

"I've heard that too. I guess I've had so much trouble getting past all of the mosquito larvae we see floating around in the well water that the taste doesn't seem to bother me," Mammy said. She made a bitter face at the thought.

"Well, you're so faithful at straining and boiling the water before we ever drink it that I hardly ever think of the mosquito larvae anymore. But now that you mention it, it's gross to think we could be drinking baby bugs every time we swallow," I said, pretending to gag.

"Ewww! I'm glad you thought to strain it, Mammy. I bet that old piece of fabric you use is as good as any store-bought strainer," Peggy piped in. "And need I bring up the other possible reason for the water's bad taste? I mean the well *is* almost right on top of the latrines. Do you think the water is contaminated by dirty bathroom *stuff?*" Peggy added saucily, swinging her legs down from the top of the *balai-balai*.

"Oh, Peggy! That's absolutely disgusting! I really don't want to be thinking about bathroom waste tainting my drinking water every time I go to take a sip," I retorted, scowling at the gall my sister had to bring up such a revolting possibility. She just laughed at me, which in turn made me laugh too in spite of myself.

***

We had worked hard in Palembang, but we were forced to work even harder in Bangka. We had new chores that were demanding, physically and emotionally. With many of the women in camp too ill or lethargic to help, those of us who could still work were forced to shoulder most of the responsibilities. Along with night watch duty, one of the hardest jobs to endure was grave digging.

People started dying in Bangka soon after we arrived. The interns had been weakened in the earlier camps, and the lack of nutrition in Bangka pushed them to extremes their bodies just couldn't tolerate anymore. Malaria and dysentery ran unbridled through camp and ended people's lives prematurely, especially among the very youngest and oldest of the interns.

The camp prisoners also fell victim to a new sickness, *beri-beri*. People stricken with this illness would swell so large that they could hardly see through their eyes, and their legs and ankles began to resemble an elephant's. Their complexions would also turn a sickly yellow color. If you pressed the skin of someone suffering from *beri-beri*, the impression would stay depressed, refusing to spring back like that of a healthy person. Mammy would tsk-tsk periodically, exclaiming again and again that the entire illness would be avoided if we were just given a more balanced diet.

Mammy no longer cooked for the Japanese soldiers. Mother Laurentia had approached her about cooking early on, but already the interns were becoming ill and dying. Mammy begged to be allowed to decline, feeling that she could be of greater use nursing those who needed help. Still, sometimes she wondered if she would have had access to nutritious food that might have helped prevent *beri-beri* had she agreed to continuing cooking.

Many of the younger interns were asked to accept the responsibility of burying the dead. In general, we were stronger and in better health than the older women in camp, and it was a physically demanding job. Grave digging was repulsive to me at first, but we soon became numb to the horror of what we were doing. The Japanese issued us wide-slatted, makeshift coffins to bury our dead, and our only tools to dig the graves were carved wooden planks. Sometimes we had only one body to bury; other mornings we worked for hours, burying six, seven, even eight bodies in a single day.

I tried not to think of the bodies as women and children we actually knew, people we'd sung with or eaten with, people with families and dreams of their own. It was too hard if thoughts like that seeped into my mind. Instead, they were just bodies . . . most of the time. There were a few instances when links to the past were unavoidable, and those connections to the corpses led to some very dismal days for me.

"Ready, one, two, three . . . lift," said my cousin Aldi, who often joined us in our grave digging duties. Aldi and Peggy were holding the two top corners of the coffin we'd been assigned to bury, while George and I brought up the rear.

"You got it, Hanny? You look a little wobbly back there." Peggy huffed as she hoisted her corner onto her shoulder. I tried to maneuver my end onto my shoulder, but it was a little unstable. I struggled to keep my corner on an even keel with the others. Just as I thought I'd secured it and we were on our way up the grassy knoll to the makeshift cemetery, I tripped over a rock, and my side of the carefully balanced coffin came crashing down like a house of cards.

"Whoa, there! I thought we were under control," George said as he tried to rescue dropping his corner altogether.

I wiped off my dirty hands. Just as I was kneeling to stand up, I looked at the corner that had landed next to my bare feet. Through the wide wooden slats, I saw an image that seared my brain. In between the gaps in the coffin, I saw the face of my old chemistry teacher from the boarding school. She was dressed in her full nun's habit, as was customary for burial. Sister Mary Catherine was her name, and she had been such a good-hearted nun, always kind to us girls. I recalled her quick smile and her quick wit to match. I remembered her blue eyes twinkling as she recounted to us a funny story she'd heard. She seemed to enjoy laughing just for the sake of laughing. We'd all liked her at school.

I'd known Sister Mary Catherine was in camp but hadn't talked to her lately because her days had been filled with caring for the many orphans we now had in Bangka. I'd heard yesterday that she was deathly ill, but I didn't make the connection until now. We were burying my old teacher. The staring of those vacant blue eyes through the wooden slats flowed like lightning through my veins. I trembled at the shock of seeing her lying there in that box, never to laugh or teach or nurse again.

"What is it, Hanny? You look like you've seen a ghost," Peggy said in a concerned voice. I took a moment to compose myself before speaking.

"In a way . . . I guess I have, Peggy. I'm . . . I'm going to need a second," I said breathlessly, turning away from my family and slumping down on a nearby boulder. I needed a minute to mourn before I could continue.

Once I had explained to the others why I was so upset, they were very sympathetic.

"Hanny, why don't you go rest for a while? We can handle it," Peggy said soothingly.

"No, no, I'm okay. Besides, we have another two bodies after this one. Let's just hurry and do this," I said, trying to sound nonchalant but failing miserably.

Peggy and Aldi started using their makeshift shovels to dig the hole for Sister Mary Catherine's coffin. It was slow going, trying to make headway through the dry, sun-baked ground with nothing but glorified wooden sticks to aid them. The wait while they dug gave me pause to try and regain my composure. I had difficulty doing so, though, when I looked out over the makeshift cemetery and saw the number of handmade crosses with names clumsily burned into them. There were even more today than when I had been here to dig three days ago. Soon Sister Mary Catherine would be among them. Just a cross with a name scratched into it to those who had never known her.

"Hanny, I'm sorry about your teacher. When I saw the blood drain from your face, I knew something was wrong," George said in a low voice after a few minutes. He put his arm around my shoulder. "I don't think I ever told you all the details, but when we first moved to this camp, I had something awful happen to me when I was told to bury a body. It was my first time, and I was petrified. The guard told me to go down to the pier where we had docked the day before and bury a body I would find lying there. I was to meet Anna and another girl from the third barracks who were to help me at the pier.

"The guards had left the body on the dock the previous morning, not taking into account the sun and the heat. Personally, I think they may have forgotten about her in all the chaos of getting people to their barracks. By the time we found her, she'd been dead for almost two days. She was bloated and smelled awful. To tell you the truth, I was so taken aback by what I saw that I actually fainted dead away for a couple of minutes.

"An old Indonesian woman came running up when she saw me pass out. 'What's wrong with you, boy?' she asked in Malay. Then she saw the decomposing corpse. 'Oh, that's so horrible. Here, are you all right now? No wonder you . . .' She never finished her thought. I don't think she wanted me to feel embarrassed for passing out. It was so disgusting, Hanny. I'll never forget it," he said, shuddering at the thought.

Now it was my turn to comfort him. I squeezed his hand and smiled. I guess we had all faced demons here in Bangka. The place stunk of death. It permeated everything, like the smell of rotten eggs that literally worms its way into every corner of a house. Maybe the place had always reeked of dying, from the time the Chinese had chosen it for a burial ground decades ago until now.

"Hey. Quit yapping, you two, and come give us a hand. Aldi and I have dug as deep as we can. We're growing blisters on top of our blisters. Do you mind trading off for a few minutes?" an exasperated voice from down in the hole yelled. We shrugged our shoulders, and George smiled wryly at Peggy as we ran to relieve her.

I let my brother and sister's playful banter wash over me, but I couldn't shake the sick feeling in my stomach as we lowered Sister Mary Catherine's makeshift casket into the ground and as I watched shovelful after shovelful of brown clay dirt slowly cover the coffin and bury my old friend from view forever.

We were in Bangka less than a year, but it wreaked its havoc on us and left a scar that would never fully heal. One morning there was a rumor we were being shipped out again to another camp, and within twenty-four hours, we were gone. We boarded the same rickety old boat to leave that we had arrived on some nine or ten months before. My mind returned to the memory of the mother's body that had followed us for miles that first day. The details were easy to recall.

Our trip to Bangka had begun with a bad omen. Like that poor woman caught in the wake, death had followed us to Bangka and hadn't let go of its viselike grip our entire stay. It made me fear what was to come next.

15

Belalau

THE TRIP AWAY FROM BANGKA on the *tongkang* was perilous. It was so overcrowded that it bobbed and swayed like a drunken man trying to keep his balance. We worried it would sink at any time. Fortunately, I saw as I glanced over the side of the boat that the water was glassy and calm. Seasickness was held to a minimum, meaning we only had to pass the old tin cans occasionally. What a difference compared to our trip to Bangka several months before.

We were weak with hunger and thirst, and the sun beat mercilessly down on our backs hour after hour. The Japanese had not issued us any food or even water since our trip began before dawn. By the afternoon, we were so parched for water that we could barely speak, although most of the talk that did make it past our lips was centered on speculating where the Japanese would land us next.

"Mammy, have you heard where they are taking us?" George asked in a breathless whisper, breaking a long silence.

"No, dear. I don't know," she replied, wiping her moist forehead with the bottom of her skirt for the hundredth time that day.

"But I thought I saw you talking to Mother Laurentia as we were boarding this morning. Surely she must know something."

"No, she hasn't heard anything either. All she knows is that they are taking us back to mainland Sumatra," Mammy said with a weak smile. For a minute, there was only the putt-putting of the boat as it moseyed down the sluggish river.

"Mammy, I'm so thirsty. Why won't they give us any water?" Justin asked with a dry cough.

"I don't know, dear. Maybe they'll pass around a cup soon."

"They better, or we'll be dried little brown raisins by the time they get us wherever we're going," Peggy said acidly.

"That or a nice pile of sand. My throat feels like the Sahara already," George added.

However thirsty we were, though, water was not forthcoming. Mercifully, we made it to the mainland without any debilitating pangs of seasickness— only those of hunger. Others had not fared so well. Before boarding the boat, the Japanese had stacked some ready-made coffins on the deck, perhaps realizing that the long trip would take its toll on women who were already seriously ill and undernourished. Sadly, several of the coffins were filled and nailed shut before we filed off the *tongkang* in Palembang.

We were so tired and weak that full coffins didn't have the same impact on us they once had. We passed them with a twinge of sadness and vague feelings of curiosity, wondering who had finally succumbed.

In Palembang, we were herded into cattle cars after relieving ourselves in the restrooms and lapping well water until we were waterlogged. The cattle cars were then hitched to trains that were already steaming and ready to bolt like bulls gearing up for a stampede. More and more women and children were pushed into each car until the claustrophobia enveloped me. Before long, the train horn blared, and we were off.

"I heard a rumor that we are going to Lubuklinggau," Mrs. Hoop shouted to Mammy over the train's rumblings. Mammy smiled in acknowledgement and then turned to us.

"Lubuklinggau is a far distance from Palembang. We could be on the train for a couple of days," Mammy said in a worried tone. Her forehead pinched together as we click-clacked along, eating up the miles while we rocked back and forth to the train's rhythm. As the time ticked slowly by, the stench of stale sweat and body odor began to overpower us.

"Mammy, I have to go," Justin said after several hours.

"Stay where you are, dear. There is nowhere to go," Mammy said, her mind obviously elsewhere.

"No, Mammy. I mean I have to go . . . go," he said, raising his eyebrows as he tried to convey to her his true meaning.

"Oh! I'm sorry, Justin. Darling, I don't think there *is* anywhere to go, if you get my meaning. You'll have to be creative. We could be on this train for a really long time," she said.

Justin glanced around. Privacy was nonexistent and clearly not a possibility anytime in the near future. I looked away and started talking to Peggy, who was stretching after having closed her eyes for a catnap.

"That was awkward. Now I have a crick in my neck," Peggy said as she gingerly rotated her head from side to side.

"You'd think we'd be used to sleeping in strange positions, but it's still uncomfortable after all this time," I said in reply.

"Ew! It stinks like a latrine in here. Now we're adding urine to the oh-so-lovely smell of sweat and body odor. Can it get much worse?" she asked under her breath, her nose scrunching in rebellion.

It did get worse. We were on the train for nearly two days straight. By the time the train slowed down and pulled to a stop, the smells of urine and excrement were all-consuming. No food and very little water had been issued to us, so we literally crawled out of the cattle cars like animals, so weak were we. Women started herding around the pump in the train yard, desperate for water.

I glanced over at Mammy, who had found Mother Laurentia in the crowd. The good sister was giving an emaciated young child the last drops of water from her canteen. She and Mammy exchanged a few words, and then I saw our mother squeeze back through the crowd of women to join us.

"Mother Laurentia heard that we are going to a deserted rubber plantation in the jungle called Belalau. She said she understands the conditions may be a little better there than what we lived through in Bangka. The downside is that we have to walk several miles from the station to get to our new camp," Mammy said, wiping the sweat from her brow and sucking in the fresh air like it was candy.

I felt so weak from sitting for two days without nourishment that my legs could have passed for wet noodles. How was I going to walk for even one mile? I felt hot tears of exhaustion and despair stream down my face. Contemplating what lay ahead of us, I felt I was almost to my breaking point, and I had to bite my lip to keep from crying out loud.

Our pathetic group of disheveled, tired, beaten-down women started the long trek to our new camp slowly. Everyone was in the same situation physically, so the occasional cries of *"Lekas! Lekas!"* from the guards went unheeded. We just kept plodding along as best we could. I concentrated on putting one shaky foot in front of the other, time and time again, focusing on that simple task alone. Peggy walked directly in front of me, so I kept my eyes zeroed in on her swaying black braid as I made my way down the jungle path.

Walking through the jungle with Peggy leading reminded me of a sunny afternoon we had passed with Pappy right before Pearl Harbor. We had ventured into the jungle near Tandjoengenim to picnic by a local waterhole in the trees. We had trailed each other in a single file to get to our destination, bantering playfully with each other all the while. Peggy's swaying hair had been my focal point then too.

I marveled at how long ago that outing seemed, but the memory still warmed me. Though no one knew how many miles separated us now, the thought of Pappy was always comforting . . . and motivating. He had trekked through the jungle alone to come home to us, sick and weary from his travels. Remembering his fortitude lit a small fire in me to keep going as we cut our way slowly through the trees and undergrowth to our new camp.

After what seemed like an eternity, we arrived at Belalau. My spirits lifted as I looked around and noticed that our new camp was nicely shaded by huge rubber trees that stood as ageless sentinels on the plantation. The late afternoon sunlight filtered in between the large green leaves to create what would have been a very welcoming scene had it not been for the ever-present barbed-wire fences that snaked around our new camp.

The next afternoon Mammy took us exploring. We found a quaint little stream that meandered through camp. It bubbled and slid over the rocks at the bottom of the bed. After a quick peek into the water, Mammy's face lit up.

"Look, girls. I see snails down there on the rocks; we can collect them for protein. What a godsend," our mother said, her thin hands clapped together in delight. *Snails! What I wouldn't give for a few of those that had plagued us in Palembang so long ago.*

After more detective work, she also found mushrooms congregating under some of the large trees and ferns growing in the dimmer parts of camp.

"Hanny, Peggy, just snip the tops of the ferns like so. The bottoms are not edible, but the tops we can eat. My mammy and pappy used to gather this type of fern leaf when I was a young girl and we would go hiking in the jungle for the day. They taught me which ones were good for you and which were poisonous," she said, examining each plant closely.

It wasn't long before Mammy had a new garden planted. She scoured the grounds in camp for seeds and soon had a type of squash called *petun* planted as well as *kankun,* the spinach we had eaten in Palembang. She situated her garden high on a knoll and close to the old abandoned house we lived in. When I asked her why she had chosen that location, she said that planting it on high ground would ward off thieves. The prison interns were so hungry now that some would use any means to get more food. Thievery was common among any little stashes of food that we had hidden. As hard as I tried, I couldn't resent hungry women who took food to try and feed their families. These were desperate times.

The general spirit in Belalau was more upbeat than in Bangka. The sun and heat were less severe. Chores still were required of those that were well, though. The grave digging continued, and we used big, two-person saws to whittle our way through the dense trees on the plantation for firewood.

"Look at my hands! You'd think I was recovering from some awful disease because there are so many blisters," Peggy said one afternoon, gazing in awe at her marked hands.

I was relaxing under a tree, watching closely for guards. We had "assigned ourselves" a short break before tackling our tree again. Manhandling that saw would have been difficult work for two grown men, let alone two teenage girls.

Justin was the foreman of our little band of teenage workers. Mother Laurentia must have seen something special in our baby brother to give him that responsibility. He was younger than most of us, but he had always had a spark in him—pluck, Pappy had called it. Whatever the name, it manifested itself in Justin's determination to get things done at all costs, a quality the camp leaders admired.

"Isn't it amazing that the boys weren't taken from us . . . again?" I asked Peggy, who was lying down rooting under some old leaves for some wild mushrooms to throw in our soup for dinner.

Periodically, the Japanese would examine the boys in camp for body hair. If any was detected, they were deemed old enough for transfer and were soon forced to leave us and live with the men in their camp miles away. We always felt the loss. Since our captivity in Palembang, many of our acquaintances had been deemed too old by the Japanese and were separated from their mothers and sisters.

With two teenage boys living in our family, we dreaded those inspection days. Knowing our fear, Mother Laurentia had stepped in more than once for Mammy, asking the Japanese guards to make an exception.

"Please, sir. These are good boys. They work long hours and are willing to take on anything we need. They cut more wood than twice the number of girls in a day, and they have the brawn to haul it all back to camp. We *need* them," I remember her saying earnestly to a skeptical Japanese soldier. Inexplicably, each time Mother Laurentia's request was granted, and our brothers were allowed to stay.

"Mammy calls it a blessing—them getting to stay with us, I mean," Peggy replied, still scrounging around the fungus-ridden ground for mushrooms.

"You know, Peggy, the first few months we were in Palembang, I prayed every day to be released from that godforsaken place, sometimes several times a day. I was starting to feel kind of discouraged, thinking that maybe God wasn't answering my prayers. Then one evening it dawned on me. Sometimes our big problems aren't taken away, but, instead, little blessings might come along to ease our burdens and help us remember He is still watching over us," I said thoughtfully.

"Now you're starting to sound like Mammy," Peggy said as she gathered five or six little mushrooms into a cloth and gently set them aside. "I guess I see your point, though," she added after a minute.

"Think about it. Just the fact that I am here with you and not with the other students in a different camp is a small wonder. Mother Laurentia told me in Palembang that they separated the boarding school students from the nuns and sent them to two different camps. That could have been me.

"Or what about the fact that not one of the five of us has died, while so many others are dropping like flies all around us? Plus, Mammy was spared in Palembang when Mrs. Schwartzkopf was trying to turn her in to the guards for smuggling," I said, counting the incidents on the tips of my fingers.

"Yeah. The boys staying with us is a real blessing. I think they are the oldest boys in camp now. Oh, and there was that time the guards gave Mammy medicine for George when he was so sick with malaria, remember?" Peggy said, getting into the spirit of the game.

"I remember. Plus, I bet there were lots of times we may not even be aware of . . . times that we were protected or rescued that we don't even really know about," I said as I stood to resume sawing.

"That's pretty deep, Hanny. Don't give yourself a brain hemorrhage. Although I guess anyone in the world could say that, whatever their circumstances. Who knows how many times we are protected from accident or sickness in a day or a week? It's kind of mind-boggling to think about," she said, picking up her side of the saw.

As if on cue, we started sawing again, the sound drowning out any possibility of conversation. We were left to our own thoughts again. I guess some of my Mammy's faith *had* rubbed off on me, because as I stood there sawing, I couldn't imagine there not being a God to watch over us or to listen to our prayers. Some might say it is ironic to hear such thoughts come from a prisoner of war, someone who had lived in captivity for more than three years and experienced deprivations of all types, but that was how I felt as I stood there pushing the saw back and forth with my sister under the thick tree canopy in a remote prison camp in the jungle of Sumatra.

***

While we did eat better than in Bangka, the interns, in general, were still weak and malnourished. Many fell prey to malaria, dysentery, and *beriberi* while we lived in Belalau. Sadly, the constant sickness in camp made our grave-digging duties a significant part of our lives. We young people were called to dig several times a week. One of the houses in Belalau was designated as the camp hospital, and many of the desperately ill were moved there and cared for by the Australian nurses and some of the nuns.

Unfortunately, many of the sick never recovered. Each day those that had passed away the day before were placed carefully in the makeshift coffins provided by the Japanese. The next morning, a call for gravediggers would ring out, and we would transport the coffins to our little cemetery outside of camp.

One day, I had just returned from planting peanuts in the camp garden when Peggy came back from grave-digging duty.

"You're home early, Peggy. Mammy is still over at House Two nursing Mrs. Hoop. They almost lost her last night," I said, using a dull tin lid to slice up some freshly picked *petun* to add to our dinner that night. As I glanced up from my task to smile at my sister, I noticed her face was ashen, and she looked short of breath. Clearly, something had happened; my sister was visibly shaken. With Peggy, it was often better to approach conversations like this from the back door instead of confronting her head on. I finished preparing the *petun* in silence, while Peggy leaned against the *balai-balai* and watched me.

I reached for her and motioned for her to kneel on the dirt floor. She did so without question because this was part of our daily routine: lice removal. I sat on the rack behind her and slid out my sister's braid, my fingers unraveling her long plait. Slowly combing my fingers through her thick black hair, I searched for the hard little round vermin that invaded our bodies on a regular basis. I felt like the monkeys I'd often seen photos of in school that would pick the lice off of their friends—a social behavior, I remember Sister Patricia saying in biology class. Here, it was a feeble attempt to keep the awful itching to a minimum and to feel somewhat clean again. Today, I hoped it would be a worthwhile cover for finding out how my sister's day had really gone.

"I planted peanuts this morning," I said, trying to start the conversation on a benign note. "Mammy says the Japanese might be growing a conscience over the lack of nutritious food we've been getting for the last three and a half years. Apparently peanuts are high in protein," I added.

"Right. Growing a conscience? More like they are secretly afraid of the retribution the Allies will dish out when they notice how skinny and sickly we all are and how many of us have . . . died," she said, her voice breaking at the end. I heard a surreptitious sniffle, but I pretended not to notice it.

"The work was really backbreaking, bending over the rows of dirt all morning. I'm glad Aldi was with me. What about you? How was your day?" I asked with false bravado. Even I could hear the artificial note in my voice, but maybe, through her tears, Peggy wouldn't.

"I *wish* I'd been planting peanuts today. Grave digging was . . . well, it didn't go as planned," she said quietly, sniffing all the while.

"What happened? Why didn't it go well, Peg?" I gently prodded, never breaking my rhythm of searching methodically through her hair for lice.

"I . . . uh, I was in the hole today. George and I joined up with two women from House Four. He started the hole, digging through the crusty surface and then down as far as he could go. I traded off with him after an hour or so. Because of all the rain last week, the ground wasn't as hard as usual, so George had made a lot of headway. I was just trying to square off the sides, so the coffin wouldn't sit in the hole slanted. We must have started digging too close to the grave next to us, because as I drove in my mallet, trying to pry out a stone that was stuck, I . . . ." She broke off then, clearly overcome with emotion.

Intrigued by her story, I tried to be patient but couldn't hold out for long.

"Well, Peggy, what happened then?" I asked, my voice dripping with curiosity.

"I . . . the mallet I was using to dig went too far, and I broke through the hole of the grave to my right. It must have been in there awhile because the cheap wood the Japanese use to make our coffins had rotted. The mallet broke through the casket, and part of the corpse spilled over into our hole," she said in a rough whisper.

She broke into sobs, at which I quickly abandoned my search for vermin and knelt down beside her, holding her head tightly in my arms. I kept stroking her long, dark hair as she cried.

"Flies actually flew out of the hole, Hanny. And . . . and the smell. I'll never forget the awful smell that came from that body. The fumes were like rotting meat but so much worse. I felt myself gagging uncontrollably. My limbs instantly lost all feeling. I crumpled to my knees as I sat staring at that dead arm lying there in the dirt. For the life of me, Hanny, I couldn't find the strength to get up and climb out of the hole. George and one of the other women finally had to haul me out. I lay on the ground dizzy for a while before I gained control again. The others insisted I go back home. Frankly, I'd had enough for one day, so I agreed. I know I'll never forget the sight of that hand. It was like a scene from the worst horror story you could imagine," she said, still sobbing into my arms.

Visions of Sister Mary Catherine's dead blue eyes revisited me, and I held my sister all the tighter. Would we ever be released from this nightmare we were living in? Or was our past life the dream? Would we ever enjoy a relaxing, civilized life again? The reds and yellows of cheerful garden flowers rose to mind and cool glasses of lemonade and strains of piano music wafting in from the parlor. Could that existence truly have been real? Or had we always lived in hunger, slept on hard racks, and felt illness and death creeping among us like thieves in the night? Shaking myself from my reverie, I swiftly kissed my sister on the cheek and gave her a last, quick squeeze.

"I'm so sorry for what you went through today, Peggy. Why don't you take it easy for a few minutes? I'm just going to go get some well water to start the broth for dinner," I said, picking up our old pot.

"No, I'll walk with you. The last thing I need right now is time alone with my thoughts," she said, more to herself than to me.

Together we walked to the well, conscious of putting one foot in front of the other, one foot in front of the other. Maybe that was the only way to survive this place after all.

A few nights later, I was assigned night watch duty. Aldi had volunteered to go out with me, but at the last minute, her sister Renie came running up from her house next door.

"Aldi's sick, Hanny. She can't watch with you tonight. She's got a fever, and Mammy's afraid she might be starting malaria," Renie said, trying to catch her breath.

"Oh. I just saw her this morning at roll call. I know how fast these things can hit, though. Tell her not to worry about it. I can go alone tonight," I said, hoping my voice sounded braver than I felt.

"Thanks, Hanny. I would offer to take her place, but Mammy might need me to run for water or sit with Aldi for a while or something," she said, the relief evident on her face.

"I'll have Mammy send up some quinine tea, just in case," I called after her as I watched her run back home. She raised an arm in acknowledgment as she raced on. I was fleetingly grateful for the boon we'd found on arriving at Belalau.

Chinchona trees grew on the plantation. These were exactly the trees Pappy had used when he'd contracted malaria on his way back home from destroying the mines. Since our arrival, Mammy had used the bark often to brew a tea for those who had come down with a fever. We even drank it preventatively once in a while, though we dreaded the bitter taste it left in our mouths. Still, malaria was worse, and we felt blessed to have the *chinchona* trees in the camp.

I went on my night watch alone that evening. Mammy was exhausted from a long stint of nursing some of the sick women in camp the night before. I couldn't ask her to come with me, and Peggy was already asleep. No, I would do this alone.

I walked outside and remembered immediately that it was a new moon. The night was completely dark. The cool light from the moon often served as a lantern for me on such evenings, but it was not visible tonight. There was a little light from the stars, but the many tree branches overhead obscured it. It was spooky—no other word for it.

The jungle was alive at night. There were insects buzzing and nocturnal birds singing high in the trees above. Normally, I found the noises second nature, but I was jumpy tonight. The loud bellow of a howler monkey left me rattled. I could feel myself start to tremble, but I resolved to keep moving ahead. I tried to convince myself that logically there was nothing to be frightened of.

We teenagers poked fun at our nightly watch duties on a regular basis. They seemed ridiculous to us; we didn't see the need. Why then couldn't my brain convince my heart? Truth be told, I was fearful. Perhaps it was a little premonition or something because not long after I'd begun my duty, I heard a bloodcurdling scream ring out in the night.

My shaking hand flew to my mouth in terror. Was someone being murdered in her bed? I gingerly called out into the night, "Who is it? Are you all right?" Fear had robbed me of my voice, though, and instead of a strong, hearty question, my words came out feeble and weak.

Clearing my throat, I prepared myself to call out a little louder when again I heard a horrible shriek cut through the air followed by sobs.

"Please . . . who is it? Where are you?" I pleaded as loudly as my trembling voice would permit.

Silence. I stepped forward to the side of the house, but I couldn't see. The black night shrouded everything. I waffled in indecision. Should I call out again? Should I keep moving forward, or should I turn back to get help? For the third time, I heard sobs coming from somewhere in the depths of the darkness.

That did it for me. I about-faced and flew back to my house like a hare fleeing a fox.

"Mammy! M . . . Mammy! Come quick! I need you," I implored, shaking her a little more than I would normally have done.

"Hanny, what's the matter? Are you hurt?" she asked, her voice rough with sleep. Her hand fluttered to my face, questioning whether I was all right.

"I heard screaming. Someone is in trouble," I said. "I can't see anything out there. It's black as tar." I heard my mother stumble out of bed and slip on her worn, brown sandals.

"I'm coming, dear." She yawned. "Are you sure it was someone screaming and not a howler monkey or some other animal out there in the jungle?" she asked—a little dubiously, I thought.

"Mammy, I *know* what a howler monkey sounds like. This was different. If an animal *is* involved, it's because it's eating one of the camp interns or something. It was definitely a woman's scream," I said decidedly.

"Okay, let's go," Mammy said, wiping the sleep from her eyes. Just as we rounded the corner, we heard it again.

The scream pierced the silence, and Mammy's sleepy pace went into double-time. I had to practically run to keep up with her.

"Stay close, Hanny! We don't want to get separated if there's danger out here," she said firmly. She didn't have to tell me twice. I was sticking to her like glue. After a few minutes of searching in the darkness, Mammy happened upon a ditch. She dropped to her knees and felt around the length of it.

"Here, Hanny! I feel some cloth and an arm."

"Mammy, be careful! Maybe some wild animal attacked her. It could still be on the prowl," I said, cautiously glancing over my shoulder.

"You there! Are you awake? Are you all right?" my mother called gently, tapping the arm she found. A soft moan rose from the ditch.

"Oh, please . . . help me! I . . . I woke, needing to use the restroom. It was so dark outside that I fell right down this hole. I must have blacked out or something," a shaky voice said.

"Are you hurt at all? I'm a nurse and can help," Mammy reassured her.

"I think I'm okay. Would you mind giving me a hand out of here, please? I am stuck in the most awkward position," the voice said. Mammy and I pulled her out, but dark as it was we couldn't make out her face.

"Thanks so much. I would have been down there until morning if you hadn't happened by," the woman said warmly, squeezing both of our hands affectionately.

"May we help you back to your quarters?" Mammy asked kindly.

"If you can just point me in the right direction, I think I'll be okay. I live in House Six."

Feeling for her shoulders, Mammy gently turned her around and said, "Can you make out that big black shape in the distance? That's the watchtower. If you keep that as your northwest point, I think you'll find home is just over there."

"I do see it, just barely. I'm fine now, really, and thank you again," the woman said with a slightly embarrassed edge to her voice.

I chuckled, shaking my head in chagrin as we strolled back to our house hand in hand. I could feel my mother's gaze on me, perhaps trying to gauge my mood through the darkness.

"Why the laugh, Hanny?" she asked curiously.

"There I go, making mountains out of molehills. If you only knew what crazy scenarios were marching through my head when I heard those screams. Tigers, hormonal prison guards, someone finally going off the deep end, just to name a few," I said, my voice clearly ashamed.

"I'm sure I would have wondered about those same things had it been me out there by myself. You did the right thing by coming to get me. We're lucky we didn't find something a lot worse out there tonight."

"Thanks, Mammy."

"Listen, I think it's close enough to the two-hour mark that we can wake Hildy and Edna to take over watch duty. I want you to get some sleep," she said, squeezing my shoulder.

We never learned whom we had hauled out of the hole that night. But, as Mammy said, it felt good to be helpful regardless of whether we knew the person or not. Little could we guess as we crawled back into our *balai-balai* that night that we would soon be called on to help two new friends in profound ways.

16

The Boys

As time went by in Belalau, more and more women had had their fill of prison life. Some refused to do chores anymore and would feign sickness. They would lounge in their houses all day and play cards or delve into dark magic or just lie there staring at the ceiling. The rest of us were expected to pick up their slack.

Other interns balanced precariously on the high wire between sanity and the black hole of insanity. One or two fell right off the edge and lost their minds completely.

"You have a new assignment, Peggy," Mammy said hesitantly one day.

"What do you mean? A new job assignment or something? Not that I would miss grave digging or anything, but . . ." Peggy questioned, a confused look on her face as she folded her blanket one morning.

"Mother Laurentia and the others have specifically asked for you. This . . . assignment is not going to be easy, but you're strong. I know you'll be able to do it," Mammy said reassuringly.

"All right, now you're scaring me. What is it?" my sister asked, her brown eyes growing wide.

"Well, you know how Mrs. Brauermann has sort of been having . . . trouble with her mind lately?"

"The woman is completely out there. I think she's losing all touch with reality," Peggy said emphatically.

"She really lost it last night. She was screaming and screaming. I'm surprised the whole camp didn't wake up," I interjected sleepily from my rack.

"She did lose it. She has completely broken from the real world now. The Japanese have moved her into the old abandoned house next door. We are to . . . watch her. We need to make sure she doesn't hurt herself or anyone else," Mammy explained, searching my sister's face.

"O—kay . . . what does that have to do with me?"

"They . . . Mother Laurentia has asked that you be one of the interns assigned to watch her. Just for a couple of hours a day," my mother said, steeling herself for Peggy's response.

"No."

"Peggy, someone needs to do this. You're young and strong. I see Mother Laurentia's point."

"No, I can't do it. I know I can't."

"Peggy, please be reasonable. This poor woman needs our help. She can't help what she is. She simply couldn't face prison life anymore, and her brain finally revolted against it. I think we've all felt close to snapping at one point or another. She finally did," Mammy said gently.

I thought I detected a small crack in Peggy's obstinacy. My sister had a very compassionate heart, despite all her bravado. Mammy knew how to reach that.

"It will only be for two-hour shifts, and if it turns out to be too much, I will personally talk to Mother Laurentia for you," Mammy said soothingly.

"Well, okay. I'll do it, but I'm not going to like it. That kind of thing scares me to death. I guess I see where you're coming from, though. It could have happened to any one of us," Peggy grumbled reluctantly.

"Good girl. I'm proud of you. Your shift starts at noon," Mammy said, clearly relieved that everything was resolved. Giving us all a quick hug, she continued, "I'm off to see the Van Hootens. Mother and daughter both have bad cases of dysentery. I've boiled burnt rice tea for them to help stop the runs."

"If I didn't know better, I'd say she gets positively excited when she can brew that nasty tea and help someone choke it down," Peggy said, shaking her head in amazement as we watched our mother stride off toward the hospital barracks.

"Mammy takes great joy in her nursing, Peg," I corrected gently.

"I know, I know. If only I were more like her, maybe I wouldn't balk at having to sit with a mentally deranged woman for half the afternoon," Peggy answered under her breath.

"You'll do great. Maybe you'll feel safer with protection. You could always ward her off with this," I said jokingly, offering her our old makeshift broom. Most of its bristles were gone, and it looked very pathetic indeed. She shook her head in disgust.

I chuckled as I left that morning for my gardening assignment. The peanuts the Japanese had given us to plant were coming along very nicely.

That afternoon, after returning from a hot morning in the sun, I sank down on the *balai-balai*. I relished the quiet I had before our quarters would again fill with its inhabitants.

"How was work today, Hanny?" Justin asked from his resting spot in the corner.

"Oh, you scared me. I didn't see you there," I said with my hand over my heart. He wasn't usually home this early from his chores.

"Work was fine, I guess. Same old, same old. And you?" I asked.

"It was good. We chopped down a huge old rubber tree on the south part of the plantation. I'm giving everyone an hour rest during the hottest part of the day before we tackle another two trees farther west," he said.

"Were you here when Peggy left at noon?" I asked curiously.

"I was just walking back when I saw her head out. Strange though, I wondered where she was off to with our old broom in her hand. She was clutching it to her chest like it was a sword and she was off to face the dragon," he said, looking perplexed.

I laughed until my brother thought *I* was the one having trouble with my mental health.

***

After picking up our rice ration for dinner one evening, Mother Laurentia tapped Mammy on the shoulder as we passed House Three on our way home.

"Tina, dear. Would you be so kind as to walk with me for a minute? I am in a bit of a dilemma. Perhaps you could help me," she asked with a smile.

"Why, of course, Mother Laurentia. What would you like me to do?" Mammy asked.

"There is a young boy and his mother who are very ill down at the hospital wing. As sick as the boy is, his mother is even worse. Mrs. Rottier is her name. She keeps mumbling in Malay, although I know she's a Dutch citizen. I think she is reverting back to her childhood language because of her high fever. Perhaps you could speak with her and see if she's comfortable . . . if there is anything she is wanting," Mother Laurentia suggested.

"I'm not sure what good I can do, but I'll be right down," my mother said. "Peggy and Hanny, will you come too? Maybe you know this woman's son and can entertain him while I talk to his mammy."

We nodded in agreement and soon found ourselves by the sick woman's bedside. Her yellow skin and vacant eyes had the look of death. I'd seen it repeated a hundred times since I'd been in camp. I turned away for a second. That glazed look was never an easy one to witness.

Mammy didn't flinch, though. She knelt down beside the sick woman and took her hand, squeezing it gently. We stood behind her after quickly determining that her son, Louis, was too far gone for conversation.

In Malay, Mammy coaxed her gently, "Mrs. Rottier, how are you, dear? Tell me what you are thinking. We only want to help you."

Fear registered in the sick woman's face. I could tell it surprised Mammy.

"You are afraid. What frightens you?" our mother asked kindly, gently wiping the perspiration from Mrs. Rottier's feverish forehead with a threadbare cloth.

Still no response, but she looked troubled. Peggy and I glanced at one another, puzzled, but not Mammy. Her mother's intuition sensed a kindred spirit.

"Do you fear for your son?" she asked quietly. The woman closed her glassy eyes that were filled with ancient sadness, and I know she would have nodded had she been able. Mammy stroked her disheveled black hair and said soothingly, "Don't you worry. I'll take Louis, and I'll do my best to nurse him and give him a good life until I can get him safely back to his pappy."

The woman's face smoothed in relief. A wan smile hovered on her trembling lips, and I knew she understood. Her son was in loving, capable hands now. It was the best she could do for him given the circumstances. We learned she passed peacefully just a few hours later. At the time, I wondered if I would be one of those asked to dig her grave the next morning. I shuddered to think about it. It always made the task worse when I thought about the people I was burying and the lives they were leaving behind.

As for Louis, he was in no position to speak either. His face was as thin as a skeleton's, and his sunken eyes couldn't focus. They kept rolling back into his head. I feared he would die before my mother had a chance to keep her promise. We transported him as gently as we could up the knoll to our house. Mammy kept feeding him her burnt rice tea with a teaspoon. He was thirteen years old, just a year or two younger than Justin, but he reminded me of a thin little bird, taking minute sips from time to time before falling back into an exhausted sleep. It didn't seem enough to sustain him, but over the next couple of days, he grew stronger.

About this time, Mammy stumbled across some eggs. Unlike Bangka, the black market existed in Belalau, but most women had nothing more to trade. Fortunately, Mammy had her homegrown vegetables, ripe and delicious, the envy of many women in the camp. Occasionally she would be able to land some goods on the black market by trading harvest from her garden.

Somehow, around the time Louis joined us, she made a deal for five very precious eggs. Protein of any kind was virtually unheard of in camp. Eggs were such rare commodities that we hadn't seen one in our humble living quarters since Palembang. Needless to say, we were ecstatic at the thought of such a feast. We held the fragile delicacies reverently in our hands and pondered the many ways we could cook them. There was one for each of us, and we thought about the boost to our energy a little protein would provide. We savored the experience.

As we pondered our culinary options, we heard a knock on our door. Mother Laurentia stood tall and regal in the door frame, asking for Mammy. Mutual regard registered in both sets of eyes as they stood talking with one another.

"I came to check on Louis's progress. How is he?"

"We're very pleased, Mother. He's sitting up again, and he asked for more broth this morning. I'm quite certain I saw a shadow of a smile on his face when the children were teasing back and forth over dinner last night," Mammy replied.

"I am so pleased to hear he's doing better. He was starting to frighten me before he came up here to you. I was afraid we were going to lose him."

"I wondered if we would as well, but he's stronger than I thought."

Mother Laurentia sighed then. "I did come to check on Louis's situation, but I've also come to ask another favor, Tina. I know you are busy with Louis and your own four, but we've got another boy who is very ill. In fact, your sons probably know him—he works on Justin's tree-cutting crew. His name is Tommy Harrevelt. He lost his mother earlier in the camps to *beri-beri* and has no one to care for him. Frankly, my sisters and I and the nurses have all we can manage down at the hospital. I wouldn't ask if we weren't truly in need of help," she ended, looking at my mother hesitantly.

Mammy looked away for no more than a few seconds and then turned back to her friend. She simply nodded, and the nun squeezed her shoulder in gratitude.

"He's very ill, Tina. He's so weak he can't walk anymore. Could I borrow your boys to help carry him up the hill to your house?"

"Of course. They can walk back down with you while Hanny and I make him up a quiet corner to lie down. Peggy, start some broth for Tommy and Louis, will you dear? Add some of that spinach I brought in from the garden to the rice. It's full of vitamins," Mammy said in full nurse mode.

Justin and George rigged a makeshift stretcher for the sick boy. They laid him on a sheet and each of my brothers carried one side of it up the hill to our home. They said he was light as a feather. Once he was situated and resting, Mammy called a family meeting. We gathered in a circle outside the door in quiet consultation.

"We need to discuss the eggs, children. We have five. Originally, I bartered so each of us would have one, but that was before the boys came along. Tommy's in a very bad way, and Louis is not much better. He could easily take a turn for the worse. I think they would really benefit from the protein those eggs provide. What do you think? Should we give them each an egg?" My mother looked around the circle at each of us.

Without hesitation, we all agreed.

She continued with a proud smile on her face, "Well done, children. Now, we still have three eggs left. Any suggestions on how we should divide them among ourselves?"

"We could make a soup with the eggs and eat that," George said doubtfully.

"Soup? Again? Can't we come up with something a little more original?" Peggy asked, shaking her head in disdain.

"What about scrambling them?" I suggested. "We all used to love Kokie's scrambled eggs back home."

"Excellent idea, Hanny. All in favor, say aye," Mammy said. We all agreed that scrambled eggs sounded wonderful.

"The ayes have it. Let's get scrambling," Justin said, rubbing his hands together in anticipation.

After feeding the sick boys an egg each and sharing the other three, we tidied up our part of the house, trying desperately to rearrange our few things to better accommodate Louis and Tommy. Suddenly, I noticed a movement at the window. A *hahok* was standing right outside, waving at me to get Mammy's attention. I was astonished to see him at the window because they were commanded not to talk to prison interns under any circumstances.

Hahoks were local Indonesians who had been coerced into working for the Japanese. They were paid a small amount of money to watch us and report to the Japanese if we disobeyed the rules. Glorified babysitting was how I thought of it. Communication between the *hahoks* and the interns was strictly forbidden, and consequences for disobedience were grave.

"Mammy, over here," I gestured, pointing to the window.

Mammy looked at the window and then glanced around quickly. Two of our housemates were well-known spies for the Japanese. They would love to sink their teeth into a juicy tidbit like this. They would probably get an extra lump of sugar or something as a reward for ratting us out. Fortunately, I spotted them lounging in the next room, intent on a game of cards.

"I'll watch for you, Mammy," I whispered quietly.

She slipped out the front door to talk to the slightly built man creeping around the corner. Within two minutes, she slid back into the room again. We were all curious as to why the *hahok* had approached her.

"Outside, children. I think there is some *kankun* that needs harvesting in the garden," our mother said, loud enough for the women in the next room to hear if they were paying attention.

Once we were safe from prying ears, Mammy turned to us. Her thin shoulders trembled, and tears welled in her eyes. She was shaking with emotion as she reached into the pocket of her worn red dress and then held her hand out so we could see what she had hidden there. There, nestled in her palms, were eggs—two of them. We looked at her with confused faces.

"Mammy, where did you get those eggs? Were you able to trade for them again?" Justin asked.

"And what did the *hahok* have to do with anything?" Peggy added curiously.

Mammy shook her head and wiped a stray tear from her cheek. "I'm completely shocked. I followed the little old man around the side of the house. Once out of sight, he grabbed me by the arm and whispered quietly, 'Say nothing! Say nothing!' Before I had time to register what was going on, he handed me the eggs and scurried away."

"Those are just like the two eggs we gave to Louis and Tommy. But . . . how could he have known?" George asked incredulously.

"I don't see how he could have known. I have never spoken to him before today. Although I always smile and nod my head when I pass the *hahoks,* I've never so much as exchanged a greeting with him," Mammy said, holding the eggs like they were two priceless jewels.

"Somehow, someone must have told him," Peggy said, shaking her head in disbelief.

"How could anyone have known? We made the decision to share our eggs just this afternoon. No one has left the house since we ate them for dinner," Mammy countered.

"What a weird coincidence," Justin said, his face screwed up in confusion.

"Some people may call it luck or coincidence, but the timing is just too perfect. *I* think it was a blessing," Mammy said, her face glowing. "I've always said, 'When you help people, it comes back to you in the end.' I really believe that."

"I think you're right," I said, squeezing her hand as we stood together in the shade of the eaves.

"That's another one to add to our list, Hanny," Peggy murmured as we turned back to go inside.

"What list?" Justin asked.

"Oh, just our 'God is watching' list," Peggy said nonchalantly.

But I knew that like me, Peggy was touched by what would always be known as the miraculous egg story. Little did we know that we would get another windfall the following day.

***

"Children, listen. The same *hahok* that gave us the eggs approached me this morning as I was leaving the hospital. He was standing behind a large rubber tree and waved me over," Mammy said in a low voice. None of our housemates were home yet, but you could never be too careful.

"Do you think he's setting a trap for us?" George asked, leaning against the wall with his arms folded.

"No, no. He'd get into a lot of trouble for giving us those eggs yesterday if he were ever discovered. Besides, I don't think we're under suspicion. We've been so careful around Mrs. Trompe and her lot. I think this man legitimately wants to help us," my mother said with conviction.

"What did he want this time?" I asked curiously.

"I joined him on the back side of the rubber tree, and then he asked quietly in Malay if there was anything at all I needed. It surprised me, and I blurted out, 'More rice. Always more rice.' He didn't even hesitate for a minute. 'Good,' he said. 'I'll be outside your barracks at midnight with more rice if I can get it.' I grabbed his arm and reminded him not to knock. 'There are women who are not to be trusted living in the room next to us,' I said. We stood thinking for just a split second, and then I suggested a plan. 'I will tie a string to my toe and throw the other end out of the window. If you come with the rice, gently tug on the twine, and I will sneak out to get it,' I said. He nodded and then turned to go. I touched his arm once again and whispered, 'Thank you so much . . . for the eggs and for the rice.'

"He smiled and nodded, his old brown face wrinkling into laugh lines. I was so grateful I could have hugged him right there, but that would have surely given us away. A second later, he disappeared into the trees. I had to pinch myself to make sure I wasn't completely dreaming the whole thing up," Mammy said, as she swept a stray lock of hair away from her face.

That evening we cared for Tommy and Louis, encouraging them to sip more broth every couple of hours. Tommy kept muttering, "I'm tired . . . I'm just so tired," but Mammy would spoon some more soup into his mouth and then gently lay him back down, whispering, "Rest now. Lie back and rest."

Louis was doing much better. He could rise for a few seconds now on his shaky stick legs, wobbling for a step or two before needing to sit down again. Peggy and I felt a little like new mothers watching their baby toddle his first steps, we were so proud of him. We clapped our hands in delight the first time he walked, and a big grin crossed his face at our enthusiasm. He knew we cared about him and his health. He was one of us now. We helped him lie back down and covered him with a worn blanket.

I saw Mammy at the window watching the sun sink slowly through the trees, her forehead lined with worry. Her hand flew up to rub the tension away. I could guess what she was thinking without needing to ask. This business with the *hahok* was a foray into smuggling again, a path she'd left behind in Palembang. Was it worth the risk, especially with two sick boys to care for? Mammy had a lot on her plate. Piling it higher with peril and intrigue would just add to the burden. Still, rice was food, and no one here in camp dismissed that lightly . . . or ever. Therein was her answer. Mammy was nothing if not practical.

"We must bed down for the night like normal. We don't want to raise any suspicion from Mrs. Trompe and her lot," Mammy whispered as she turned back from the window, her aura one of briskness, a throwback to her underground work in Palembang. *I guess a zebra never really changes its stripes.* I shook my head in admiration.

We puttered around like normal for the sake of the spies playing bridge next door, although the tension was as thick as butter in our room. Peggy and I checked one last time on our two patients, ensuring that they were comfortable for the night. Then we sank into our own racks, feigning sleep. I wanted to stay awake to see what transpired during the night, but a busy morning cleaning bathrooms and weeding peanut plants made me tired and susceptible to sleep's siren call. The next thing I was aware of was my mother's gentle pressure on my arm shaking me from my dreams.

"Hanny! Peggy! Wake up, girls." Mammy was frantic in the dark.

"Mammy, what time is it? Did we nod off?" Peggy mumbled, her words thick with sleep.

"The *hahok*'s been and gone. I was worried the informers next door would never call it a night, but they finally did. Just in time too. Soon after I heard them bunk down, I felt a tug on my toe. Our ruse worked! I crept outside, careful to avoid the creaky plank near the door. There was our friend, the *hahok,* kneeling around the corner with a huge bag of rice. There had to be twenty-five pounds inside. I stared at him holding the bag, completely appalled. 'How are we going to hide all this rice?' I thought to myself. He was so pleased to be helping us, though, that I managed a smile and a very sincere handshake. 'Thank you,' I mouthed to him in the dark. He grinned and was gone without another word—eerily fast, really.

"Anyway, what are we going to do with all this rice? I thought he might give us a can or two, but this is so much," Mammy whispered, clearly dismayed at our boon.

"We'll hide it," Peggy said. She slid silently off the rack and sidled to the door that separated us from the women in the next room. She put her ear gently to the door and then tiptoed back.

"They're either fast asleep or *very* good actors. Let's use this time to hide the rice in everything we can think of. Wake the boys," whispered Peggy, already reaching under the *balai-balai* for her case.

In less than a minute, we were all hunting for any kind of containers we could find, tin cans, cups, our old shoes, pots, and even our pillowcases. By the time every grain of rice had found a home, we felt like we'd run a marathon. Justin acted as lookout near the partition separating us from our treacherous neighbors. Miraculously, none of the women next door awoke, even though we were pouring rice into containers and hiding them as inconspicuously as possible for more than an hour. As we lay our heads back down to rest for a short while before daybreak, we realized that our pillowcases may not have been the best choice to hide the rice. They wriggled and moved like they were alive!

"What in the world?" I whispered incredulously in Peggy's ear.

"Rice beetles," she said, punching her pillow softly. Of course. Our rice in the camps was often riddled with beetles. Most of the time, they died and were sloughed off the top by the cooks before they served us our dinner, so no harm done. But with hidden raw rice, we were not so lucky. Sleep evaded us with no way to forget the bugs crawling under our heads as we tried to rest.

The following morning as we walked tiredly back to the house after roll call, Mammy said, "The more I think about it, the more I'm convinced we need to distribute that rice as soon as possible. Who knows what kinds of prying hands and eyes might discover it if the rice stays hidden at our house? Let's wait until the ladies in the next room leave for their jobs in the Japanese hut, and then we can begin to share it around."

"You're right, Mammy. I wouldn't trust Trompe and her cronies if my life depended on it," Justin said emphatically.

"It does depend on it! If we are discovered with that rice, it will be our heads—and the *hahok's* too, if they learn he's been involved," Mammy added.

"I think we should give a big portion of it to the hospital. If anyone needs extra food, it's the sick and the nurses who care for them," I said.

"And we should give some to the sisters. They've taken all those orphans in to live with them since their mammies started dying. Little bodies need nutrients to grow," Peggy added.

"Well, there is certainly enough to go around," Mammy sighed as we walked up to our door. We stopped talking immediately, not knowing who might be listening from the open window. Our worries were unwarranted. The women next door and all our other housemates had left for the day, off to work their various jobs around camp.

We had just checked on Tommy and Louis, who had managed to eat a little rice, when there was an angry knock on the door. Mammy jumped, turning cautiously to us with her finger to her mouth in warning.

She cautiously opened the door to find a Japanese sergeant standing on the step with his arms folded. Mammy stepped back in surprise. The guards generally didn't come into our living quarters unless they were performing a search of some sort. He strode into our room and turned to face Mammy. We quickly bowed as was required when confronted by one of the Japanese.

Before we had risen all the way, he began in a harsh voice, "A bag of rice was taken from our storehouse last night. We are going house to house to discover if the prisoners know anything," he asked.

My heart, which had been racing since he appeared in our doorway, hiccupped momentarily at his question and then began beating double-time. I was sure I would pass out from the stress, but I willed myself to stand quietly next to Mammy so I would not arouse any suspicion. I looked at my feet until I could control my nerves. Then my eyes moved to her face. Only someone who knew her as well as I did would be able to detect the pulse in her forehead that ticked away nervously and the beads of sweat that slowly budded on her face.

"Why, no. I went to sleep early last night and heard nothing. Children, do you remember hearing anything unusual last night?" she asked evenly.

"No. We were out digging at the cemetery all day, so we were pretty exhausted. We all went to bed before usual too," George said, looking the sergeant squarely in the eye, his gaze not wavering.

Please, don't look around. Please, don't start searching, I pleaded in my mind. All the guard would have to do is turn to his left, his right, look under the bed. He was literally surrounded by the rice he was seeking. It was hidden in the old pot next to his foot, the shoes behind the door, the suitcase under the rack, the pillowcases under the blanket in front of him.

"Trompe lives in this house, doesn't she? Is she here now?" he asked, glancing at the closed door next to us.

"That's her room there," Mammy answered, nodding in the direction he was looking. "She and her friends are gone for the day, though. In fact, I think they are working over in your barracks," she added conversationally.

I hoped the sergeant would chalk up my mother's nervous smile to him standing in our living space and not to fear for something we had done wrong.

"Hmph! Well, I don't suppose she knows anything about the rice, or no doubt we would have heard about it by now," he said, more to himself than to us. He nodded briskly and then departed, leaving the door open behind him.

Mammy closed the door gingerly and sank down behind it. I ran to her and put my arms around her neck, pulling her close.

"If he would only have glanced around, he would have seen the rice. It was everywhere. I was praying frantically the whole time he was here," she murmured wearily.

"I know. I felt this urge to look around and make sure all our hidey-holes were covered well enough. It took everything I had to keep my eyes trained on him and look as wide-eyed and innocent as possible," Peggy said, joining us on the floor.

"It's a miracle Trompe wasn't here when the guard came. She has just the type of suspicious mind that would plant a seed of doubt in his head. The gig would have been up for sure," George said.

"Well, in a way, her living here might have actually helped us today. Once the guard learned she bunked in the room next door, he quickly dismissed us as possible suspects," I said thoughtfully.

"That's true. I guess having the old hag living next door does have its advantages," Justin said from his perch on the edge of the rack.

"I just can't believe the *hahok* pinched a whole bag of rice from the Japanese. I thought he'd get it from somewhere outside the camp, the next village maybe. I never *dreamed* he'd take it from the storehouse," Mammy said shakily.

"Yeah, that does take nerve." George admired, shaking his head in amazement.

"Or insanity," Peggy added sarcastically.

"Well, regardless, we need to get rid of the rice today. Let's get moving," Mammy said as she stood up. She wiped the perspiration from her forehead with a shaky sleeve, and I knew in that moment that the scene we had just witnessed had taxed her more than I'd initially thought. If not for the grace of God, we would all be facing the captain and a certain death sentence right now. We had cheated death yet again. I silently prayed that it would be the last time any of us would ever need to.

17

Guards

THE NEXT FEW MONTHS FELT like torture through monotony. Each day was filled with chores, sickness, death, and more death. We felt like the zombies we had heard about on the radio programs at home, walking but not thinking, sometimes not even feeling. The Japanese devised a new method of working us to the bone in Belalau: stone removal. According to our captors, we were supposedly clearing a path around the camp so they could construct a road, for what we were never told.

As interns, aka slave labor, we were ordered to remove all the rocks embedded in the path so a road would lay smooth. It was backbreaking work. We tried to pry the rocks loose with wooden mallets, inching them out of their centuries-long resting place. Then we toiled over loosening the rocks even more, bending in half and wedging our chafed fingers into any nooks and crannies we could find to further dislodge the stones.

We spent hour after hour laboring over our chore, sometimes making very little headway. At the end of each day spent road building, we were exhausted. Finally, after a couple of weeks, we completed the space we had been told to clear.

"Report back here tomorrow morning," a stocky young guard said, standing at attention with his hands crossed behind his back. He made no eye contact with any of us. To him, we were nuisances, and he was disgruntled that he had to babysit us.

"But . . . but, sir . . . " George started incredulously, his hand directed toward our finished work.

"Shh, George! Let's just go. We'll find out what this is all about tomorrow morning," I said, grabbing his hand firmly and pointing him toward home.

I was afraid George's questioning would anger the guard. He was one who reached a quick boil, and more than one intern had felt his wrath since we had arrived in Belalau. Among other things, he had a reputation for beating and kicking interns who were belligerent enough not to understand his orders barked in Japanese. We knew enough about self-preservation to give him a wide berth.

"But, Hanny, what more is there to do here? We've wrestled out every stone bigger than a walnut," George asked, under his breath.

"I don't know, but just humor him . . . and me, okay?" I said quietly in my most soothing voice.

He shrugged and walked on, but I suspected this wasn't over.

***

The sun dawned earlier than it normally did the following morning—at least it felt that way to me. I dragged out of bed, untangling myself from my threadbare blanket, my back muscles screaming for me not to misuse them like I had the day before. I tried to stretch away the ache, but it stuck like a burr under my clenched muscles. Peggy was just rolling out of the *balai-balai* as well, but Justin and George were still snoring away, oblivious to the world.

"Good morning!" Tommy said from the corner.

I stared at him, fascinated for a moment by his towhead blond hair, so different from our shiny, black mops. His hair stuck up in all directions just then, and it usually shone in the sun like spun gold. Thankfully, he and Louis had fully recovered from their sicknesses. Mammy's nursing prowess had set them right again.

I had stood by, interested to watch how the two boys would fit into our family once they healed. Tommy and Justin were close to the same age and had hit it off like old friends. They were as thick as a couple of thieves, always volunteering to work together or eat side by side.

Louis, on the other hand, was naturally more shy and reticent. We would often find him staring wistfully out the window. He seemed lost in some scene in his mind, one starring his mammy, I imagined. We learned from Louis that he and his mother had been very close, particularly since they had been separated from his father and forced into the Palembang camp soon after the Japanese invasion. He missed his mammy every day, almost as if half of him had been injured beyond repair when he learned she had died. Mammy believed that he would feel complete again once he was reunited with his father after the war. I certainly hoped so.

Louis was a tenderhearted boy, and I felt the urge to mother him like I would a stray animal fighting its way back to health. I resisted coddling him too much, though, as I felt that the only loving hand he truly craved was his own mother's.

After shaking the boys back from oblivion and tidying up our living quarters, we all set off for roll call. We would meet Mammy near the guard tower since she had been out all night nursing some of the sick women in the hospital.

Roll call was routine this morning, thank goodness. Everyone trickled into the old tennis court area and was accounted for, with the exception of those who were ill. The nurses submitted a list naming those who were too sick to stand for roll call. This captain in Belalau was a little less strict than the ones in Bangka and Palembang. He accepted the nurses' note with no problem and proceeded with the roll call. After all, if we were to run, where would we run to? We were in the middle of an unfamiliar jungle. It would be suicide to try to escape on foot. The captain must have realized that early on because his restrictions were more lax than we had experienced in the earlier camps.

After roll call, we all went our separate ways. Mammy ambled back to the house for some well-deserved rest. Tommy, Louis, and Justin were on tree-cutting duty in the northwest corner of camp, and Peggy, George, and I headed toward the gate to learn what we were to do on the road-building project.

"Whatever they ask us to do, *don't* cause a scene, George," I chided him as we approached the other ten or twelve interns assigned to the work crew.

"Maybe they'll want us to lay the tar," Peggy said. "That should be lovely, considering it *is* already 110 degrees outside."

"Don't exaggerate. At least we have the tree cover to protect us from the sun," I said, trying to sound positive.

As we joined the group, we saw the stocky guard from yesterday afternoon approach. We all bowed to him, as was expected.

"Today, you will take the rocks there in the truck and put them back in the road," the guard said, his arms crossed. The look on his face challenged us to defy him. A low murmur rose from the group. Clearly, no one was happy with our directive.

"Silence! Do as you are told," the guard said, clapping his hands sharply. We stared at him incredulously.

"That's ridiculous! What was the whole point of last week's chores?" an English woman I recognized from the vocal orchestra grumbled.

"Busy work," another woman muttered under her breath. I looked at my brother and sister. George was staring at me with a penetrating glare.

"What?" I mouthed to him, shrugging my shoulders. I wasn't happy about it either.

The guard's cries of *"Lekas! Lekas!"* got us moving. We'd heard those words so often over the years; I think we were conditioned to respond, like Pavlov's dogs or something.

Peggy, George, and I worked out a system. One of us would dig the holes, while the other two lugged the rocks from the wheelbarrows nearby. The ground was soft from the last few days when we had loosened soil from around the rocks, so the work was a little easier than previously.

Still, we fumed as we worked. What a complete waste of time and, more importantly, our energy, which was limited to begin with. Busy work had been the right way to describe our day's labor, and we stewed about it from the time we started until the time we left.

I was proud of George though. His face was livid, but he channeled his frustration into the work. No one lifted the same amount of stones he did or worked at a faster pace. The guards must have thought he was simply a diligent laborer, but I guessed that he was pushing himself to avoid a confrontation with the Japanese.

***

Not all the guards were like the stocky one from the road-building project, although many were. There were a couple of exceptions. One guard in the Palembang camps was always quick to smile. His eyes often followed the children as they played, and as they did, I imagined he might be thinking of his own little ones back home in Japan. Once or twice, he handed out a pocketful of candy to the youngest in our camp. The children looked at the sweets like they were made of gold and at him like he was Midas. One little girl got up the nerve to timidly take a piece of candy from his hand. He smiled at her, and the rest flocked to him like birds looking for breadcrumbs.

Another guard, a younger one, began smiling at Peggy and me every time we passed. He had smooth skin and playful, black eyes that crinkled in the corners. His smiles didn't feel sinister like some of the other guards' who routinely leered at the interns. What was attractive to them I will never know. We looked bedraggled and exhausted, sick and starving. Our clothes were faded and tattered, and frankly, most of us were a mess.

One morning as Peggy and I were walking to our chores in the camp garden, the playful young guard stepped in beside us. He startled us, but we smiled back at him tentatively.

"A couple of us are having a little soiree at our barracks tonight, and we are asking some of the young girls to come and join the party. There will be dancing and food. Are you interested?" he asked, looking at our startled expressions with inviting eyes.

"Um, I don't know. We'll have to ask our mother," Peggy answered cautiously.

"Try and come! It will be fun," he said, falling out of step with us and entering the guard tower.

"Imagine that! Invited to a dance party," Peggy said eagerly once the guard was out of hearing range.

"I've never been to a dance party. I'm not even sure I know how to dance," I said, bewildered at the thought.

"We've got nothing decent to wear. Our liberation dresses are too short now, and everything else we have looks like it's been run through the mill," Peggy commented, her mind racing.

"Peggy, I'm nervous. Are you?"

"Of course I am. But a dance party, Hanny? Think about it! When will we ever get a chance like that again?" my sister asked, excitement raging in her rich brown eyes. I squeezed her hand tightly. I felt bubbly inside too. Nervous but bubbly.

That afternoon, as Peggy and I were walking home from the garden area, we picked up the discussion again.

"Let's go home and rest for an hour and then run over to the bathhouse and get cleaned up. As good as we can anyway," Peggy said, looking dismally at her chafed hands and dirty, bare feet.

"Peggy, let's not jump the gun. We've still got a big hurdle to get over . . ."

"Mammy!" we both said in unison.

"Well, we could go for the practical approach. Getting on the Japanese's good side could have its advantages," Peggy said, looking thoughtful as we walked.

"I think we should reassure her that it is just a harmless party and that lots of other girls are going too. After all, we *will* be right next door to the house. I bet she'll be afraid the Japanese will try to do a little more than just dance with us, though," I said. I could feel a tiny seed of uneasiness start to sprout in my very active imagination.

"Like there are not enough willing participants for that type of thing. There are more than enough spies and informants to choose from. You know those women will do anything to impress the Japanese . . . and I do mean *anything*," Peggy said with her eyebrows raised.

"Agreed. I'm just trying to figure out what Mammy will say," I said, feeling slightly more reassured by Peggy's confidence that tonight was purely about wholesome fun.

"Well, we're about to find out. We're almost to the house, and Mammy's sandals are lying right by the door," Peggy said, sighing loudly. We walked in feeling momentarily blinded by the sudden change in light. The room was dim and peaceful after the bright afternoon sunshine we had just come from.

"Hello, girls. How was work today?" Mammy asked as she brewed some of her quinine tea.

I decided to try the direct approach. "It was fine. Mammy, you'll never guess! We were asked to go to a dance party over at the Japanese barracks. Most of the young single girls were asked. I think the guards are just throwing it to break up the boredom a little bit," I said breathlessly, realizing at the end that I was starting to ramble. It must have been the nerves.

"Pleeeease, Mammy. Can we go?" Peggy pleaded, her hands knit together as if in prayer. Mammy was completely silent as she turned toward us. Her eyes were hidden in shadow, so we sat in suspense, wondering which way the coin was going to drop. After a full minute of not talking, she stood up and gazed out of the window. I detected a pulse beating quickly on her forehead, generally not a good sign.

Peggy and I glanced at one another nervously.

"Girls, I have a question for you. Where is your father, and who put him there?" she asked, turning to look at us, her eyes penetrating and dark.

The whole world seemed to crash around my ears in images and memories as I contemplated what she had asked. The Japanese. They had done it all—our separation from Pappy, the deprivations, and the death. How could we ever have considered doing anything with them voluntarily? It was inconceivable. The look on Peggy's face told me she had reached the same conclusion.

"We're so sorry, Mammy. What were we thinking?" I asked, amazed at my own cluelessness.

I felt as if I had betrayed my father, whom I loved and respected like no other. He was stuffed away in some Japanese prison camp, or worse, for all we knew, and I had been ready to run off and revel with his captors. I felt like the lowest worm alive.

"We're idiots, Mammy," I heard Peggy say in a very small, strangled voice.

"Come here, you two," Mammy invited, walking over to the *balai-balai* and patting the rack next to where she stood. We did as she requested, sheepishly and not meeting her eyes, but still obediently. She knelt down in front of us.

"I want to talk with you for a minute, girls." She sighed. "Look, I know it's hard. The Japanese have not only robbed us of Pappy but also you of your youth. At sixteen and seventeen, you should be attending parties with friends, going on dates . . . maybe even sharing your first kiss. There has been no possibility of any of that here in the camps. But I promise, you will have all of that one day. The war won't last forever, and when we are free, there will be lots of chances to make new friends and be young again," she said tenderly, squeezing us close.

We melted into her embrace.

"Accepting invitations from the Japanese is not the answer, though, girls. Just be patient, and your time will come," she added, kissing us each on our heads.

Her kindness was enough to guilt us for life. A harsh lecture wouldn't have had nearly the potent effect our mother's love did. We both burst into tears.

"Shh! Shh! It's all right," she gently whispered into our hair. She held us like two little girls for what seemed like hours. Soon I realized my tears were not manifestations of my shame anymore. They were for my father and for unfulfilled dreams. I jumped when I heard Justin's voice as he shoved through the door.

"What's this all about?" he asked, looking a little embarrassed. Tommy glanced at us quizzically too as we wiped our eyes hastily on the bottom of our skirts.

"Uh, girl stuff, you know," Peggy muttered, purposefully nondescript.

"Okay. Sorry I asked," Justin retorted, clearly not in a hurry for more detail. He and Tommy shook their heads in unison, probably feeling infinitely glad they were not girls, and hurried to the corner to play a game of rocks, which resembled checkers, on the floor.

"Should we go next door to the Japanese barracks and tell them we won't be coming?" Peggy asked Mammy in a low voice.

"No, I don't think that will be necessary, especially since many of the other girls were invited too. Just do nothing, and maybe you won't be missed," Mammy replied thoughtfully.

***

The next day after roll call, though, as everyone was bustling to their different workstations for the day, the young guard again surprised us by falling into step with us as we walked, his hands in his pockets and a twinkle in his eye.

"We didn't see you two last night. You missed a good party. What happened?" he asked curiously.

"It was loud enough that we didn't miss a thing," Peggy murmured, still disgruntled that our sleep had been interrupted by the noisy get-together next door. I sighed.

"Look, we were told to ask you this: where is our father?" I asked quietly.

The young guard didn't say anything for a few seconds, and then he stopped and turned to us. His eyes looked sad, or maybe I just imagined they did.

"I understand. Good day, ladies," he said as he about-faced to return to his post at the guard tower. That was the last time he ever singled us out again. I'd like to think it was out of respect for what we had said, but more likely there were just too many easy targets to stay disappointed for long.

18

Liberation

NOT LONG AFTER MY EIGHTEENTH birthday, on an August day scarcely unique from any other, Peggy and I were scrubbing the bathhouse, a truly horrific job, when we heard the whistle blow several times. Curiously, we rose to our feet and peered outside. A table and stool were being pulled onto the old, dilapidated tennis courts where we attended roll call each morning. Odd. Something out of the ordinary must have happened because this broke routine, and the Japanese were vigilant about staying on schedule. Again, the whistle sounded, and we saw dozens of women warily approach the court area.

"Line up! Line up!" the guards ordered.

"What could have happened?" Peggy asked in a concerned voice.

"I'm not sure. Maybe someone got caught smuggling or . . . I don't know. Maybe someone tried to run," I suggested, at a loss myself.

"Let's go. We don't want to get punished for showing up late," my sister said, striding briskly toward the tennis courts.

Once there, we joined Mammy, with Mrs. Hoop at her side. Our old friend was just recovering from a very grave illness, a virulent form of malaria, Mammy had said. This afternoon was the first time Peggy and I had seen her out of her living quarters since her sickness.

"Mrs. Hoop, how are you? We have all been so worried," I said, approaching her with a smile.

"I've had some dark days, girls . . . dark days. I honestly wasn't sure if I was going to pull through," the frail lady said, shaking her head.

She looked stooped and worn, like a crumpled, older version of the spry, cheerful woman we had all grown to love in the earlier camps. Her sickness had definitely aged her. Peggy and I smiled at her sympathetically.

She grabbed each of our hands. "Your mammy is a dear, you know? I would never have made it back without her kindness. She sat by me and nursed me through some of the worst of it." Dewy tears formed in her earnest blue eyes. She rubbed them away with a gnarled finger, bent with arthritis.

"We're biased, but we think she is pretty wonderful too," Peggy said sincerely, glancing over at Mammy who had turned to greet Tommy and Justin. They had just walked up from hauling wood on the north side of camp.

We were milling around, waiting for the remainder of the prison interns to filter in from their various workstations, when the whistle sounded once more. We started lining up in our usual formations—by house—thinking that perhaps an impromptu roll call had been issued. Curiously, the Japanese seemed less strict about the usual protocol, although each guard was clad in his full dress uniform, complete with all his ribbons and medals. Regardless of their formal dress, if I didn't know better, I would have called the guards distracted. They were whispering among themselves, something that virtually never occurred when their superiors were present.

The captain himself left the guard tower as we assembled into our groups. When we were finally situated, he calmly strode up to the center of the commons and, with the help of a subordinate, stepped first on the stool and then up on the table. That got our attention. We were silent as we bowed quickly to the captain. He stood ramrod straight, his hands folded formally behind his back and his gaze far over our heads as he prepared to address us. The other guards also stood behind him, straight and formal.

"*Perang habis,*" the captain said simply. It was Malay for "the war is over." Peggy looked at me in confusion.

"What was that he said?" she mumbled.

"He said, 'The war is over,'" I repeated dully.

Though I had heard the words, I did not comprehend the meaning. We had all anticipated this day for more than four years, and now that it had arrived, we couldn't register the magnitude of the moment. Low whispers swept through our ranks.

"Did the Allies win? The captain never said in his announcement."

"Yes! It must have been the Japanese who lost, or our captors would be celebrating."

"Can you believe it?"

"What does that mean for us now?"

"I think it must mean we are going home!"

"Thank God! Oh, thank God!"

Amidst the murmuring, the captain quietly dismounted his makeshift riser and marched back into the guardhouse, followed by a string of underlings. While many of us, myself included, stood in shock, others were quicker with their shouts of jubilation. Some of the Dutch sang out strains of "The Wilhelmus," and the British anthem, "God Save the King," rang across the camp as well. Other women just stood in place and wept as they slowly took in the news. Mammy looked tenderly into each of our faces and held us close. I could feel her heart beating wildly through her thin blue blouse.

"We are *free*," she whispered.

My mind still balked at the idea. How could it be, after all this time, that we were suddenly free? The very word seemed foreign to me. I looked uncomprehendingly at her as our eyes met and she stroked my hair. Hand in hand, we turned from the commons area and walked back to our house on the knoll. Later, we learned the date was August 24, 1945—a full nine days after the armistice had been signed.

***

The next day, we woke up early as usual and set about doing our chores. Peggy and I weeded and watered the peanut plants in the camp garden as we had been scheduled to do the morning before the captain's news had changed our whole world. Maybe it was just too momentous an announcement to be reckoned within such a short amount of time. We stuck to our routine as a safety net to shield us from our utter disbelief. If it hadn't been for the fact that no roll call had been whistled for that morning, I would have considered yesterday's news that the war was over a beautiful, surreal dream.

The following day, food and supplies we had yearned for over the past four years began to roll into camp: sugar, meat, fruit, and medicine. It was like Christmas a hundred times over. It was then, as the trucks drove in and were unloaded, that the news slowly seeped into my system, like water flowing through a tired, dehydrated body. We were going to be rescued. We would soon be free. Why it was taking so long for the Allies to arrive, I did not know, but I finally started to believe that at some point it was going to happen.

Later that morning, angels fell from the sky. Paratroopers dropped in, four of them from the Dutch Special Operations, *Korps Insulinde*. The

Allies had been searching for the Japanese prison camps for days. A tip had led the troops to Lubuklinggau, the nearest village to Belalau. The camp proved hard to locate in the dense jungle climate, so jumping in seemed the easiest solution.

The looks on the soldiers' faces as they landed and stepped out of their gear spoke volumes. Their expressions mutated from pleasure at finding us to shock and then pity as they scanned our group and saw the pathetic condition we were all in. We were so delighted to see the paratroopers and to realize that the world finally knew where we had been stashed that we didn't care what an alarming sight we made.

The food and supplies kept rolling in over the next few days, and with them came our men and boys from surrounding camps. They looked skinny and unshaven, as bedraggled as we did. Many had been lost to sickness and starvation, but we would not know how many for days and weeks. With every transport, we searched for our father. He may not have been housed with the regular population of prisoners, we kept telling ourselves. Having committed crimes against the Japanese army, he would likely have been detained in a more restrictive camp, like a prison.

Memories of our time in the jail cell in Moeara-enim came to mind, and I shuddered at the thought of my poor father forced to live in such deplorable conditions for years on end. I prayed he had been spared that type of living arrangement, but a tiny voice in my brain said it was doubtful. The enemy would have been furious with him for thwarting their plans to capitalize on Sumatra's resources. His punishment would have been unforgiving and relentless.

While we waited for our first sighting of Pappy, we reveled in the reunions of others. Husbands and wives smiled through their tears as they held each other and stared in dismay at one another's awful conditions for the first time. Children bashfully welcomed their fathers and brothers, loved ones they had not seen in a handful of years and sometimes did not even recognize. The early days of liberation were bittersweet.

Many families were reunited, but almost all of them had lost one or more members, and we wept at the loss. Still, there were happy moments.

"Mrs. Londt-Schultz, is it?" a tall, blond-haired man asked, leaning down to speak with my tiny mother as she stood in the doorway of our house.

"Why, yes. I am Tina Londt-Schultz. Do I know you?" Mammy replied. Before he could respond, Tommy came careening out of the house and into the man's arms.

"Father! Father, is that you?" Tommy asked, tears welling in his eyes.

"Yes, my boy! Yes, I am here to meet you," the man said, weeping into his son's shoulder and stroking his unruly, golden hair. He looked as if he had found his precious lost treasure after a long, grueling search.

"She's gone, Father. Mother died in the camps. *Beri-beri* killed her," Tommy explained after several minutes.

"I know, son. I heard this morning from the head nun in the hospital. I'm . . . I'm so sorry I wasn't here with you when it happened," he whispered, his face distorted in regret.

"I would have died too if it hadn't been for *Tante* Tina," Tommy said, looking into his father's face.

"Yes, the good sister told me all you've done for my boy. I thank you. There are no words," the man said, ripping his eyes away from Tommy and shaking Mammy's hand as if he were pumping water from a well.

"My children and I were happy to do it, Mr. Harrevelt. Tommy fit right in with our family and became close friends with our Justin. What are your plans now the war is over?" Mammy asked, tousling Tommy's hair affectionately.

"I'm not sure yet. I think we must go back to Holland. Rumors in our camp hinted that there is unrest among the natives here in Sumatra. The Japanese have filled their heads with thoughts of independence, and they no longer want to be beholden to the Dutch for anything. I fear things could get violent, so I think Tommy and I will take the first ship we can back to Europe," Mr. Harrevelt said. His voice was uneasy and his blue eyes troubled.

Mammy nodded, and I thought I saw a telling look pass between Mr. Harrevelt and my mother as they ducked inside to gather Tommy's small parcel of clothes and belongings. Apparently the unrest between the local Sumatrans and the Dutch was more dangerous and relevant than Mr. Harrevelt had wanted to share in front of us teenagers.

A few short hours later, a similar reunion took place between Louis and his father, Mr. Rottier. Louis's father had just been trucked in from the men's camp with his two older sons who had been held captive there with him. Coming to fetch Louis was their first priority upon arrival. He was quieter than Tommy had been, but a profound aura of relief enveloped him as he embraced his father and two older brothers. Father and brothers wept as they learned of their mother's death in the camps. A tender reunion, laced with sadness, so similar to hundreds of others that took place that week throughout Sumatra.

19

News

THE NEXT DAY, AFTER A mouthwatering meal of fish, rice, and mangoes, I was walking back to the house by myself, musing about why Peggy had missed lunch. It was very unlike her. In fact, I hadn't seen her since right after breakfast. It occurred to me that she may be visiting with our cousins, Renie and Aldi, in their quarters. More Allied troops had arrived earlier that morning. Perhaps the girls were checking out the new prospects. I smiled at the thought.

As I passed through camp, I noticed Justin and George chatting with old friends from Tandjoengenim. They were laughing out loud as I passed, apparently over a story one of the other boys had told. My brothers had enjoyed very little contact with boys their own age during the last few years and were basking in it now that many interns from the men's camp had united with ours.

I was just topping the knoll leading to our house when I looked ahead and saw my mother talking to a tall, regal-looking man in front of our door. He had the tanned, tired look of a camp intern but still held his head high and exuded an air of authority. Where did I know him from? Mammy looked thin but attractive in a faded yellow dress, a color I always thought suited her tan skin and dark brown eyes. Her arms were folded in front of her as if she were listening most intently to whatever the man was telling her. Who was that man? I vaguely recognized him but couldn't seem to put my finger on exactly how I knew him. Maybe he was one of Pappy's old friends from the mines.

As I was contemplating the possibilities, something unexpected happened. I saw Mammy put a shaky hand over her mouth and stumble dangerously before catching her balance against the wall. The man had relayed something to my mother that had completely thrown her. She gazed at the man with a haunted expression in her eyes before crumpling in a dead swoon. The man caught her nimbly in his arms right before she fell to the ground.

I stopped, unable to take a single step more. A brick wall had risen between me and the rest of the world, and I had slammed right into it. A truth I knew more clearly than if someone had spoken the words aloud crashed into me like a freight train. Pappy was dead.

The tall man with the mustache had come to break the news to Mammy. I don't know how I knew; I just did. As weak as it may seem, I turned and ran. A small part of me registered that my mother needed me now more than ever, but a bigger part balked against that. I needed to be by myself, to lick my wounds alone. I ran down to the stream where I could cry without anyone interfering.

My father was dead. Dead. How could I ever wrap my mind around that horrible truth? I was never to see his warm smile again or hear his words. Never to smell his aftershave or crawl into his lap like a little child. I yearned to be able to hold his hand once more or watch him walk, hands in his pockets, as he searched the trees for birds. How could I bear so many "never agains"? He was gone, yet try as I might, I just couldn't seem to comprehend those three little words.

When had this happened? How could I not have sensed that my beloved Pappy was no longer with us? Shouldn't I have somehow known? But none of us had ever suspected he was dead. We had never even entertained the thought that he had passed away in the camps. With death looking us in the eye day after day, how could we not have considered his passing a possibility? Maybe the others had in some small corner of their brain, but I never had. Not once.

I had believed in happily ever afters, just how the fairy stories always ended. No one good ever dies in the end. Isn't that the way it was supposed to be? Not this. Not the best man alive dying alone in some godforsaken prison camp. I felt my heart cracking and breaking into a thousand painful shards of grief, and there was nothing I could do but cry and feel it. I felt acutely every one of those stabs of anguish over my father and cried a tear for each one. I don't know how long I lay there weeping by the stream. Dusk was falling when I finally came to myself again.

My swollen eyes burned. My tears had run dry hours ago, but the racking sobs had gone on and on. My head hurt like a wrecking ball had swung right through it, but it didn't touch the pain I felt in my chest.

As I lay there, spent, I heard footsteps slowly walk down to the streambed, hesitating a few feet away from where I had fallen. I couldn't find the strength to turn and see who had discovered me. Suddenly, familiar hands gently lifted me up and held me. They were hands I would know anywhere—Peggy's hands. I would have cried fresh tears if I could.

"When did you find out?" I asked her in a tired, raspy voice after a long moment of silence.

"This morning after breakfast. One of the men from the Red Cross told me," she whispered, her words laced with pain and resignation.

I nodded, realizing that explained her absence from lunch that afternoon. She stroked my hair and rocked me back and forth.

"I'm sorry I wasn't the one to tell you. I . . . I couldn't," she said, her voice breaking. I could feel her warm breath in my hair.

"How's Mammy?" I asked.

"Not good. I've put her to bed, and George and Justin are watching over her," she replied quietly.

"I couldn't go to her, Peg. I saw it all unfolding, and I knew what that man was telling Mammy, but all I could think to do was run," I said, hoping for absolution.

"She's been worried about you. You've been missing for hours, Hanny. I told her not to be too concerned. I figured you needed time to grieve by yourself. That's where I was all morning, hiding behind a vacant old house, letting it all out," my sister replied, compassion in her voice.

"Help me up, Peggy. I need to go to Mammy," I said, pushing my own pain aside for a time.

Arm in arm, we walked up the bank toward our home. Stars were peeking through the darkening sky, but they had lost their appeal for me. I couldn't look at them without thinking of Pappy.

***

The next morning, I was ready for answers. Mammy looked pale but resigned. She had cried many tears the night before and would surely cry many more, but she was strong to the core. She woke up, smoothed her dress, and ran a comb through her hair. She met us in the doorway as we were walking back from breakfast, looking frail but resolute. She reminded me of a reed that bent daintily in the wind but never broke.

Peggy and I had brought her back a breakfast of papayas and bananas. After asking Mammy how her night had been, I sat down next to her on the rack. Justin and George were sitting across from us, their heads resting on their arms. Justin's face was streaked with dirt and dried tears, his eyes strangely vacant. George's looked dewy, as if tears were forming just below the surface, ready to spring to life at the smallest provocation.

"Who was that man who brought us the news yesterday?" I asked hesitantly, trying to gauge my mother's emotions.

"That was Baron Von Asbeck, a dear friend of . . . of your father's and mine before the war," she said gently. "He was the leader of the men's camp, the equivalent of Mother Laurentia here, I guess. It was very kind of him to come tell us the news himself." I sat for a moment in silence, trying to absorb what she had said.

"Did he know anything more about Pappy's time in the camps? I mean, we know nothing about how he lived . . . how he died. I suppose in the end it doesn't really matter, but it would still be nice to know," Peggy said, sighing as she leaned against the door frame.

"The baron said that Pappy was held in a prison in Soengailiat on the island of Bangka."

"What? But that was so close to where we were . . . at least for a while," Justin said incredulously.

"And we never knew," Peggy said in a daze.

"Go on, Mammy. What else did he say?" I prodded.

"He . . . he said that there were eleven men in the prison cell all together. Your father was one of those eleven. By the end of the war, only one had survived, a Mr. Kajado. The rest had slowly starved to death. The surviving man told the baron that most days they had lived on ten kernels of corn each," she said quietly, staring down at her hands as if hesitant to meet our eyes.

"Ten kernels a day! That's torture! That can't be right under the terms of the Geneva Convention," George roared, his face raging with indignation and anger.

"I don't think much of how we've lived for the last three and a half years would make the cut for humane treatment of prisoners, George," Peggy responded gently.

"Ten kernels? How long did he last?" I whispered, appalled at the thought. "Do they know for sure when he died?"

"Yes, Baron Von Asbeck kept accurate records. He died August 27, 1944, almost a year ago to the day," she said. Her lip quivered as she fought for control.

"Did the baron have any more information he could share with us?" Peggy pressed softly.

"I was curious about his wedding ring. I would have loved to have had that back. But Baron Von Asbeck said that near the end Mr. Kajado sold Pappy's ring for food," Mammy said quietly, tears dewing in her eyes.

"How could he do that? The ring wasn't his to trade," Peggy said impetuously.

"Your father would have given it to him, Peggy, if it had meant the difference between life and death. As disappointed as I am that we won't have that part of him, I can't fault the man for trading it to survive. In fact, the baron mentioned that Mr. Kajado offered to pay us back the cost of the ring when he gets back on his feet. I appreciated the gesture but asked that he decline. I don't have it in me to put him to that trouble now," our mother said, brushing a stray tear from her cheek.

"You're right, of course. He would have given it to his friend for food," Peggy agreed, rubbing the moisture from her own eyes.

Our conversation broke up soon after that. Each of us was glad we knew a little more about our father's last days, although the news did not ease the ache we felt for him. Not one little bit.

It occurred to me that maybe the fissure I felt in my chest would never fully heal. Perhaps it was too deep and too broken to knit back together. The news of Pappy's death had been too life changing not to leave a permanent scar in the fleshy tables of my heart. Maybe that's the way it always is when someone you love leaves you. The loss brands you with an indelible mark that stays with you, a permanent reminder of that person and the love you'll always feel for them.

20

Departure

OUR TIME TO GRIEVE WAS abruptly interrupted. The next phase of our liberation took place soon after our conversation about Pappy. The Allied troops were separating us again to transport us to hospitals and holding places before we were free to either stay in Sumatra or travel back to England, Australia, Holland, or wherever our motherland might be.

The Australian nurses were among the first to leave Belalau. Their numbers had been greatly depleted in the camps due to sickness and death, but the troops from Australia had been overjoyed to find them. They had been searching for the nursing corps for weeks. It was a day of teary good-byes as we all separated and went our different ways.

How can you contemplate saying good-bye to people with whom you struggled to survive for years on end? These were the few individuals on the planet who actually understood the hell in which we had been living for the last three and a half years. The bond was strong and the feelings deep and profound as we parted.

My family and I were driven by truck to a holding place—an old hotel, really—with a group of other Dutch interns, waiting for transport back to Holland. The unrest in Sumatra was too mercurial and dangerous to consider going home to Tandjoengenim, a fact that saddened us incredibly. We were not to see our garden again or our home, the place of our last happy memories with Pappy.

The end of the war had ignited the locals' thirst for independence from Holland. In that way, the Japanese had brought home their point. Having Dutch citizenship in a country where Holland had overseen the locals, we were particularly afraid of becoming targets of mob violence.

We were escorted to the hotel by only a small handful of Allied troops. My family was assigned a nondescript room to share, reportedly for only a few days, until the ship manifests back to Holland were finalized. A couple of hours after we arrived and got situated, Peggy burst through the door.

"You'll never believe this!" she began, her face flushed and her eyes wild.

"What? What's happened?" Justin asked, jumping off the bed. Mammy glanced up from the letter she was writing to Kokie, telling her of our plans to return to Holland and wanting to hear the news about Pappy as well.

"Well, I was down in the lobby chatting with Aldi and Renie when we struck up a conversation with one of the Dutch *Jonge*. Andrew, I think his name was. He was quite good-looking too," Peggy said. The Dutch *Jonge* was a group of youth who had enlisted to help the Dutch troops during the war. Two or three had been assigned to our group to assist the regular troops in keeping us safe.

"Okay. So, don't keep us in suspense. What did he say that was so interesting?" George said anxiously.

"He told me something that gave me the chills. He said the Japanese were only days away from shooting at least some of the prison camp interns. They had mounted machine guns on the tops of the guard towers in many of the camps, and ours was one of them. They even had a date set," Peggy said breathlessly.

"I don't believe it! I mean they neglected us and everything, but I can't imagine them going *that* far," George said in disbelief.

"No, it's true. Andrew said that the date was set for Queen Wilhelmina's birthday, August 31. We barely made it out alive, with only days to spare," she said.

"I don't know about that. What proof does he have?" George asked skeptically.

"Look! I believe him because as we were standing there being told the war was over, I caught a glimpse of something shiny and metallic on the roof of the guard tower. It glinted in the sun. At the time, I barely had the energy to even wonder, let alone care, what it was, but I *do* remember seeing something shiny up there. It must have been a machine gun," Peggy said. At George's dubious look, she cried, "It's true, George. I wouldn't make something like that up."

"I believe you, dear. The Japanese must have known things weren't going well for their cause. It makes sense that they would try and retaliate somehow. Opening fire on us would have been a blow to the Allies . . . like they couldn't save us in time or something. And to schedule it on Queen

Wilhelmina's birthday would be like pouring salt in the wound," Mammy said from her desk.

Although we never received a firm confirmation that the Japanese had been planning to slaughter us, we were all convinced it was true.

We had a savory chicken dinner that evening. Oh, how succulent and delicious the meat tasted in our mouths. We couldn't get over the variety of food we now had to choose from. What an improvement over the rice and spinach we were used to eating!

Bedding down on comfortable mattresses felt wonderful, if not a little surreal. It felt like ages since we'd nestled into a soft, cushy bed with fluffy feather cushions. I think I was out once my head hit the pillow. It had been a taxing couple of weeks, and I was exhausted.

***

Crash! The sound of splintering glass woke me from my slumber. I opened my eyes to darkness, although I couldn't tell what time the clock read. More falling glass and shouts met me as I tumbled out of bed. I shook away my grogginess and bounded to my feet.

"What's going on?" I asked, confused.

"I don't know. I think we woke up at the same time," Peggy said, rolling out of bed.

"Children, stay here while I find out what's happening," Mammy commanded firmly as she slid on her sandals and smoothed her hair. Opening the door, she shook her head as George slipped out of bed to follow her.

"Stay here, George. Please. I am just going to talk to the Dutch soldiers and see what is going on. I'll be fine," she said reassuringly. Peggy and I sat on our bed and waited, flinching every time we heard a bottle smash into the walls outside or heard the angry cries of people below.

George and Justin were trying to peer out of the window in our room to see if they could discover who was behind the assault on our building.

"I see torches down below, but it's such a cloudy night. I can't make out who is throwing things at the hotel," Justin said.

"I think they're talking in Malay down there," George said in surprise. "I half thought it might be the Japanese back to take one last go at us."

"Step back from the window, you two. What if they see you and start aiming at us?" Peggy cried, biting her thumbnail nervously.

"I see a dozen or so of them throwing rocks and bottles, and a couple of them are pounding the walls with sticks. Whoever they are, they're *really* mad," Justin said, giving us the play-by-play commentary. Clearly, he was intent on ignoring Peggy's advice to back away from the window. "Oooh! They just shattered a window on the ground floor. I think I see the soldiers moving in to try and fend them off with their batons. Do you see them, George?"

"Uh-huh. Ouch! One of the mob just took a blow to the head. I hope the soldiers will be okay."

"Soldiers! I think only five or six escorted us to the hotel, and two of them were Dutch Younge. How can they possibly protect all of *us* from all of *them*?" I asked dubiously. Just then Mammy slid through the door.

"Away from the window," she said, pointing to the boys.

"What's going on, Mammy? Who are those people down there, and why are they so angry?" I asked. I was speaking the questions on all of our minds.

"They're local Indonesians. Somehow, they learned that Dutch citizens are being housed in this hotel, and they are protesting. They want us out of Sumatra so they can have their country back."

"We're not the ones they should be protesting against. We have nothing to do with the government and its decisions. This is our home too," retorted Peggy.

"They don't see it that way. The Japanese have empowered them with the belief that all we've done is control them and ship their resources back to Europe. They think the Dutch have been taking advantage of them all this time." She sighed, slid off her sandals, and placed them by the door.

"In my opinion, this has been coming for a while," Mammy added, sitting on the bed across from us.

"Mammy, how can you say that? The locals are our friends. That's Kokie and Nanny you're talking about," Peggy said.

"Yes, Kokie and Nanny *are* our friends. And there are many other local Indonesians who are kindhearted and feel fine about sharing their country with Europeans. Others are not okay with it anymore. They want to be free of us."

"I guess I kind of see their point," George said. "I mean, how would you like to live under the thumb of another country, helping them get rich while you end up doing their menial labor?"

"Hmph! Well, I don't see anything wrong with sharing the country. Sumatra is a big place," Peggy said, crossing her arms in front of her.

As I sat there listening to the shouts of the men below, I felt scared, really scared—perhaps more frightened than at any time during our stay in the camps. The mob seemed so reckless and out of control, a stick of dynamite on the verge of igniting.

After awhile, the chaos outside finally seemed to die down, but clearly, the protestors felt strongly about their cause. I thought about what my brother had said, and a glimpse into the lives of the locals we knew whispered to me that he might be right. Maybe the Dutch powers had oppressed the Indonesians for long enough. Maybe it *was* time for us to leave the country and let the locals make a fresh start of it.

We sat on our beds listening in the dark for hours after the protestors had lost their fire and left, the breaking glass and bangs of angry sticks fading in the distance along with them. Sleep had fled us for good, so we were up and dressed when the soldiers gathered us together early the next morning to announce a change of plans.

"So sorry for the scare last night, ladies and gentlemen. We'd arranged with the staff to stay here at the hotel for several days, but, frankly, it's just not safe. A repeat of last night could easily happen again, and this time someone could get hurt. Our officers have agreed to move you all to a camp in Palembang. You'll wait there until your transport ships arrive," one of our protectors announced.

He was a tall, weathered man of about forty who looked as if he'd seen his share of wartime during his stint as a soldier. He was one of those men who had an aura of resourcefulness about him. You got the feeling you were in safe hands regardless of your circumstances.

"We'll be safe wherever you are driving us?" one older woman asked, looking for reassurance. Her worn face was etched with fear and exhaustion.

"Yes. There are just too few of us soldiers to withstand any kind of assault here. The camp in Palembang will be better protected. Pack your things, ladies and gentlemen. We'll eat breakfast and move out in about two hours—once the trucks show up."

Packing took all of about five minutes since we had so few possessions left after our time in the camps. Breakfast was a solemn meal, although we still relished the variety of fruits and breads we had to choose from. Conversation at the tables centered on our experience of the night before. We realized that, like us, the other members of our group had been truly shaken.

"I was so worried those heathens would climb through the windows and start attacking us," one young women said acidly, stirring cream vigorously into her tea.

"I must say I have never been so frightened in all my life. At least in the camps, the Japanese kept their distance—from those of us who wanted them to, that is. I felt like that mob last night could have killed us outright," her friend responded as she nervously tore her croissant into tiny pieces, her agitated fingers twitching mechanically.

"I think it's right to move us. We're in good hands with our soldiers," a mild-mannered grandmotherly type said reassuringly. Smiling, she took a bite of her piping hot oatmeal.

"Yes. It wouldn't be safe to stay here another night. I wonder if we'll end up back in one of our first Palembang camps," Mammy mused. She turned from the women's conversation back to us.

"I guess we'll soon find out. Just another leg on our scenic tour through the prison camps of beautiful Sumatra," Peggy said in the same chipper tone you might hear from a travel guide.

21

Good-Byes

THE TRUCKS CAME ON SCHEDULE. The urgency with which we were loaded spoke volumes about how anxious our protectors were for our safety. As we drove quickly away from the hotel—every bump reminiscent of our other truck rides over the last three years—I couldn't help but wonder where this trip would take us, literally and figuratively.

Mammy had warned us the night before that Holland probably wouldn't be the utopia we sought. Our motherland had also been ravaged by war, and the people were heartsick and struggling with loss just as we were. It may be difficult to find work, but at least we had Pappy's papers still nestled safely in their hidey-hole at the bottom of Mammy's old suitcase. For the hundredth time, I thanked him silently for his forethought. Mammy also cautioned us that there may be prejudice in Holland, as there was in many other European countries.

"Our tan faces may be difficult for many of the fair-skinned Dutch to accept. Unfortunately, I have heard from others that we may be looked down upon because we have Asian features and dark skin and hair," Mammy warned us gently. That was something I hadn't really considered. Here in Sumatra, there were so many nationalities represented that differences were the norm for us.

"I hope this doesn't prove the case," Mammy continued. "I have always reared you with the knowledge that God loves all of his children, regardless of the way they look on the outside. I just want you to be prepared in the event that we do encounter racism, although I pray we don't." Her words left me with food for thought, and I continued to gnaw on them as we traveled to our new camp.

That evening found us unpacking our few belongings in one of the houses of a Palembang community that had been abandoned. We were free in some sense of the word, but the ever-present soldiers reminded us that all was not well in Sumatra and our safety was still in jeopardy.

The soldiers were able to scavenge some old mattresses that they laid out on the wooden floors. They found a couple of actual bed frames for the elderly in the group. We bunked down, more familiar with these circumstances than the cushy beds in the hotel the night before. Our experience at the hotel would have felt like a dream had it not been for the fear tasting bitter in my mouth each time I recalled the glass shattering and the shouting. The sound of bamboo sticks knocking against the brick walls of the hotel still rattled in my brain.

For a week we wandered around the camp, renewing old acquaintances, hearing their stories of survival, and mourning for those we had lost. We strolled through the camp and relished the fact that we could walk through the gate if we wished. We didn't dare, though, not without a military escort, for fear we'd meet with some overzealous locals bent on our demise. To our relief, there were no more incidents like the protestors at the hotel. We felt protected and anxious to be embarking on the next leg of our journey, the boat ride back to Holland.

One afternoon we had a surprise visitor in our little corner of the makeshift neighborhood in Palembang. There was a gentle knock on the door, and the Dutch soldier standing there when we opened it stepped away to reveal none other than our old friend and cook extraordinaire, Kokie. I wondered how she knew where to find us after our hasty exit from the hotel. Luckily, my mother had been able to send off her note that last morning before we left. I bet Mammy had quickly scribbled a postscript before handing her letter to the hotel receptionist to mail.

Kokie was a sight for sore eyes. Her dark hair was dusted with a little more gray than I remembered, and there were a few more wrinkles around her eyes. Besides that though, her trim, petite figure looked the same, wrapped in a cheerful peach-colored sarong. She enveloped us in one of her tight, heartfelt embraces, and I felt love and concern emanating from her pint-sized form.

"My, how you children have grown! You're head and shoulders taller than me now," she exclaimed, tiptoeing to give me another hug.

I smiled at her exaggeration. It was so typical of her to try and make us feel older and taller than we really were. Three and a half years ago the compliment would have made me blush with pleasure. Now I simply sighed wistfully at the memory.

"We are going back to Holland, Kokie. Come with us," Justin said, his eyes sparkling.

"I can't, dear. Sumatra is my home. My parents are elderly now, and I have nieces and nephews that would miss me if I left. And we can't forget Ape and Knorrie. What would they do if I sailed away to Europe?" she asked, patting his hand as she explained.

The next part of her visit was laced with sadness as we told our old friend about our father's death. Mammy had forewarned her in the note she had sent, but in hearing the details of his starvation in a camp far away from everyone who loved him, she flicked away tears from her cheeks as she listened.

"He was one of the best and kindest of men. Never a harsh word to me or Nanny in all the years we worked for him," she said, shaking her head sadly.

Seeing her reaction, I felt the longing for my father that I desperately tried to shove away most of the time seep into my heart. The ache was always there, but I made a valiant effort to keep it in check. There was just too much to deal with to add grieving to it. There would be ample time for that when we finally made it to our new destination in Holland.

"Thank you for agreeing to take our animals, Kokie. I still miss them, even after all this time. Say good-bye to them for me, will you?" George asked as he cleared his throat of emotion.

Kokie rubbed his arm affectionately.

"I'll take good care of them, and they will always remind me of my second family," Kokie said as she rose to leave. "By the way, I brought the jewelry you left in my care, Miss Tina."

"Kokie, you remembered!" Mammy exclaimed, her hand flying to her mouth.

"Why, of course. I couldn't let you leave without your family heirlooms," our friend said with a smile.

She reached into her woven bag and extracted a linen cloth. As she unraveled it, the gleam of my mother's best gold jewelry shone from its wrapping. Inside were the chains and rings Mammy had once sewed into our dresses before we had been captured. She had unpicked the hems when we had been in Tandjoengenim during our short reprieve from the camps and sent the jewelry to Kokie for safekeeping, not willing to risk detection from another inspection by the Japanese. There were also some heirloom pieces from our *Oma*, which were said to have been passed down from mother to daughter for generations. After losing so many other possessions that had had sentimental value, the recovery of these jewels that had been given to Mammy by her mother was a treasure like no other. Mammy gingerly touched a gold bangle and looked up at our friend, her eyes glistening with emotion.

"Thank you so much, Kokie, for all you've done for our family over the years. And bless you for bringing me my jewelry. It must have been a hardship getting here, with the Allied troops stationed on every corner," Mammy said. Her dark eyes were bright with tears as she realized this was probably a last good-bye.

"It was nothing. I couldn't let you all leave without trying to see you one last time," Kokie said, shrugging her shoulders and smiling.

We each hugged her warmly and watched as her trim figure walked down the street and finally out of view.

***

One aspect of camp that was new and exciting for the young women was having Allied soldiers everywhere. Many were young and unattached and, after long stints in battle, were starved for female interaction. They were anxious to be acquainted with the young ladies from the prison camps, especially now that we were cleaned up and starting to put meat on our spindly arms and legs. Personally, I felt a little wary of being thrown into the company of so many men after having lived without them for more than three years. It had been a virtual famine for all of us, and it would take me awhile to adjust. Perhaps my natural shyness was rising to the surface again. Regardless, a number of soldiers requested the presence of Peggy and me at many of the dances the troops pulled together at the local dance hall.

"What are we supposed to wear, Hanny? I'm literally willing a new dress to magically pop into my suitcase. Barring that, I guess I'll be forced to settle for my faded old blue one." Peggy grimaced and shook her head doubtfully.

One of the soldiers' makeshift dances was scheduled for the following evening, and the all-important question of dress was foremost in our minds.

"I have absolutely nothing to wear either," I lamented, glancing ruefully through my small collection of dresses for the hundredth time.

"Well, you're in luck," Mammy said from behind us, a smile evident in her voice. I turned to see her perched on the edge of the bed with her hands behind her back.

"What do you mean, Mammy?" I asked, excitement welling in my chest at the mischievous look on her face and the twinkle in her dark eyes.

"You know I was pretty severe about your invitation to dance with the Japanese awhile ago. I'm not sorry for what I said at the time. It was wrong to attend a social gathering with the enemy under any circumstances. But now that the war is over, this is your time to have fun, girls. That said, I have a surprise for you," she said, glee evident in her voice.

From behind her back, she withdrew a large canvas bag. Inside were two dresses, and not just any dresses—two silken dresses of the finest, most luxurious fabric imaginable. Mammy handed me a deep rose-colored dress with burgundy piping, and she drew out a shimmering, mint-colored dress with forest green trim for Peggy. I glided the smooth cloth reverently across my cheek and reveled in the touch of silk against my skin. It reminded me of the softest rose petal or the creamiest cream my mind could imagine.

"Mammy, how in the world . . . what did you have to do to get these amazing dresses?" Peggy asked, a staggered look on her face as she too stroked the beautiful sea-green fabric with her hand.

"Well, I am not supposed to say, but you can thank Oom Piet from the dress shop for the dresses. He approached me on the grounds soon after we arrived in Palembang, and I was so pleased to see my old friend from before the war. We'd had many business dealings in our time, as I dearly love to sew and he owns the best material warehouse in Palembang. After wringing my hand and hearing all of our news, he drew me close and whispered behind his hand, 'Tina Londt-Schultz, I've heard all about the good you did in the camps. My niece had much to tell me about you. Anything you want for those girls of yours, my dear, anything at all, you tell me and I'll get it for you,' he said, his old face breaking into a wide grin. I could see he was sincere, and I knew you both could use a new dress, several new dresses really, so I told him some colors you might like and your sizes and *voila*! Here they are," she said, her brown eyes dancing.

"They're *gorgeous*, Mammy! Just gorgeous," I said, holding mine against my chest as I danced around.

"Thanks so much, Mammy! I've always loved this shade of green," Peggy said, eyeing her dress dreamily.

"Well, there are more clothes coming in a few days, hopefully some more practical ones. Oom Piet got a little extravagant with his choice of fabric, but they will do just fine for the dance tomorrow night. He may not be your real uncle, but Oom Piet has taken it upon himself to outfit you girls with a couple of fine dresses each before we set sail. I've offered to do some of the sewing, and, to be honest, I'm excited about working on something new for a change instead of all the mending I've had to do for the last few years in the camps. That's such tiresome work," she said, folding the canvas bag and stowing it in her suitcase.

"Without your talent for mending, we'd be in rags right now," Peggy replied with a smile.

"Regardless, it'll be nice to take on a new project. Now about your hair, Peggy . . ." Mammy began, reaching over to touch my sister's unruly black tresses.

"Well, I've got to go. Fritz asked this morning for another lesson in Malay. A promise is a promise," Peggy said, hastily jumping off the bed and narrowly evading my mother's hand.

She smiled at me nervously before flitting around the corner and out of sight. After all she'd been through, the thought of shears in Mammy's hand still sent her running for the door. I chuckled at the thought.

***

"My hands are so sweaty, Peg," I said, wringing them together as we approached the door to the dance hall the next evening.

"It's just nerves. Aren't you the least bit excited, Hanny?" my sister asked, her face glowing with anticipation.

She looked beautiful tonight, her normally wavy, untamed hair coiled into an elegant twist at the base of her neck and the sea green of her dress accentuating her dark skin and eyes.

"Does nauseous count?" I asked dubiously, hearing the big-band music blaring just behind the closed door in front of us. The laughter and conversation of a hundred voices greeted me like a flood of new opportunities.

"You look amazing, Hanny! Every boy in the room will want to dance with you," Peggy said offhandedly. She tweaked one of my curls before grabbing the door handle to pull it open.

"And that is supposed to make me feel better?" I sighed under my breath as I followed her into the cacophony of sound and reveling.

Actually, the dance wasn't as bad as I had anticipated. It was fun to see the soldiers in their uniforms twirling and swinging their partners to the beat. The excitement of the evening was contagious.

The only nail-biting moment I had was when one of the Indian soldiers bowed graciously in front of me and asked me to dance. There were soldiers of many nationalities present in Palembang—all those helping the Allies regain control of the area. The British Indian Army was no exception. The young officer before me was tall and dashing in his soldier's uniform, his white teeth flashing me an inviting grin as he waited for my reply. I swallowed anxiously and then attempted a timid smile as I nodded my assent. He was a most considerate partner, recognizing my nervousness and smiling kindly at my reluctance to meet his eyes.

He talked to me in English, a logical choice, as it was the language most frequently shared in camp. Unfortunately, my English was limited to a children's storybook about daddy longlegs that I had studied in the Palembang barracks camp and the few phrases I'd managed to pick up working side by side with the English interns.

At one point, during a particularly loud part of the song we were dancing to, I thought my Indian partner asked me something about where I was staying. I meant to say in the white houses nearby, but I realized right away I'd misspoken and said something about a white elephant. I blushed in confusion as I met his quizzical eyes. He looked a little affronted, and then I remembered that white elephants were sacred animals in the Hindu religion. Perhaps he thought I was mocking him. I tried desperately to explain my mistake, but the damage had been done. The words I was trying to conjure out of thin air were so beyond my limited abilities that I finally shrugged and shook my head in defeat.

At the end of the song, he guided me back to my table then bowed politely and left, glancing back at me once, a puzzled expression crossing his face. I tried to smile my thanks for the dance, but the embarrassment I felt at hurting his feelings must have been apparent on my face. I sank into my chair and hid my face in my hands. Maybe it was too soon to start socializing and dancing, no matter how much fun it sounded like on the surface. The dating scene was stressful, and I greatly doubted that my limited social skills stretched far enough to bridge the awkwardness I felt with members of the opposite sex.

I spent the remaining hour sitting quietly on the sidelines, watching my sister and cousins dance with some very enthusiastic soldiers. They had a wonderful time, and I thoroughly enjoyed myself watching them. I was completely content playing the roll of spectator the rest of the night until our escorts arrived to take us back to the camp. I'd had my fill of male/female bonding for the evening.

***

Less than a week later, the Dutch guards informed us that it was our turn
to ride to the dock and catch a boat to our new home. Again we assembled,
clinging to our few possessions, and boarded the truck that took us to the
train station. After arriving, we were quickly shepherded aboard the train
already sitting in the yard. We all sat rigidly in our lush passenger cars as
we pulled out of the station. Wisps of previous train rides wafted through
my brain when accommodations were not so genteel, or even humane for
that matter. My experiences in the cattle cars during the war made me
appreciate the comfortable benches and the bright windows all the more.

After watching the familiar scenery of the Sumatran countryside
quickly slip by for several hours, we started to see the telltale yellow of
sand dunes intermingle with the foliage, and I knew that the ocean was
drawing near.

The train pulled to a halt, and we gathered our bags once again. Mammy's
battered brown suitcase caught my eye, complete with its secret compartment,
and I felt a pang in my chest for my father. He should have been with us, sharing
in the bittersweet taste of a new beginning as we crossed the train platform and
stepped down onto a sandy path that led to the docks. I missed him.

I choked back emotion as I walked the pier to the ship to which we were
assigned. Would I ever return to Sumatra again? Was this a last good-bye?
I scanned the countryside greedily, trying to drink in the green landscape.
I willed it to memory, promising to remember how the air smelled that
afternoon—like fish and lemon trees and briny seawater. I could feel the
slight breeze coming off the water and watched it waft playfully through
the treetops like wind through a girl's hair. I didn't want to forget the
noises of the island I loved so much either—the birds singing, the insects
clicking, and the occasional guffaw of a jungle monkey. They were all
familiar to me. They were the sounds of home.

The boat's horn bellowed just then, and I turned reluctantly to
embark on the ship we were to ride to our new life. The *Klipfontein* was
the ship's name, and she was a huge battle-ax of a boat, a former luxury
liner converted to a trooper ship in WWII. She bore the scars of a handful
of skirmishes at sea and reminded me of an old woman who had lived
a debutante's life as a youth, only to be weathered by life's trials and
challenges in her later years. We climbed the ship's wooden plank and
entered the vessel on the port side.

Dutch soldiers gestured for us to walk down the stairs to a berth in the
belly of the ship. It was an old barracks-type room with racks stacked one

on top of the other for the soldiers who occupied it. It was dark gray and dank, with the overripe smell of vomit permeating the air. After choking down a dinner of rice and spinach that evening, we met back downstairs to get ready for bed.

"Ugh! The smell in this place is enough to make me lose my dinner," George spit out disgustedly.

"You mean the rocking of the boat hasn't already done that?" Peggy asked, looking a little green in the face. I felt too nauseous to put my two cents in, and Mammy was already lying gingerly on one of the bunks, holding her stomach as if that would help her keep things intact.

Justin had met an old friend from Tandjoengenim at dinner. Before parting, they'd arranged to meet on the upper deck for a catch-up session before bed.

"You know, I think Justin may have the right idea," Peggy said. "This room is not helping the seasickness at all. Why don't we just sleep on the deck tonight? We may manage better up there."

"I'm not sure if we are allowed to. What do you think, Mammy? Do you want to try resting upside?" George asked gently, concerned about our mother. She just shook her head faintly, her eyes still shut tight, and waved us away.

"She may just need some time by herself to adjust to the rocking ship," I whispered, trying to reassure my brother.

"So, Hanny, are you in? Do you want to sleep on deck tonight?" Peggy asked, kissing Mammy lightly on the forehead as she passed.

"I'm in," I said, mustering some enthusiasm. I was game for anything that would get me out of this oppressive berth.

"Mammy, we'll check on you in a couple of hours to see if you need anything. If we don't catch Justin on deck, can you tell him where we are?" I asked gently, handing her a damp cloth for her forehead. I gathered the thin blanket I'd been issued from my cot and followed Peggy and George up the stairs, happy to be away from the noxious odors that were wreaking havoc on my system.

The smell of salt air bombarded my senses as we walked along the deck. I thought it might be chilly outside, but the cool night breeze felt soothing on my clammy skin. I glanced into the sky and saw that we had a full moon to light our way. Its silver light washed over the deck, and we could make our way very clearly through the bodies milling about. Apparently we weren't the only ones who had traded our bunks for a bit of space on the deck that evening. Dozens of people were chatting and relaxing, some leaning over the rails enjoying the view . . . or taking care of business. I wasn't sure which, and I wasn't about to slow down to find out.

We found a nice sheltered space by some tables to rest. After enjoying the night air for half an hour or so, George's eyes slowly began to close, and within a few minutes, he was out for the night. Peggy rearranged his blanket to cover his shoulders.

"I hope he'll be warm enough," she whispered.

"If we get too cold, we can always go back down below," I replied.

"I'd have to be darn near frozen to venture down there to sleep," Peggy said under her breath. I smiled—my sentiments exactly. After a few minutes spent silently contemplating the stars and realizing they still reminded me of Pappy, I turned to look at my sister who was staring out over the waves.

"What do you think we'll do in Holland?" I asked.

"What do you mean?"

"I mean, according to the soldiers, Holland got hit pretty badly during the war. It's not like people are going to meet us at the dock and offer us a house or jobs or even food on a silver platter. I'm worried," I admitted. Peggy's eyes kept roving across the scenery as she considered what I had said.

"I don't know. I guess I haven't thought much about it. Whatever we face can't be any worse than what we left behind, can it?" she asked. Thinking back over our time in the camps, I shook my head.

"You're right, I guess. Can I ask you something, Peg? It's kind of personal, but do you want to get married right away? I mean, you're seventeen, and judging from the number of partners you had at the dance, you could be in big demand once we get to Holland," I said, curious to hear her answer. She chuckled.

"No, I am in no hurry to get married. I figure there will be time enough for that later. You know what I really want to do, Hanny?" she asked, looking at me, a glimmer of excitement in her eye. "I want the chance to go back to school, to get an education. I feel like we missed out on that in the camps, and there is so much I don't know," Peggy said earnestly.

I could see the fire in her brown eyes, even by the dim light of the moon.

"I want that too. I feel like I was just starting my education when the Japanese bombed Pearl Harbor, and there's still a lot I want to learn. There will be opportunities for boyfriends down the road . . . maybe, hopefully. After the dance last week, I'm not so sure," I said skeptically. "Have you thought about what you want to study?" I asked, watching her profile carefully.

"Well, music for sure. That's my passion. But I want to learn languages too, and I want to travel. Maybe because we were forced to stay confined in one place for so long, I have this desire to see the world," Peggy answered, staring off into space as if she were picturing herself on some far-off continent.

"I want to be a nurse," I said quietly.

"Really? I think you'd be a great nurse, Hanny. When did you decide that?" Peggy asked, smiling at me quizzically.

"In the camps. I would watch how Mammy nursed the interns who were ill. She knew so much, and she was so kind and gentle with them. I guess I want to help people on that kind of basic human level too," I said, fiddling with the edge of my blanket. Peggy nodded.

"We're starting down a new path, aren't we?" my sister asked decidedly. "Not just this boat ride to Holland but a new journey in our lives. I used to think that the camps were like a journey, traveling from one prison camp to another, all part of some morbid trek across Sumatra. But now we've set off on a different course, and I have to admit, I'm kind of excited," Peggy said, shivering a little at the thought. She swung her blanket over her shoulders and leaned against my side for warmth.

"Is our journey ever really over, Peggy? I mean, life is what it is. There are always going to be new hills to climb. I guess it's what we do with the challenges we face that matters most. If nothing else, life in the camps taught me that."

"Stop with the philosophizing already. My brain is too tired and fuzzy to focus on all those deep ideas this late at night," Peggy chided, shaking her head. I laughed, pulling my sister close. Together we looked out into the night, listening to the waves crash and break against the ship, both of us glad to have a tomorrow and each wondering what it might bring.

EPILOGUE
Three Lifetimes

"Look at how green everything is, Peggy! Do you remember it being so green here in Sumatra?" I asked, admiring the mossy lichen growing on the trees and the almost neon green of the grass underfoot.

"Of course I remember it being this green, Hanny. It's practically subtropical here. If there is one color I identify with Sumatra, it's the color green," my sister retorted, playfully "tsking" under her breath as she walked on. I smiled as I followed her down the path. Some things never change.

"Look, the dahlias are out and blooming. Mammy would be ecstatic. They were always her favorite," I said nostalgically, trying another conversation starter.

"Yes, they really are such lovely flowers. I never see them without thinking of Mammy," Peggy replied, her tone softening considerably at the thought of Mammy and her beloved flowers.

"She would have loved to have been here with us today, wouldn't she? I think it was a high point in her later years to be able to come and say good-bye," I whispered reverently as we entered the cemetery gate.

"I know it was. It was a sacred thing to watch her talk to him like he was right there next to her. Somehow, they maintained their connection throughout time and space," Peggy said, wiping a stray tear from her eye.

"I'm glad I could be here with you today, Peg. I began to think I would never get to visit him, and it made me sad," I said, squeezing my sister's hand tenderly.

"It only took sixty some odd years, Hanny, but here you are. You made it. That's his gravestone up ahead to the right there," she said, nodding to an area in a quiet corner of the cemetery.

Emotion coursed through me, deeper and more profound with every step I took toward the grave my sister had pointed out. Tears filled my eyes and fell in undisturbed streams down my weathered cheeks. I had imagined this day my entire adult life. A chance to see him again, to finally say good-bye. No words were needed as we picked our way across the cemetery to the quiet corner where he lay.

I looked at my gnarled hand, freckled with age spots, as I placed it shakily on the marker with his name engraved. It seemed to me just yesterday that my hand was smooth and tan and safely enfolded in his larger, stronger one. In some ways, I still felt like that fourteen-year-old girl that had been ripped away from her father for all time. Some wounds crust over but never truly heal.

I knew my sister well enough to know that she was shedding tears too. She'd been with Mammy to visit his resting place a decade before, but the emotion was still strong as we stood together—two bent, wizened old women wishing for one more moment with their father.

After what seemed an eternity, I turned to smile at my sister. Her brow was still furrowed as she looked back at me.

"You know, Peggy, it seems to me like we've lived three lifetimes," I said, formulating a thought that had been slowly percolating in my mind for sixty years.

"What do you mean?" my sister asked, her eyes still young and curious in her lined face. She knelt and lovingly placed a bouquet of purple orchids on Pappy's grave while she waited for my reply.

"I mean we've lived three lifetimes, you and I . . . the one before the war with Mammy and Pappy, the one in the camps with all its trials and challenges, and the one after the war. Each one was like its own separate universe," I said. "Most people only get to live one existence. They settle in their comfy homes, sometimes in one town all their lives. They know the same people; they go to the same places. Ours has been nothing like that. We've lived enough for three people, wouldn't you say?" I asked thoughtfully, running my hand across the smooth white cross of my father's headstone again.

"Yes, our lives have been full . . . a grand adventure, I guess you could say," she replied, nodding her head in agreement as a smile played on her lips. "Would you have changed it if you could?" she asked, eyeing me with interest.

"Hmmm. There are parts I would change. Pappy's death. Mammy's struggle to support us after the war. My husband's early passing. All the death, the sickness in the camps . . . *that* I would change. But for the most part, no. There is not a lot I would change. You?" I asked in return.

"The same, I guess. I can't imagine living a different life, despite the challenges. I've seen so much. I've traveled to so many different places. No, I'm content," she said, looking out over the trees.

"It's only you and I now. We're all that's left of our generation. I don't want our experiences to die with us. I want our children to know what happened to us as girls. Maybe in some way, what we lived through will help them with what they face in life," I said, glancing over at my daughter who had traveled with us to Sumatra. She was standing by the cemetery gate, her arm around her own daughter. Together they had agreed to give Peggy and me some time alone with our father before paying their respects. A thoughtful gesture.

"It's part of their heritage too. My son asked me awhile ago to write down my stories of suffering through the camps. It's difficult, though, to remember all of the details these days. The memories used to be crystal clear in my mind. Now there are fuzzy edges around the stories and the people we knew back then."

"Maybe that is why I feel such an urge to share what happened to us before it is too late. I'm eighty, Peggy. Life is winding down for both of us. It's now or never, you know?" I smiled, playfully elbowing her arm.

"For you, maybe, my beloved *older* sister. But I plan to live for many more years, my dear," she said with bravado.

I chuckled. "I think Laurie and Rachel are waiting to have their time with Pappy too. Why don't I walk back to get them and give you a few extra minutes alone with him," Peggy suggested considerately.

"That would be nice," I replied, smiling my thanks. I watched her bent frame meander back up the path toward the gates, my heart brimming with love for the sister who had been with me from the beginning. Then I turned to my father, emotion rising in my chest again.

"I kept my promise, Pappy," I whispered tremulously. "The one I made to you all those years ago before the Japanese came for us. You asked me to watch over Mammy . . . and I did. I stayed with her for her whole life. Even when dementia snatched her memories and age bent her in half," I murmured, hoping that wherever he was, he heard me. A gentle breeze picked up and caressed my cheek as my fingers lovingly traced his name engraved on the marker.

"I love you, Pappy," I mouthed. Tears found their way down my wrinkled face, and I thought I heard a familiar voice whisper back through the breeze, "Remember."

***

Hanny and her family immigrated to Holland from Sumatra in April 1946 via the *Klipfontein*. The old, battered suitcase with the secret compartment at the bottom accompanied them, and the papers inside were instrumental in helping the family get a start in their new country, just as Hanny's father had hoped. Tina Londt-Schultz received her husband's life insurance benefits and pension shortly upon arrival, while thousands of other post-war refugees, whose papers had been lost, waded through a quagmire of red tape and bureaucracy before acquiring compensation.

Unfortunately, shortly after the war and upon Tina Londt-Schultz's request, Hanny's uncle unburied the treasures hidden beneath the cement slab at their home in Tandjoengenim only to find that the dishes had broken and the jewelry and silverware buried there had corroded beyond recovery. In that instance, Alex Londt-Schultz's careful preparation for his family had come to naught.

The benefits from the papers Hanny's father had hidden in the suitcase assisted the children in paying for their education once in Holland. There, Hanny attended nursing school and worked as a nurse until 1958, when she, her mother, and her two younger brothers left Holland for a new beginning in the United States. Hanny was later informed that their father's heroism in WWII opened the doors of immigration for them faster than for most wishing to leave the overcrowded and war-torn country. The family found sponsors in New Jersey, where Hanny was offered a job in a nursing home. She worked there for nearly a year. She and her mother then moved to Rochester, New York, where Hanny was finally licensed as a nurse in the United States in 1959.

Hanny was first introduced to The Church of Jesus Christ of Latter-day Saints in Holland a few months before she left for the United States. Her mother, Tina Londt-Schultz, and her brother George joined the Church before they immigrated, but Hanny had only received four discussions and wanted to complete all six before she committed to baptism.

While living in Rochester, she saw two elders riding by her home on their bicycles. When Hanny recognized them as representatives of the Church, she ran out of the house and flagged them down. She told them she had been hoping to find "Mormon missionaries" since her arrival to the U.S. She promised them during that first meeting that if they would teach her the last two discussions, she would get baptized. She officially became a member of the Church on October 3, 1959, in Palmyra, New York. Peggy and Justin never joined the Church but continued to live with the faith their mother had instilled in them during their time in the prison camps.

Hanny met her husband soon after her baptism and was sealed in the Salt Lake Temple on October 23, 1960. The newly married couple later made their life near Syracuse, New York, where they were blessed to become the parents of three children. Hanny lived with or near her mother for her entire life, even working at the nursing home she was admitted to in her last years after being diagnosed with dementia.

Hanny currently lives with her daughter, Laurie, and her family in Oregon.

***

As an interesting aside, in a conversation with one of her associates after the war, Hanny's mother learned that a certain questionable socialite by the name of Mrs. Schwartzkopf appeared at a black-tie function in Singapore a few months after liberation, donning an exquisitely beautiful diamond necklace with a very familiar description. There was no doubt in the minds of Hanny and her family as to where their old acquaintance had acquired such a singular piece of jewelry.

Street in Sawah Loento

Alex Londt-Schultz

Justine Londt-Schultz
with two-month-old
Hanny

From top: Hanny, Peggy, Justin, George

Alex and Justine Londt-Schultz with Hanny

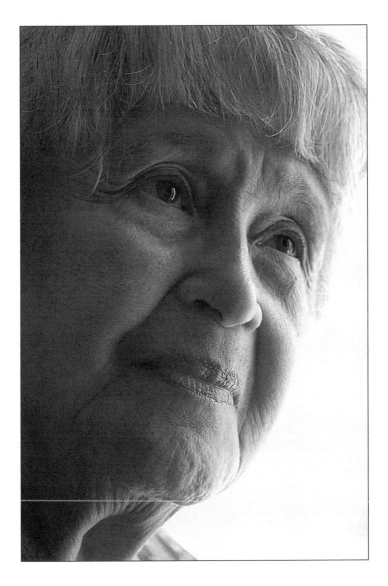

Hanny Londt-Schultz Smith, 2008

Peggy, Hanny, and Rachel (Hanny's granddaughter) in
Bandung, Java, at the gravesite of Peggy and Hanny's father,
Alex Londt-Schultz in 2007

Peggy (left) and Hanny (right) Londt-Schultz

Kelly DiSpirito Taylor (middle) with Peggy and Hanny

ABOUT THE AUTHOR

A graduate of Brigham Young University, Kelly DiSpirito Taylor lives with her husband, Alan, and their five children in eastern North Carolina. A few of her favorite pastimes include exploring the beaches of the Outer Banks with her family, reading, and writing. Her day job consists of teaching at East Carolina University in the Department of Child Development and Family Relations, an endeavor she enjoys. Along with her children, her students keep her young at heart.